A Journey in Ladakh

Andrew Harvey

A Journey in Ladakh

WITH

A NEW AFTERWORD

A MARINER BOOK

HOUGHTON MIFFLIN COMPANY

Boston · New York

First Mariner Books edition 2000

Afterword copyright © 2000 by Andrew Harvey
Copyright © 1983 by Andrew Harvey
All rights reserved

Visit our Web site: www.hmco.com/trade

Library of Congress Cataloging-in-Publication
data is available.
ISBN 978-0-618-05675-0

Printed in the United States of America

EB 10 9 8 7 6 5 4 3 2

To Iris Murdoch

Contents

Acknowledgments

To Caroline Blackwood.

To my friends Ann Wordsworth, Simonette Strachey, Jim Crenner, Gillon Aitken, Iain McGilchrist, and Eirian Wain, for their help.

To Liz Calder, most encouraging of editors.

To Sally Purcell, for her typing.

To Shambhala Publications for permission to print excerpts from *The Hundred Thousand Songs of Milarepa*.

To Uwe Gielen, for permission to use one of his photographs.

To Nawang Tsering, of Leh, for his patience with my ignorance.

To the Warden and Fellows of All Souls College.

To the XIIth Gyalwang Drukchen.

To Thuksey Rinpoche, to whom nothing I have written or could write could express what I owe.

I have changed most of the personal names in my account. I have shortened slightly some of the Teachings I was given without, I hope, falsifying them. The Tibetan tradition is one of direct oral transmission and so my account of these Teachings is, necessarily, limited.

'Rinpoche' is pronounced 'Rinpochay', with the accent on the first syllable.

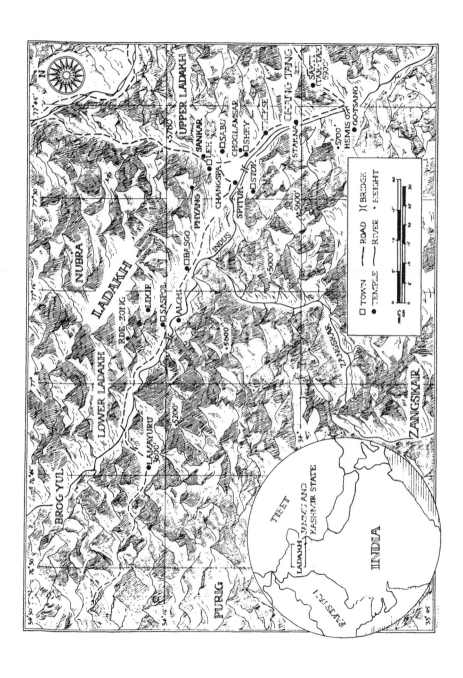

1

The Beginning

I shall never forget the four photographs. They were in the same khaki-coloured encyclopedia that taught me the names of supernovas, the uncanny oddities of the duck-billed platypus, and the colours of the snakes of India. I have seen them in dreams, enlarged and animated, and coloured fantastically; I have searched bookshops on three continents for them, as if they could bring me happiness and good luck. They were photographs of Tibet.

In the first, a man is sitting on a horse looking away at a line of snow-fringed mountains. His shoes are fat, and turned up at the end like Aladdin's.

In the second, a priest is sitting on a throne. He has a hat of huge feathers on, bound in bands of thick gold; his feet are wide apart in shoes that the blurred photograph makes seem like puffs of smoke; on his robes you can just make out three twisting fire-breathing dragons.

The third photograph is of the Potala in Lhasa, the palace of the Dalai Lama. To a child growing up on the flat hot Indian plains there could be nothing as extraordinary as this building, climbing up its small mountain and ringed by larger ones; I peopled each of its rooms with magicians and Oracles; each of its ascending levels became the stages of different miracles, of monks sitting in clouds of fragrance and changing at will into diamond or light, of serene and ornate ceremonies with bells and chants and waving coloured silk.

The fourth photograph is the simplest. It is of mountains, a semi-circle of completely snow-covered mountains, enclosing a desert of rock with one man in it and a yak; the man is so still and expressionless he seems another rock. I would stand at the large window of our house in the evening and look out on the shanty town we lived opposite, its rotting roofs and puddles of filth the children played in, all its noise of radios and dogs, and try to build in its place, slowly and painstakingly, that desert and those mountains. Once I succeeded; for an instant, in the middle of a monsoon downpour, there was nothing but rock and snow and a cold wind.

It was when I was up at Oxford in the early 1970s that I became interested in Buddhism. My life was full of confusion and distress of every kind, and I found in Buddhist philosophy a way of thought that enthralled me by its calm and radical analysis of desire, its rejection of all the self-dramatising intensities by which I lived, and its promise of a possible, strong, and unsentimental serenity. I read everything I could — the Dhammapada, the Heart and Diamond sutras, the books of Conze and Watts and Herrigel, the essays of Suzuki, texts from all the different Buddhist traditions; I talked often of Indian thought with a young tutor of mine who later gave up his academic career to live in an ashram, and whose happy breadth of mind moved and inspired me. It was a long time before any clear picture of what I was looking for even began to emerge; although I read widely I understood little of what I read; I was still too fascinated by the turbulence of my own life to want — or be able — to take on the responsibility of living a philosophy as exacting and un-self-flattering as Buddhism; I found no Teacher and followed no discipline.

In those years of haphazard enthusiasm for Eastern philosophy I had two experiences, both aesthetic, which have lasted in my imagination. In the Ashmolean Museum at Oxford there is a Khmer head of a Buddha; it is small and broken and now rarely on display. While I was an undergraduate it was always to be seen and I would visit it regularly, three or four times a week. What drew me again and again to that face, that smile, those lidded and quietly shining eyes, was the peace that their contemplation gave me, a peace I had rarely found in Western art, that I could love with my mind but lacked in my life, and so

4

needed, I knew, if I was to achieve any spiritual or emotional maturity. How to practise what I had begun to learn from that head I did not know, but I understood that I would one day have to, or wither in the bitterness and solitude of my life.

In the summer after I took Schools, when I was living in Oxford, there was an exhibition of Japanese and Chinese paintings by Buddhist masters in the Ashmolean, a small exhibition of which I can remember now only one painting. It was of a butterfly about to alight on an open flower. I came back every afternoon for three weeks to stand before it. Slowly I realised that what moved me was not merely the dazzling and delicate artistry of the work, but the attitude of clear joy, of tender, precise and unselfconscious wonder at things, that had created it. That wonder and unselfconsciousness were so far from anything I felt, and so excluded from any of the poetry I was writing, that I was amazed at them and frightened at the lacks and absences they exposed in myself. I realised as I contemplated that painting that its power was the reward of many years of spiritual discipline; I did not feel fit, at twenty-one, for that discipline, or know, in any sense, what it might entail.

In the turmoil of the years that followed, fragments of my reading in the Buddhist scriptures and my glimpses of Buddhist awareness through the Khmer head and the painting of the butterfly would surface in my mind to remind me of what I had left unexamined and unlived. At twenty-five I decided to leave Oxford and return to India for a year. I felt frustrated by my life and the limitations of my poetry, its obsession with irony and suffering, its largely unremitting anger and hopelessness; I wanted, at last, to explore the world of Indian art and thought without any possibility of distraction. The project I set myself was to study Buddhism in all its forms and places. I never completed the project; but a growing involvement with it and with the new forms of thought and understanding that it uncovered has taken me, since 1976, to many of the Buddhist shrines, in or around India, to Sri Lanka and Nepal, to Sarnath and Bodhgaya, Ajanta and Ellora, to Sanchi, and, eventually, in 1981, to Ladakh, one of the last places on earth, with Sikkim and Bhutan, where a Tibetan Buddhist society can be experienced.

5

I went to Ladakh because I was going to Nepal. I found out about Ladakh because I wanted to go to Nepal. It was in January 1978. I was in India for the winter. I was in Delhi and looking for a travel agency a friend had told me would help me trek in Nepal the next summer. Eventually, through endless side-streets, swerving phut-phuts, klaxons, bullock carts, I found it. It was a tiny, untidy room with peeling walls and two old tattered posters of the Himalayas, at the back of an office block.

There was no one in the room but a young Frenchman reading. He looked up as I entered, smiled, and said, 'No one has been here for the last three hours.'

We talked all day. His name was François. He was about thirty, a schoolteacher in Provence. The man who should have been at the desk never came and no one rang. Slowly, we took over the office, chatting with our legs up on the desk, smoking all of the cigarettes that had been left on the table beside a pile of out-of-date cinema magazines and travel brochures.

We talked with the intimacy and abandon of two people who felt at ease with each other and who would never see each other again. We talked about France, about sex, about Descartes, about Indian lavatories and officials and bedbugs, about Theosophy and Zen, and, all evening, before he left on the night bus to Khatmandu, about Ladakh.

'You have not heard about Ladakh? How is this possible? You have been so many times in India and no one has told you that you must go? Well, you are lucky today. I am telling you. You must go. It is necessary that you go. Ladakh is the last place where you can see something of what Tibet must have been like, now that Bhutan is open only to the very rich. And Ladakh is a wonderful world in its own right too . . . If I had a group of gangsters and a plane I would kidnap you and take you there myself . . . Through Ladakh, I have come to see everything differently. If you have felt anything in these hours we have been together, any intensity, any truth, think that it was not just

6

from me or from us, but from Ladakh too that they came. I know that sounds strange . . .' He stopped. 'I haven't been so vehement for years. I did not realise I felt so absolutely about the place.' When we parted he said again, 'You must go to Ladakh. It will change your life as it has changed mine.'

I did not go to Ladakh for several years although I could have done. I was a little frightened, I suppose; I thought, 'The Frenchman was beautiful but mad.' I thought, 'What helped him will not necessarily help me.' My life was full of other plans, other obligations.

One night, about a year afterwards, I dreamt about François. He had a long red robe on, and was sitting on a rock in the middle of a stream. He waved to me to come and join him. I stepped out towards him. As I did so, he laughed, 'So you have come after all.' I felt flustered and a little angry. 'No, I haven't come,' I said. 'This is a dream.' But I kept on walking.

I n 1980 I visited Sri Lanka and made friends there with Ananda, an old German painter who had become a Buddhist monk.

I remember with especial vividness our first conversation. We met at the house of a friend in Colombo. It was a hot January afternoon and we sat by the fishpond in the garden, talking while everyone else slept.

'Are you nostalgic by nature?' Ananda asked me. It was a strange question.

'No,' I answered.

'Good,' he said. 'I hardly think of the past at all. Anneliese, my wife, came to see me last week. She flew out to try and get me back. She comes once every ten years. She always says the same thing. That I am a fool, an idiot, that I am ruining her life and my life, that I am ruining my career . . . And I told her what I always tell her. That I had always been unhappy as a painter, and that what fame it had brought me had given me nothing but pain. That I believed what the Buddha said in his fire sermon — that the world is on fire and every solution short of liberation, of Nirvana, is like trying to whitewash a burning house. She cried a great deal, and then dried her tears, and looked at me very hard. Do you know what she asked me? She asked me, "Will you at least give me all the paintings?" '

Ananda paused and looked down at the fat goldfish circling in the pond. 'She wanted the paintings. She wanted the money. She is in her seventies and she wanted the money. I said she could have everything she wanted if she promised never to see me again. I have nothing now. Not even any books. I feel happier than I have ever felt.'

'I have lived vainly and carelessly,' Ananda said, after a long pause, 'but perhaps now I am beginning to understand something.'

Then he asked me what I knew of Buddhism.

'I have read a lot,' I said, 'but is that knowledge?'

'No. But it is a beginning.'

'A beginning of what?'

'How can I say? When you are ready, it will happen. But you must want to be ready; you must put yourself patiently, again and again, in a position for it to happen. You must study, and meditate, and travel, above all perhaps travel, so that you will meet someone who can give you what I can only tell you about.'

'Did you travel a great deal when you were young?'

'Yes. As much as I could. I travelled all over the East — China, Indonesia, Malaya, Burma . . . And I went to Tibet. That changed my life.'

'How long were you there?'

'Three years.'

All afternoon Ananda talked of his time in Tibet: of travelling on yaks over high mountain passes; of Lake Mansarovar and its clear green water; of the long pilgrimage to Kailasa and the first view of the sacred mountain; of harvesting with the villagers; of staying with poor Tibetan families all winter; of meetings with the Panchen and Dalai Lamas; of Tibetan gentleness; of the light breaking over the mountains at dawn; of his grief that the Tibetan world he had loved had almost disappeared.

'If Tibet does not open,' he said, 'go to Ladakh. You must see and experience some last part of Tibet. What I learnt in my three years there has lasted my lifetime. Although I have not chosen the Tibetan Path — I am a Hinayana, not a Mahayana monk — I have no doubt that for many it can offer great help. It is a very rich path, a path that excludes no energy and banishes no perception. You may find that it is what you need.'

The last time I saw Ananda we talked at the top of a mountain, in his cave of meditation, on a wild spring day, looking across the plains to the sea. He lived in a cave in Kataragama, the sacred shrine at the heart of Sri Lanka. He said he would not leave it now that he had found everything he wanted. His last painting was the blue rainbow that he had painted in colours from earth and stone over the doorway to his cave.

I had walked for hours to see him, through a jungle of white butterflies. It was a month after out first talk. His face had lost its look of sadness. He was thin and tanned. He took me into his cave, and we sat in the soft dark for a while without saying anything.

'There are cobras here, you know,' he said. 'But they do not bite if they know you are harmless. Sometimes as I sit here in meditation they come and brush past me.'

I gave him a copy of the *Sonnets to Orpheus*, by Rilke. He handed it back to me, gently. 'I do not read any more. You keep it.' Then he took me up to the top of the mountain, just above his cave, and we walked slowly round the small bo-sapling he had planted there.

Just before we parted, Ananda said to me, 'I had a dream about you last week. I saw you in a small room, sitting quietly. Out of the window behind you I saw mountains, snow-covered mountains. You will find that room.'

'I hope so.'

I must have sounded doubtful, because he said again, 'No. I am certain you will.'

'Was there anyone else in the room?'

'Yes. Several people. They were sitting with their backs to me and so I couldn't see who they were.'

'Do you have any idea where the room was?'

'No. But it was very like a room I once stayed in in a monastery near Lhasa. It was definitely a Tibetan room. There was a large painting on the wall, but it was in shadow and so I cannot tell you what its subject was. You have an inner relation with Tibet and Tibetan philosophy; you will have to explore it sooner or later!'

I walked down the hill, sceptical and amazed at what Ananda had said. He called after me, 'Be happy! Be happy!' and I turned and saw him high on his rock, a small orange bird.

The next winter Sarah and I were walking in Sarnath. Sarah is seventy; Sri Lankan; a Buddhist. It was in her garden that I had first met Ananda. Now we were meeting each other in December in North India to make a pilgrimage to the Buddhist Holy Places of Bodhgaya and Sarnath. Sarah wanted to see them before she died.

Sarnath is where the Buddha preached the Deer Sermon, the sermon of the Law. There are deer there still, and the remains of a huge stupa.

As we walked slowly in the winter sunlight over the ruins of the Deer Park, Sarah talked — about the misery of her husband's life and suicide, of the unhappiness of her children, of her own long unhappiness. She wore the white sari of a widow and looked old and stricken.

'When I was a child I would anger my mother by shouting at her, "I do not want your peace. I do not want your calm." And now that I long for that calm of heart I have neither the strength nor the will to attain it. I believe in reincarnation — but what kind of a consolation is that? To feel that I will return in life after life to endure the same restlessness, the same misery . . . Sometimes I feel there is only one Nirvana and that is death — to be nothing any more, to feel nothing for ever. But I do not believe in death.'

We walked into the museum of Sarnath. On the left wall as you enter there is a row of Buddhas. We stood in front of them.

There was one that Sarah loved especially — of the Buddha in the lotus position, stretching one hand down to the ground in the gesture that says, 'I have mastered the earth.'

Sarah said, 'The Buddha does not have to beat the ground. He only has to touch it delicately with one of his fingers.'

Then, standing in front of that Buddha with her hands in prayer, she turned to me and said, 'Ever since I have known you you have talked of wanting to go to Ladakh, of your long fascination for Tibet and Tibetan philosophy. Why do you never go?'

'I still feel so ignorant. I still know so little.'

'That is not the real reason.'

'No. I am frightened.'

'Frightened? Why? What have you to fear?'

'Disappointment. Change. Both possibilities are frightening. We imagine we want to transform ourselves and our lives, but do we really? Do I? I am not sure.'

'You must go and find out. You must go and discover whether there is anything in that world for you. I am too old and broken to come with you. Promise me that you will go. Promise me in front of this Buddha that you will go.'

'I promise.'

We stood in silence. Winter sunlight fell across the Buddha's lap, one half of his smiling face.

The next year, 1981, I taught and travelled in America. I read what little I could find on Ladakh. I read Moorcroft, De Vigne, the *Gazetteer of India*; I read some of the Tibetan scriptures; I read badly printed books on cheap paper on Himalayan fauna and flora. I amassed files of half-interesting facts, quotations; I almost succeeded in killing the lure of Ladakh altogether.

I decided I would have to go to Ladakh that summer, or never go at all. Although I knew a little Ladakhi and a little Hindi, and had some small grounding in Buddhist philosophy, I knew that I was not prepared. Even after I had bought my ticket I still did not know whether I would go. I had a book of poems and a thesis to finish; I had friendships to re-establish that I had let slide over years of frenetic travelling . . . So many reasons not to go, and they nearly held me back. But the voices of the Frenchman and my Sri Lankan friends were too strong, and my inner need for change was too insistent and so I caught the plane for Delhi in July 1981, with a copy of the Heart and Diamond sutras, and four empty notebooks marked 'Ladakh' in shaky black letters.

I am in a friend's flat in Delhi. I am going to Ladakh tomorrow.

There is a copy of Dhammapada on the shelves.

I take the book down. What I read is not encouraging:

'A careless pilgrim scatters the dust of his passions more widely.'

'Not nakedness, not plaited hair, not dirt, not fasting, or lying on the earth, not rubbing with dust, not sitting motionless, can purify a mortal who has not overcome desires.'

'By oneself the evil is done, by oneself the evil is undone, no one can purify another.'

'Men who have not gained treasure in their youth, perish like old herons in a lake without fish.'

'**D**on't forget,' the Frenchman had said. 'It is essential you go by bus. It takes two days to Leh from Srinagar. You will be tempted to fly there. Don't. I have been down the Amazon; I have walked across the Kalahari; I once spent five weeks in the Sahara . . . and they are *nothing* to those two days going up from Srinagar to Leh, up the Kashmir valley into the mountains of Ladakh. Find a patron saint and pray to him; don't look too closely at the side of the road or you'll faint or be sick; pray you don't get the same drunk dishevelled unshaven Kashmiri driver I did who swigged from a bottle of gin and sang and giggled to himself the whole way. You'll be all right. You're British, you have the stiff upper lip, you'll be all right. Take opium if you can get some. It helps. The greens and purples and browns in the mountains sway and tremble and sing if you do and you giggle with the driver and do not mind that on that corner the bus was an inch from a three thousand foot drop.'

I did go by bus, but without opium. On one side I sat next to a fat German lady in her forties who kept clutching my knee and screaming, 'I can't look! I mustn't look!' On the other there was a young green-faced Frenchman reading Kierkegaard in between puking very softly and politely into a puce plastic bag.

What did I know about Ladakh? I knew facts only — that it was the highest, most remote, most sparsely populated region in the Republic of India; that its climate was extreme even in summer, when hot days were followed by freezing nights; that it was cut off from the world from November to May by snow; that it was of great strategic importance, bounded on one side by Tibet and China and on the other by Pakistan; that it was part of Jammu and Kashmir State and had been the focus of political controversy and strife for twenty years between Central and State Government, between Muslim and Buddhist; that its cuisine had names like 'mok-mok' and 'thuk-pa'; that one of its queens had once had earache and designed the first ear-muffler in the Himalayas as a result; that an English traveller, Moorcroft, had once seriously proposed to plant its deserted plains and slopes with rhubarb to steal the trade from the Chinese. I had noted with relish this sentence from Cowley Lambert's book of his trip to Kashmir and Ladakh (1877): 'The prevailing features of this country are bare rocky mountains, bare gravel slopes, and bare sandy plains, with not a green thing, not a tree, not a bush, not even a blade of grass, excepting a kind of grey prickly grass that crops up here and there.'

I had written this paragraph in Delhi:

'Dry; stark; remote; harsh in climate, topography and altitude, this country of rock has yet been adorned by many names. It has been known as Mang Yul (the country of many people),

Naris, and Kha-Chum-Pa (the land of snow); Fa-Hien, the great Chinese traveller, who visited the region in A.D. 400, called it Ma-La-Pho (red land). Its present name, Ladakh, comes from La-Tags, in Tibetan the land of the la, the land of the high mountain passes; and it is the best name of all.'

Why did I write, 'and it is the best name of all' so confidently, when I had never been there? A vague erudition had turned, somehow, for a phrase, into a kind of prophecy. Ladakh *is* the land of high mountain passes; my experience of Ladakh and its people was to be, for me, a pass, into another awareness of reality.

Nothing I had read or imagined prepared me for the splendour and majesty of the mountains that first day; that was the first gift Ladakh gave me, a silence before that phantasmagoria of stone, those vast wind-palaces of red and ochre and purple rock, those rock faces the wind and snow had worked over thousands of years into shapes so unexpected and fantastical the eye could hardly believe them, a silence so truly stunned and wondering that words of description emerge from it very slowly, and at first only in broken images — a river glimpsed there, a thousand feet below the road, its waters sparkling in the shifting storm-light, the path below on the bare rocky surface moving with sheep whose wool glittered in the sunlight, small flowers nodding in the crevasses of the vast rocks that lined the road, rocks tortured in as many thousand ways as the mountains they are torn from, sudden glimpses of ravines pierced and shattered by the light that broke down from the mountains, of the far peaks of the mountains themselves, secreted in shadow, or illumined suddenly, blindingly, by passing winds of light. And there is no reason in the images, no demure and easily negotiable order, because they emerge from a silence and a wonder so full that they each seem to exist in a time of their own, in a silence of their own, remote from all thought, glimpsed purely as they are, as they are in their essence, in some final purity words do not reach. As the bus creaked and wheezed its way slowly up that vast winding pass of Zoji-La, I found my mind falling silent, becoming as large and as empty as the spaces between the mountain faces, as wide as the skies above the peaks of the mountains; for long moments I felt as if everything that happened, the passage of a lonely bird across a ravine, the glint of sudden sunlight on spray-shined boulders far below, a wash of wind through a field of small purple flowers on a ledge above, happened within me also, within my mind that had become as large as the landscape, as airy, as silent. That silence! It is the quality of that silence that no words can convey, that silence sustained over millennia, that silence of snow and rock and water, in which every sound and movement was contained, with which every object in that world was bathed, as if with shining water. I had never felt before as I felt on that first day the transforming power of silence, its genius of giving everything back to itself. Each mountain existed in its unique contortion; each crag of purple rock, each landslide of scree, each winding dark stream, each small shrub clawing the sides of the road, each bird, seemed to be so full of its own essence that it hovered on the brink of dissolution, so brimming with energy that I feared often it could not survive itself, and I would not survive feeling its radiant danger, and my own, so acutely.

My mind kept returning on that journey to a painting I love — Claude's last painting, that hangs in the Ashmolean Museum. It is of a classical myth, Ascanius killing the stag of Sylvia; Ascanius in the foreground lifts his bow to shoot at a stag that is waiting in a kind of noble daze to be killed, on the right. The true subject of the painting, however, is not that myth, not the expression on the stag's face or the psychology of Ascanius — but the landscape, the lake beyond, and the one mountain beyond that, its sheer white face glittering in late sunlight. Claude seems to be saying, with the clairvoyance of the dying, that it is not the details of history or biography that are important, not the violence that happens in time that is the true source of joy and creation, but those apprehensions of the timeless, those sudden initiations into silent joy by a wind on a lake, a light shaking on the face of a mountain, that are the real biography of the spirit, its true life, a life which art can only hint at. Again and again, in that first day in Ladakh, as light touched the peak of a mountain, as I looked over the side of the road at a stream leaping over its darkly shining rocks, I thought of that painting, of the secret knowledge of the spirit it so delicately celebrates, of the tender silence that illumines it. I had been Ascanius or the stag so long, trapped in the turbulence of my life; now the bus was carrying me slowly into the background of the painting, away from the ruined classical temple, the Oxford walks and Italian trees, all the complex civilised ironies and melancholies of Europe, towards the silence of the lake, the white light on the mountain, the happiness of those solitary sails opening so completely to the wind bodying them that they seem only slightly heavier than the wind itself.

I was asleep; I awoke; on the bare flank of the hill opposite there was a mani stone, the first I had ever seen, a large black stone with OM MANI PADME HUM ('Praise to the Jewel at the heart of the Lotus') vivid in dark bold stripes on its surface. It was early afternoon, and the rock shone from its bed of dust and wind-swept grass.

As I watched them in that light, the syllables of the sacred mantra of Tibet, the mantra of Avalokiteshvara, the Bodhisatva of Compassion, seemed to become alive, as if the rock itself had written them, as if that great mountain silence of purple and brown rock, of stream and scrub and long wastes of shining sand had formed them slowly over millennia and was now speaking them from the rock, and would go on speaking them steadily without interruption, as long as the rock lasted. The whole landscape, or so it now seemed, was speaking that mantra; the small fast yellow stream was speaking it, and the wind, and the flurries of dust the wind raised from the grass, and the yellow flowers scattered in the grass, and the three hawks circling silently above the rock, and the bus also was speaking it in its wheezing over that winding road. Everything in that world was linked by the sound of the mantra; everything in that world was created from the sound of the mantra. Suddenly, even the long line of mountains ringing us seemed as transparent as breath.

16

The farm I saw later. It was twilight and for an hour already a darkening gold light had suffused everything, made everything, the small twisting streams, the mountains with their fantastical balconies and surreal staircases of scrub and colour, even the filthy windows of the bus, tremble and burn. I had seen a wild horse running alone down the whole length of mountain stream, kicking up the white dust behind it, flinging back its head and neighing in the pure frenzy of its solitude, a small mountain horse, tough as the Ladakhis are tough, tough and hard-limbed and very fast; I had seen a man on the other side of the river, in a brown robe that was almost the colour of the wall of rock he was walking down, walking slowly with a donkey, as if he had always been walking and had another eternity to reach the place he was going to, gathered up completely into the rhythm of the silence that contained, ennobled, and shielded him. And now the bus stopped. We were only an hour away from Kargil, where we would spend the night; the driver wanted to make himself some tea; everyone wanted to get out and stretch and stand quietly in that glowing waste of rock and evening. A small mountain farm faced us, from the far side of the valley. There was one stone house, stones clumsily stacked on each other, with three gashes for windows; there were three horses standing motionless in pools of dark gold light, their manes fretted by the wind; there was a thin burning crescent of wheat above and around the house. I write 'wheat', but there is no word for that gold brilliance; all the power of the landscape, of the running streams and rock and silence, seemed for that moment to concentrate itself and break into flame in that wheat burning against the dark mountain. So much of what I came to experience of Ladakh was contained in that image of the wheat of the isolated farm burning in the last light — so much of what it held for me of courage and joy and revelation — that even now when I think of Ladakh the first thing I see in my mind is that farm, those windows, those horses, that crescent of wild gold.

These too are Ladakh for me: the spray of gentians I saw between two ear-shaped rocks; the yellow Iceland poppies glimpsed in a field at the top of Zoji-La; the one purple orchid blossoming in the dirt by the side of the road; the small brilliant daisies covering the rocks of the descent from Zoji-La; the large rose-bush, alone and dancing in the wind, its flowers alive in the light like large red butterflies, that I saw standing on a small hill before the bus entered Kargil.

Kargil is the second most important town in Ladakh after Leh. You have to stay the night there when you go up to Leh on the bus; it is the penance, the mortification, for so much wonder. The walls of my hotel room looked as if excrement had been smeared over them; there was no bed, just one tattered mattress in a corner, dancing with fleas. There were three posters in the room, all with a corner torn off or some unintelligible writing scrawled over them. One was Mohammed Ali grinning; one was Mohammed Ali waving his fists in the face of the photographer; one was Mohammed Ali looking very grand and grim in a black suit, with the Ka'aba tucked away in the right hand corner, surrounded by Arabic lettering and small pictures of oil derricks. Kargil is Muslim, and everywhere there are pictures of the Muslim Boxer Prophet. A Ladakhi Buddhist friend said to me later that whenever he hated anyone he prayed that they would be reborn in Kargil.

I was too excited to sleep, even if I could have done so on that mattress. I roamed the streets, just missing being run over by car after car without lights; I walked to the end of the town and beyond into a few moonlit fields, to look longingly into the valleys we would reach in the bus tomorrow; and I bought a bottle of gin from the fat German lady who had clutched my knee all day (she had eight bottles of gin in her trunk, and three translations of the Dhammapada), and spent the night and morning under the bare swinging light-bulb in my room, reading De Vigne's *Travels in Kashmir and Ladakh*:

'The merchandise that passes from Yarkund, via Ladakh to Hindustan, consists of gold, in ducats from Russia, in old coins from Bokhara, and a small quantity also finds its way from Bultistan; silver, silks, and porcelain from China; musks, furs . . . From Hindustan to Yarkund are carried madder, pearls, English calicoes, Dacca muslins, chintzes, kimbals or golden cloths of Benares, shields, indigos, henna, spices, sugar, taba-shir . . .'

I would never see the markets of Leh full of kimbals, indigo, calicoes and tabashir; I was half a century late. It did not matter. Nothing mattered that morning but beginning a new stage in the journey. The bus started out in darkness, the driver singing a slow ghazal under his breath. I asked him what the words meant.

'I lost my beloved, I looked for him everywhere.
I looked for him in the hills, I looked for him by the sea,
I found him at last
In the corner of my own house.'

The first mention of Ladakh seems to have been made by Herodotus, who describes in his history a land of wonderful ants. As they burrowed out homes in the earth they threw up gold. These ants were nearly as big as dogs and even more ferocious, very fast and with a keen sense of smell. It was hard for the Indians who wanted to get the gold. They had to fetch it by day when the ants slept, and carry it away on especially fast horses.

Tibetan nomads who belonged to the Bon religion were the first inhabitants of ancient Ladakh. They wandered about the immense upland plains of the Himalayas with their large flocks of sheep, goats, and yaks, moving on from pasture to pasture as

19

they still do. Some rock carvings that survive show that the nomads chased *kiang* or wild sheep.

There are now three different ethnic groups in Ladakh — Mons, Dards, and Mongols of Tibetan origin. The Mons were the first immigrants. In the Mahabarata there is a reference to Tibetan gold dust that must have been brought as a present by the Khasas or Mons from Tibet. The Mons were Buddhists, and have remained so.

The Dards came from Baltistan. They were more warlike than the Mons and occupied the cultivated areas. The Mons were compelled to accept a lower status. The original nomads, who were of Mongolian-Tibetan origin, did not resist the colonisation of Ladakh by the Mons and the Dards. The last Mongol migration occurred as late as the tenth century A.D.

What happened to all the gold? No one could tell me at Leh. Back in Oxford, I went to look up Ladakh in Thornton's 1854 edition of the *Gazetteer of India*:

'Gold has been found in the sands of the river Shy Yok, but its collection is discouraged by the authorities, apparently for combined motives of policy and superstition. Some Lama predicted that unless the pursuit were discontinued, the harvest would fail; there is also a belief that the gold lying in the soil belongs to local deities, who would inevitably inflict dreadful misfortunes on such as should sacrilegiously seize it.'

On the bus, the German lady was ecstatic. She kept seeing faces in the rock: 'Look, over there . . . that looks like the Cardinal of Munich! I hate him! Such a stupid man! He believes that pre-marital sex is the ultimate sin! Can't you see . . . nose, eyes . . . mouth . . .'

And once, in the pass above Lamayuru, she saw Beethoven, glowering out of the swarming limestone.

'Yes, I promise you! It is Beethoven! The young wild crazy Beethoven! The Beethoven of the early portrait!'

The Hebers, who lived in Ladakh in the early twentieth century, had seen faces in the rock too. 'We constantly noticed

20

fantastic shapes in the rocks on the other side. There was a realistic statue of Judge Cockburn, a certain outline of Cardinal Wolsey.'

The German lady says, 'I suppose you are the rationalistic type! You don't even see shapes in fires!'

'I never see shapes in fires,' I said.

If she sees any more faces she keeps them to herself.

B uddhism first came to Ladakh through India and not Tibet. In fact, Ladakh was Buddhist, of the Hinayana, 'Lesser Vehicle' school for about eight centuries before Tibet was converted.

Buddhism was introduced into Ladakh in the third century B.C. by the missionaries of Asoka, the great Buddhist Emperor of India, whose empire included the whole of non-Tamil India, besides a large portion of Afghanistan and the valleys of Kashmir and Nepal as well. In A.D. 400 the Chinese traveller Fa-Hien observed the use of the prayer wheel and noted that there were two relics of the Buddha in Ladakh — a bowl and a tooth.

Later Ladakh came under the influence of Tibet. Its form of Buddhism became Mahayana, 'Greater Vehicle' Buddhism, Tantric Buddhism.

François had said in Delhi, 'The mountains of Ladakh have been the setting for Buddhist meditation since three centuries before Christ was born.'

A fter Kargil the Frenchman made an almost miraculous recovery. He went on reading Kierkegaard, but he no longer puked at intervals into his plastic bag. Today he looked ten years younger and, although he was reading Kierkegaard, managed to chuckle to himself a great deal.

Near Lamayuru he turned to me and said, 'I am very frightened. I have a very erratic temperament! I am a mathematician, yes, but a very erratic mathematician! Have you read Restif de la Bretonne? No? You should! What is your favourite line in Baudelaire? I have a very erratic and tender temperament! I believe anything! Worse – I want to believe everything! I want to believe in flying lamas, levitation, the raising of the dead, everything! It is a great problem, this desire to believe everything. Perhaps I should never have come. Perhaps I should have gone walking in the Hindu Kush. Perhaps I should have stayed back in Paris and done maths problems all summer. You like maths? It is so cooling.

'I would like to levitate. Not just a few inches but right to the top of the room. I'd like to go and visit my mother in Provence. She is sitting by the window sewing. She has her usual sour, resigned expression. I go up to her. I say Hello Maman, I hope you are well, I hope the neighbours are as awful as usual, I hope your shares are still rising. And then we sit on her sofa and then . . without any warning . . . I float to the ceiling. I float very softly. Maman starts screaming. She clutches her heart. At last, after so many years of saying she is suffering from a bad heart, she has a real heart attack.'

I t is good that the journey is so slow and awkward; you lose, you have to, all sense of time and urgency, all calculation, all sense of past or future. You may get to Leh after two days; you may get there in the afternoon or late at night; you may not get there for three days or even longer if the bus you are on breaks down and the buses following it are full, as they may well be. You do not know when you will get to Leh, and after a while you do not even know whether Leh itself exists; the existence of a fertile valley and a town in all this wilderness of rock is so improbable that Leh seems as mythical as the Golconda of Marco Polo, an imaginary city you will spend the rest of your life travelling towards, in this bus, with the German woman and the Frenchman. And that Leh should be mythical does not disappoint you. I had been on this journey to Leh for several years now, I realised, and I still was not ready or anxious to get there; it had been the journey that was Leh's gift to me, even if Leh itself turned out to be a fiction of De Vigne and Moorcroft and Indian gazetteers, malicious on local rot-gut and exile.

The journey itself is a rite of initiation. You pass from the lush green valley of Kashmir up the long winding granite sides of the mountains to Zoji-La; then, at the heart of the Kara-korams, you pass again through ring after ring of mountains, each more spectacular, tortured, brilliantly coloured than the last; then finally, when you are half-frightened and exhausted by the raids so much magnificence makes on your wonder, you move, by slow degrees, into the plateau of central Ladakh, edged and cradled by the Indus, and from that into the long, fertile valley of Leh and its surrounding villages and mona-steries. It is an education in wilderness, this journey, a progress into a bareness that at the last moment breaks into the flame of wheat-fields and prayer flags; it is the penetration of an enor-mous Mandala with Kashmir for its lush and dangerous sur-round, the Karakorams for its walls, and Leh and its long valley for its inner room, the room where the creator of the vision of his own inner making is seated in meditation and where the Gods can appear, shielded from cynical eyes, by walls of burning rock and snow.

I n Leh, at last.
The Frenchman: 'If night has fallen it is for a purpose. If we are not allowed to see Leh it is for a purpose.'

I had been wondering for two days what the first glimpse of Leh would be like, and now — darkness, a few lights, a large hill with, I could see, dimly, a 'castle' on it . . . the main street . . . low dark shops . . . turning left down a hill . . .

And we get out of the bus, raddled by the journey. It is nine o'clock. No one has any idea where they will sleep. The town is so dark that no one can see anything. The only sound is the large ugly throb of a generator.

Then an arm grabs me in the confusion. I see now, about four inches from my face, the grinning, slightly pitted face of a young Muslim.

'Welcome, dear sir. Many welcomes. Here am I. Here you are. This is Leh. My name is Ahmed. I am very trustable. I am coming from the best hotel. It is near river. It is quiet. Very good people, dear sir, best people. Only thirty rupees one night. Very good room. All glass room, sir. View of mountains. Bath nearby.'

I accept. He slings my filthy plastic case on his shoulders and starts off down the hill to the river. 'You like a cigarette, sir?' Ahmed says, sad when I show him by my answer I haven't got any.

Leh will have to wait until the morning. As we are walking to the riverbank to the hotel, an old Ladakhi woman crosses our path. Her hair is very white in the moonlight. She has no teeth. She looks into my eyes and smiles. For the first time in Ladakh I hear the word 'Jullay', that will be the refrain of every day and nearly every meeting. It means 'Hello', 'Welcome', 'God bless'.

2

An Exploration

Ahmed knows everything about Leh. He is in league with every dealer, Kashmiri shawl-seller, mok-mok maker, restaurateur, tourist guide, defrocked lama, lamp-fixed, out-of-work folk singer, in town. He grins, 'Sir, I am not boasting, dear sir. But you name it, I am knowing it very fully. This is truth, sir.

'You see, dear sir, I am a Muslim boy from Delhi. I am working here in summer. Tourist season. I have to make much money. Old father, old mother, sir. Very old. And I only son. So I must know everything, no?'

He grins again and fingers my sleeping-bag. 'How much you want for this?' I say I need my sleeping-bag, and he looks sad.

'Since you know everything, Ahmed, tell me where to eat.'

Leh is no longer imaginary.

'Breakfast? Best place Pamposh. Muslim brothers. To left of main street, wooden. Eggs, chapatis, coffee. All Europeans are going there. Some of them very funny people, sir. You cannot say girl or boy. Lunch? All are going to Tibetan Restaurant. Down street from Pamposh. On the corner. Very good woman, very pretty lady, sir. I am not liking Tibetan food. It is making me sick, sir, but you will like. Dinner? I am always saying, go to Dreamland. It is next to generator. It is good. Tibetan and Western. Young Tibetan girl, very pretty, with her brother, very thin. Same food — mok-mok, Lhasa chow-mein. I am sick for this food. But you are Christian, you will like.'

Pamposh is hardly a café at all. It is a shack, a rickety wooden shack, open on all three sides to the street. It has coffee so bad, so old, and so thin, you have to be a caffeine addict to get through it at all. It has an owner so absent-minded that he poured salt into my coffee instead of sugar. It is where All Leh goes, as Ahmed said, toute la cirque of bandana Italians, Australian sannyasins . . . On one wall there is President Carter, three smiling portraits of Mohammed Ali (again!), two posters of Donna Summers (one moustached), and Botticelli's 'Birth of Venus' (no moustache); on the other are a fat Indian male film-star in gold lamé trousers walking in the gardens of the Taj Mahal, Indira Gandhi as Mother Kali, Avalokiteshvara with his thousand orange, red, and purple arms, Evel Knievel leaping through a hoop of flame in Colorado on his super-bike, and Cranach's portrait of Martin Luther with 'Io t'amo Martino', signed Giovanni Maria Claudio e Pietro in the corner.

Crazy though this debris of images is, I feel at home, amused, and exhilarated. A German lorry-driver is haranguing me about Rimbaud; a Kashmiri salesman is trying to squeeze the knee of the Italian girl with the red bandana, to my left; in the corner an old, dignified Ladakhi is sipping his tea noisily; a young girl, slightly pockmarked, in a dark woollen skirt and peaked black hat, stares in at us all from the street, intently, yet without malice or fear. Ahmed had said, 'Go to Pamposh, my dear sir, and everything you will see. You will see girls. You will see Kashmiris. You will see lamas. You will see foreigners. You will hear all languages, dear sir. Every smell of the city you will smell. Everything I am telling you you will see.'

'What do you think of Leh?' the Italian girl asked me. 'I am fascinated . . .'

'You are fascinated. How stupid! There is nothing left in Leh. Look at the Palace. It is ruined. Look at the Gompa. It is modern. Look at the main street. It is the only street. It is ugly. Look at the shops. What do they have? In the Tibetan shops everything is fake; in the Kashmiri shops everything is fake and crazily expensive. Leh is a place where foreigners get fleeced, that's all.'

She stared in front of her bitterly. 'Tomorrow I am going back to Goa. At least there's sea there.'

She was wrong about Leh. It is true that it is no longer the exotic market town with Chinese, Yarkandi, Tibetan and Russian traders that De Vigne described; it is true that there is only one main street with an ugly inefficient post office, an ugly Cultural Academy, and two rows of ugly tumbledown over-expensive under-stocked shops; and there is no graceful order to the streets or houses, that run into each other haphazardly. Yet Leh does have charm.

There is nothing whatever to do. That is Leh's charm. There is a cinema, but it is down the hill, about a mile away, and shows nothing worth seeing; there is a Gompa, but once you've walked round it, making all the prayer-cylinders round its walls shake and whirr, you've seen it — there are no ancient frescoes, no old sculptures to be seen inside; there is a Cultural Academy but nothing happens at it, no Dance Meetings, no Evenings of Ladakhi Songs, no displays of tankas, or half-learned talks on Buddhas and Bodhisatvas; there is a market in the evening of fruit and vegetables along the main street, and another market all day in a side street, where bells and tankas and turquoises are sold, along with cheap sweaters and sleeping-bags and pots and calendars, but neither are so arresting and colourful that you long to return to them. There is nothing to do but to slow down, relax, laze, to become one vast transparent eye.

The solidest joy of Leh is seeing its Palace from every angle and in every light; from below, as it stands in the full dazzle of the morning sun; from the side, in the afternoon from the roof of my hotel, as one of its sheer sides ignites slowly in the dusk; from behind, on the road to Leh from Sankar, as it rears, ghostly in the moonlight, hardly distinguishable from the massy dark rock it is built on. You are haggling for vegetables in the market at sundown, and suddenly you look up and see the last sun catch the top of one of its balconies; you are talking to a friend in the evening, walking up the main street, and as you talk you see that the moon has risen above the palace, and seems to be wearing it like a vast earring; you turn a corner of one of Leh's innumerable labyrinthine streets and for a moment a whole flank of the palace stands in front of you, bare and stark as the mountains that surround it. The Queen and her family now live in the smaller palace at Stok, ten miles away; the Palace of Leh is empty and crumbling. When you walk through its large vacant rooms, fat tame mice come out of the dark corners to be fed.

E very morning I pass the slaughterers at work under the bridge.

There are four young slaughterers, young Muslim Ladakhis with red faces and big arms, and two older ones, one of whom wears a filthy red bandana and has only one eye. They whistle, and chatter, and sing. This morning the youngest slaughterer was singing a ghazal — a slow, melancholy lovesong. I remembered some years back rowing on the lake of Pokhara in Nepal with a young Iranian. He had been tortured under the Shah, kept in a room where he could not stand up, had horsehairs shoved up his penis. He stooped, had terrible insomnia. And he sang as beautifully as the young slaughterer. The slaughterer and the tortured boy sang together in the morning.

The Iranian had sung me a ghazal by Rumi:

'Sufi, why are you standing before the door?
What are you looking for?
I am looking, my friend,
For what is impossible to find:
I am looking for a man.'

And he had wept as he sang.

The odour of blood is in everything. In the flowers by the

river, in the current of the river, in the wind blowing down-river from the mountains.

The sheep wait huddled by a small stone shack on the other side of the bridge. They make no noise. They look at their killers with hollow eyes. They hardly even twitch as their throats are cut.

There are always spectators. There is an old woman or two; a few ragged children; an old man smoking and contemplating, whirring his prayer wheel round and round.

'Every object in the light of Ladakh seems to have something infinite behind it; every object, even the most humble, seems to abide in its real place.'

François's words and his voice came back to me as I walked, in the early evening light, to the stupa at the edge of town and sat down in its warm shadow. A stupa is a building of plaster and brick that has four stages: a large cubic foundation, rising diminishing cubes that support a wide, empty, bun-like middle portion, which supports in its turn a long spire that comes to a point in the symbol of a crescent moon cradling a sun. It is a building in which relics are kept, the relics of saints or kings or very holy teachers, and each stage of the building symbolises a different state of consciousness. All over Ladakh, there are stupas of every shape and size; in mountain passes, on the long slopes up to monasteries, along the banks of rivers, at the entrance to secluded villages, sometimes with small shrines attached to them, as in the stupa at the entrance to Sankar, where a few badly painted smiling Bodhisatvas raise their hands in blessing. Wherever you walk in the lower parts of this landscape, you are never far from the softly rising brick-red spire of the stupa, from the flash of its crescent moon and sun in the light, from the eye, the Bindu, at the centre of that union of sun and moon, that is an ancient symbol of Universal Consciousness, of the Awareness that is Nirvana. Wherever you walk, you are reminded, in the carefully calculated shape of the stupa, of the different stages of illumination that end in the experience of liberation; each of its different parts is dedicated to a different element, a different Buddha, a different ecstasy. It is a simple building, but its shape represents a whole philosophy, *is* that philosophy in one of its purest statements, crumbling white plaster and brick, against rock and sky.

The stupa at the edge of Leh stands separately on a small raised hill. I noticed as I walked up to it, seeing it against the wide spread of the Karakorams, that its shape was a meditation on the wild forms of the mountains behind it. The stupa echoes the mountains and the mountains are stupas also. Everything in this world is linked.

Everything is dark by ten. Leh is given over to the night, vast, cloudless, soaked in moonlight and starlight, the Milky Way lustrous in this high mountain air, each cluster of stars, each swirling nebula, precise and dazzling . . .

You walk into the main street and look up at the palace, that by day looks so dilapidated. At first you can hardly tell it from the rock it stands on. Then slowly its walls emerge; night gives them back some of their old grandeur. Starlight salts them brightly . . .

Hardly anyone in the street. A few Kashmiris sitting under an extinguished street-lamp talking in low voices and smoking. An old woman who passes and stares at you, her face mysterious and sibylline in that light, until she smiles. A dog you cannot see, that brushes past you suddenly and barks in fear.

There is one café that is always the last to close. It is at the beginning of the main street. At the time I go there, usually about nine, there is no one else there except the young Sikh who is sitting on a table in his dirty yellow turban, making samosas for the next day. We are friends. He has taught me how to make samosas, how to mould the batter, how to fill them with vegetables. But I am ashamed of my slowness, my lack of expertise. He can sit and talk and laugh and his hands move instinctively, shaping, filling, conjuring samosa after samosa out of the chipped white bowls of batter and vegetable . . . I have to watch all my movements. My samosas are lumpy. He laughs at me gently.

Sometimes when I come back to Leh late I pass him sitting alone in the window of his café, making samosas by lamplight. His fine, sad face shines in the yellow light; his hands, pianist's hands, move with an almost magical delicacy and precision . . . He looks up, calls me in, and we talk. An hour or two later, I walk back to my hotel. I can never sleep at once; my mind is too full to read. I lie on the roof and look up at the night, breathing in its mist of stars.

You see and hear water everywhere in Leh. Under all talk, every silence, all slow, sensuous watching runs the murmur and flash of water. Every street glitters with snow-water, racing from the mountains into the ragged stone channels that lead it though the town into the fields below.

I wake up and walk to town. The first thing I see is the morning river, leaping in the light over its smooth rocks. I walk up to Pamposh; water, noisy and brilliant, runs down the hill on both sides of the street. I sit in Pamposh and look out at the old lama passing, or the woman sitting on the corner selling cabbages, or a young Kashmiri squatting outside his shop and singing, and in everything I see there is a flash of running water. I walk in the late afternoon to the Tibetan Restaurant, just down the street from Pamposh, and wait for friends, and try to write; every time I look out of its wooden windows on to the street I see the small turbulent stream outside with a child dabbling in it, or a dog wading through it, or two old Muslims sitting by it under a tree and smoking their evening hookah. And when at night I am walking, alone or with friends, through Leh, up the small streets behind and round the main street, or outside to Sankar or Changspa, the villages that are only a few hundred yards away, it is always to the noise of water, shaking in moonlight and starlight, coursing in untidy channels through darkening corn, between moon-washed poplars and willows, bringing a flickering life to paths lined by shrines and small stupas that in the moonlight seem hardly more solid than the stream that runs by them.

Surrounded by so much water, the mind itself becomes water, hindered by nothing, abandoned, happy.

On the way to Stok, the village ten miles outside Leh, there is a suspension bridge that spans the Indus. From the distance, it looks like a circus tent, it is so covered with prayer flags of every colour. I am sitting on the seat next to the driver, a young Ladakhi, and I ask him, 'Why are there so many prayer flags?' He looks at me as if I am mad. 'If there were no prayer flags, the river would get angry.' Then he adds, 'The bridge is nearly at the middle of the valley. The wind there is very strong. The prayers can be carried down the wind on the back of the river all over this country.' It is such a festive and exuberant gesture, covering the steel lines of the bridge with scarves and mantras and holy dragons, that I want to sing. As the bus crosses the bridge, the prayer flags flap against it. The driver turns to me and smiles. 'Every time I am crossing this bridge I am saying my prayers. It is holy, this bridge.' How old is the bridge? He does not know. It is as if it had always been there — like the piles of stones in the mountains, like the stupas, like the small wayside shrines. The spirit of Ladakh has changed it into a shrine, an object of worship! Does the bridge have its guardian Buddha? The driver smiled and did not answer.

I have come to Stok to see the Palace of the Rani of Stok, but as soon as I am standing in front of it I do not want to go in. To be out here, in this light, with all the day before me, and to go into those small rooms . . . I want to walk, to walk up the trail in the mountains, to be alone with the mountains and the summer streams in the valley.

I walked all day higher and higher into the mountains. It is strange no longer to be looking at them, across the shifting lights of the valley, against the brilliant emptiness of the sky, but to be walking in them, at last, surrounded by them, travelling their inner paths. The rocks on the sides of the paths are sprinkled with small blue flowers; a fierce wild green grass grows between the boulders; with every quarter of an hour the heat increases and the rocks change, growing more and more fantastical, wings of cathedrals, falling into the river below, large fluted columns, like the hermit perches of Cappadocia, with golden moss spilling over from their height . . . and yet it is not the rocks and their dazzling forms that move me most; it is the signs everywhere, in this wilderness, of human companionship. Two men pass me on the path with donkeys laden with brushwood; they smile at me broadly and pass on. They have been working high in the mountains, getting wood for winter from the small tough bushes that grow in the ravines just below the tree-line. Everywhere along the track there are mantra-stones, stones with the letters OM MANI PADME HUM carved on them, breathing their sacred words silently between rocks, or at the side of a stream, or in a bed of flower-sprinkled moss. There are latos, shrines to the spirits of the rock and air, with dzo horns and bones in large whitening piles on them, shrines to the gods of this landscape, that are older than the Buddhist Gods but have been reconciled to Buddhism, Gods of tempest and avalanche, Gods of the streams that carry wealth to the valley. There are prayer flags, lonely, ragged but enduring, high on pinnacles of rock above me; they flap in the wind, breathing everywhere the words of the Buddha. This wilderness of rock and light has not been tamed; it remains exalted, and sometimes frightening. But it does not have the inhuman solitariness of Antarctica or the Sahara; everywhere there are small marks of human love and prayer. Resting on the top of a mountain pass, I found that the rock I was sitting on was ringed by white stones, heaped there by travellers over many years; walking on and on into the highest part of the pass, I found, just as I was too tired to go any further, that there was a deserted shepherd's hut, with its roof torn off by the wind, and a small

35

rose-bush growing in the shelter of one of its walls. I sat in it and ate my bread and cheese. On the wall the shepherd had written with charcoal from the fire, OM, just the one letter, again and again. And under each letter, he had sketched a rough Buddha's face.

I returned to Stok the next day from Leh. That night I had a dream of the shepherd's hut. Ananda was in the dream, and François, and a friend from Oxford who had been killed a year before in an accident, and we were all sitting in the hut, laughing and eating. My dead friend started to dance, a dance I had never seen before, very slow, with his eyes closed, and some mountain flowers in his hand. 'What are you dancing?' I asked him. He looked at me and smiled and said nothing. I asked him again, 'What are you dancing?' and again he smiled at me and said nothing. But the second time he came over to where I was sitting, with an empty plate in front of me, and from one of his sleeves took an apple and put it there.

The driver said, 'You are looking happy this morning.'

I told him my dream.

He thought for a moment and then said, 'This is a very good dream. If I had had that dream I would be happy. Sometimes in Ladakh we say that when a dead friend comes to you in a dream he is bringing you news of a new happiness, a different life.'

'What do you think the apple means?'

'How should I know?' he smiled lazily. 'I am not a priest. It is good whatever it is. That much I know.'

'Did you dream last night?'

'I dreamt that my wife had another child. A daughter. I have five children already. It was not a good dream.'

Then he said, as the bus came into Stok, 'Where will you walk today?'

'I want to walk up to the pass that leads down to Spituk.'

'It is a long way, but if you walk well you can get there. But you should take someone. Why don't you take my brother Wangchuk? He knows all the paths!'

36

And so I took Wangchuk, and for that day he was my companion. I still tired easily at that height, and he was patient with me, looking at me often to see if I was tiring, and sitting down first on a rock on a patch of moss, tactfully. That was gentle of him — not to mock me for my European lack of fitness but to sit first and save my face. He carried a bag of tsampa with him, and at noon, when we reached the shepherd's hut, he divided it with me equally. Tsampa is ground cooked barley. I offered to pay him for my share. He would not hear of it. We ate in the warm shadows of the hut. Every time I looked up he was looking at me, with his deep intent eyes, crouched like a large kind animal in the corner. His eyes had no judgment in them; they were as deep and still as a deer's.

After our frugal lunch he said, 'You must visit my uncle's family. They live up here all summer because there is good grazing for the animals.'

'No one could live this far up.' ·

He shrugged his shoulders. 'You will see.'

We walked for an hour, up a slow winding ravine, lined with wind-gnarled rose-bushes and a small stream. Before us, the sheer and jagged face of Kangri loomed in the afternoon sun, entirely covered with snow, and dazzling. The air at that height was very thin and so full of light that I felt dissolved in it, a moving body of light, with only my breathing and the exhausted buzz in my head to tell me I was human. All around us the rocks were in flower, and seemed at moments so transparent I felt I could put my hands through them. Wangchuk walked in front of me singing, turning round from time to time to see that I was safe. A large dzo walked dazedly past us, brushing against us both peacefully with its vast body. In that light and silence, with the rocks burning softly around me, and Wangchuk's rough strong voice ringing off the rocks around me, I lost all sense of time or urgency; I felt bare to Ladakh at last, present at last in that world without fear or armour.

'What song are you singing?' I asked Wangchuk.

'I am not singing any song,' he said. 'I am just singing.'

Wangchuk pointed silently, and there two hundred yards above us, on a crescent of high green grass, was the hut. It was long and squat, made from rough boulders, with only a canvas covering for a roof. A woman was sitting in the doorway; her two daughters were standing on either side of her, looking down at us. When they realised that it was Wangchuk their cousin who was visiting them they started to shout and jump up and down.

'Wangchuk! Wangchuk!'

Wangchuk pretended to take no notice, but he was smiling. How beautiful and poignant a human name sounded in all that silence!

'Wangchuk! Wangchuk!'

The mother was standing in the doorway now, shading her eyes from the sun and calling down to us.

'She is saying', Wangchuk said, 'that she will be very angry with us if we do not stay for some tea with her.'

I knew this meant that we should not cross the pass before nightfall, and so would have to return to Stok, but I did not mind.

We sat in the shadow of the hut and drank tea, and Wangchuk's aunt gave us tsampa and old biscuits that tasted of soda and cardboard, and two wrinkled sweet apples, and she and Wangchuk talked. And then one of her daughters danced for us.

'Dolma is the best dancer in my family,' Wangchuk said.

Dolma said she would not dance for us in front of the house; we would have to come into the field by the side of the small courtyard in which we were sitting. There, with Kangri and a cloudless sky behind her, Dolma danced. She was shy at first, shy and fumbling; several times she stopped altogether, hiding her face behind her sleeves, but Wangchuk spoke to her gently and she went on; slowly, the dazzle of the snow behind her, the great swathes of warm and lengthening light on the grass around her, possessed her and she danced wildly, throwing her head back and laughing and shouting and clapping her hands, her bare feet flashing on the grass. I remembered my dream; but her dancing was more abandoned than the dancing in my dream. As she danced, I saw the mountain behind her go gold, turn in that late light, for a moment, into a great heap of corn.

Wangchuk and I did not go back to Stok that night. We stayed in the hut of his uncle, sleeping with all the others in a pile by a small dung fire.

Everyone was already up when I awoke. Wangchuk and the two little girls were sitting around me, watching me. As soon as I was awake, Wangchuk made some tea and brought it to me.

'You'll need this,' he said. 'It is a cold day.'

Stumbling to the door of the hut, I saw what he meant. The hut was surrounded by the thickest mist I have ever seen — a silent sea of mist that blocked out everything, every peak, every valley. The mist had eaten even the small courtyard to the side of the hut.

'How long do these mists last?'

'Sometimes three hours. Sometimes three days. Who can say?'

It didn't matter. It was good to be there. We sat in the hut all morning. The two girls danced for us again, more quietly this time, a slow Ladakhi dance, and when they had finished came and sat by us and leant against us and slept. Wangchuk took Dolma into his arms and rocked her like a mother.

At about twelve, the mist retreated, leaving everything fresh in its wake. The sky and the rocks shone; the green of the short lush grass around the hut glowed deeply; the great white knife of Kangri turned dangerously in the new light. It was almost frightening, the intensity of this new world that the mist had been preparing, and the first time I saw it, from the door of the hut, I tottered slightly.

Wangchuk stood by me. 'When the mists go, the mountains are young again,' he said. 'Everything is young again.'

Then he said, 'This good weather will not last long. If you want to climb to the top of the pass, we had better start now.'

We climbed steadily up a steep smooth flank of mountain. Wangchuk was right: the weather did change. Dark threatening clouds massed above us and the air chilled, and the grass around us shivered and darkened.

'It is coming,' Wangchuk said.

'What is coming?'

'Hail is coming.'

No sooner had he said this, than the hail started. Small sharp pieces at first, then larger and wilder. The rocks around us crackled and spat.

'Hurry! Hurry! I know a ledge we can hide under.'

Panting, we ran up the last hundred yards to the top of the pass. There was a small ledge there and we sat under it, pulling Wangchuk's canvas coat over our heads to have some protection. Before us, through long half-parted curtains of rain and hail, we could see the valleys folding down to the great long valley of Ladakh. We were sixteen thousand feet up.

Wangchuk started laughing.

'It is very funny. Here we are and we have to sit under a canvas coat. We have come all this way and we have to sit here like sheep in the cold. It is very funny.'

His laughter was infectious. We laughed together. To be the kings of the mountains, the eagles . . . and to be sitting huddled freezing together under Wangchuk's coat.

When the hail cleared and the sun came out again, we walked slowly down the long stony gorges to Stok. Across nearly every gorge there shone a large rainbow. I counted nine.

'When there is a rainbow in the mountains,' Wangchuk said, 'we say the mountains are dancing. The rainbows are the scarves they wind round their wrists.'

Hans stretched his long thin lop-sided body in the chair and looked at me as he would often look at me, quizzically, suspiciously, but kindly. He was in his late forties, a professor of psychology in New York, a frequent visitor to Ladakh. I'd met his sister Helena at Pamposh's. 'Come and see my brother,' she laughed. 'He's been here every year for three years. He has theories about everything.' I liked him the first time I saw him — his long body, with slightly stooping shoulders, his myopic suspicious intelligent eyes, the thick swath of slightly greying hair that flopped down his forehead.

'I am not a Buddhist,' he said. 'I have never managed to be anything with any conviction. My mother wanted me to be a priest, dreamed of having a son in black talking sublimities from a pulpit, but I disappointed her. I'm not a Buddhist, but being here I have come to love and admire Buddhism. Does that sound strange? Should I just say, "I am an academic voyeur and I am enjoying studying a phenomenon"? Perhaps so.' He laughed shortly.

'My research takes me every day to a new village to interview someone, to talk with a family. And I have seen people of nearly every kind now. I have been to the most remote villages, I have talked with lamas and Westernised Ladakhis and old women and young shepherds. I ask all sorts of questions. It is strange for a cynical psychologist to spend every day with people that seem, as far as I can judge, to have little interest in deceiving or impressing you . . . And it is strange for me too to be among people who for the most part are happy. Don't get me wrong — this is a harsh land, It is hard to get the crops to grow here on the rocky mountainsides, it is hard to survive the solitudes of the winter and the lonely places . . . In Zangskar I met a woman with no teeth, with dugs as long and withered as any Calcutta beggar, who had lost all her children, all her money, and who lived alone and raving in a small hut outside the village . . . But most of these people live simply and unsentimentally, they live with few needs, few prides, few vanities. They are tolerant to their old people, to their children, to each other. You know what they are taught by their priests? They are taught that every living thing has been their mother in a previous incarnation, and so they must respect it as their mother. I have seen very little cruelty. Once I saw a child tormenting a dog. That's about all — in three years.

'Everything is religion here in one way or another. I don't mean that everyone is a mystic. In fact, when I first came here I gave one of my questionnaires to a Ladakhi scholar to translate. He had very high notions and spoke beautiful English. He translated it in a way that my Ladakh guide assured me no Ladakhi would understand. The religion of the Ladakhi people is practical, down-to-earth — it has very little to do with the complex refinements of the lamas. One of the questions I asked in that questionnaire was, "Is it a good thing to have pride?" Everyone answered "No", without fail, and many added that pride was the root of all evil. Nowhere, in any of the replies to any of the questions I asked, was there a suggestion that competition and struggle were central to life, that one man should win out at the expense of another. A boy of ten will tell you seriously that it is wrong to hurt anyone or anything, and that if you do you will pay for it, in one life or another. An old woman who has been a wife and a farmer all her life will say to you, "Everything is empty, everything has only a relative meaning. Why then hurt anyone?" And yet this fear of pride, this absence of any sense of competition, has not made the Ladakhis soft, or inefficient — you have only to look across the valley from this window, at all the fields scraped from the rock, to realise how hard they work . . .

'The Ladakhis are linked together by their faith in their Rinpoches, their head lamas. It is easy to look at this faith and say, it is superstitious, it absolves them from all the responsibilities of thought. But they do believe in the power of their holy men, and not only in a supernatural sense. They will go to the Rinpoche when they are sick, when they have family disputes, when they are arguing over a field — and they will accept his decision, which, in all the cases I've been able to judge, is usually a wise enough one. And this belief gives them peace. It is hard to say "And this belief gives them peace" without being either patronising or sceptical . . . but when you see and feel this peace, this dignity, day after day in the most ordinary situations, in the way in which an old woman will make you tea, in the way she smiles at you from the fields, in the frankness of her answers to your questions . . .' He waved his hands in the air and shrugged his shoulders. 'I do not understand it but I am moved by it.'

We sat in silence. Then Hans said, 'I am aware that whatever "answers" there are going to be, if any, to the strife and terror of our industrial society, are not likely to come from the very different problems of an idyllic rural one, protected for centuries from the modern world. But there is a beauty of life here, and perhaps some people will derive faith in the West from seeing that people *can* live sanely. I love these people. I want to commemorate something I have seen and felt in them. I don't know whether that can help anyone, even myself. I don't know whether it will help them in their fight, either, against a world that threatens their identity, their existence. Perhaps the Ladakhis cannot survive as they are, perhaps they will have to perish as an ancient Buddhist culture and just accept the fragmentations and competitiveness of the modern world they are being propelled into . . .' He looked away sadly.

I went with Hans that afternoon to interview a local boy in a small house in Sankar. The boy was about twelve years old. We sat and listened in a small smoky kitchen. The boy was told a story about a Kashmiri tradesman who sold a cheap shawl to a Ladakhi woman at a very high price and then was asked, 'Which of the two should be punished, the woman or the tradesman?' 'The woman,' the boy replied. 'She should have known better.' Everyone laughed, and the boy surveyed us with the tolerant worldly gaze of the accepted comic. It was not just a sharp answer, it was a very revealing one. 'The Ladakhis are a shrewd, practical people,' Hans said. 'They have to be, living as they do; they value awareness, the kind of awareness that knows when to sow a field, how to conserve water, how to tell the quality of a sheep or a shawl; they are tolerant of weakness, but they call it by its true name.

'For a community like the Ladakhis to survive intact, in the face of so many dangers and disadvantages, no one can be allowed to take themselves too seriously. Not even the monks are exempted from mockery — their pretensions to power and holiness are satirised, sometimes sharply, in the comic interludes of the dances. In Ladakh people are not seen as isolated individuals with rights to self-fulfilment but as living parts of a whole, with responsibilities to that whole, that they must not shirk or enact with too vivid a sense of self-importance.'

Walking back to Leh, Hans went on, 'Ladakhi humour is not merely a product of social exigencies: it is rooted in the practice and philosophy of Buddhism. There is a humour in Buddhism which has too often been ignored by Western writers, prone, like Schopenhauer, to see the Buddha as a kind of world-weary super-sophisticated victim of accidie, and Buddhism as a philosophy of sad negation. In fact, the Buddha lived a very active life, thoroughly involved with his world. The Buddha even made a joke on his deathbed. When one of his disciples came to him and asked how the world should commemorate him after his death, the Buddha, who had always taught the vanity of fame and the Non-Existence of the Self, took two wooden bowls and put them on top of each other, meaning, "To commemorate any man is to heap the emptiness of fame on to the emptiness of selfhood, to pile one emptiness on another." Being omniscient, he would have known that the man would take the shape of the two bowls and make out of it the Buddhist stupa . . .

'Buddhism is, in fact, essentially "comic", in the highest, philosophical, sense. The Buddha taught that all phenomena are, from an "absolute" perspective, non-existent, "empty", that they are all projections of desire, creations of a fictive neurotic Self that can be cured by realising that it does not "exist", that its true nature is "empty", that all mental, emotional and spiritual constructions are false. The nature of all things and all actions is "dukkha" — suffering, or "unsatisfactoriness" — and it is by realising, by awakening to, the emptiness of phenomena, that what the Buddhists call "sunyata", freedom from suffering, can be attained. Freedom from suffering, from *all* suffering, *in this life* is the aim of Buddhist philosophy and practice. The Buddha did not want men to rest in a mournful clarity about the vanity of the world and the futility of all perception; he wanted them to be "awake", to be "buddha" (the word means "awakened" in Sanskrit), to be free from all hopes and fears, from all desires and constructions of desire. Such a vision is in the deepest sense comic because it denies any final significance to individual striving or tragic awareness, any ultimate importance to the agonies and vicissitudes of the Ego.'

'You said you were not a Buddhist, Hans.'

'I am not.'

'You talk like one.'

'Ladakh does that to you. You'll see.'

I have been waiting for Ahmed's omniscient lecture on the Ladakhis, and it has come.

'Very good people, sir. I am not understanding all the Gods, sir. In Muslim religion only one god, Allah. He is everything. In Ladakh too many Buddhas, this Buddha, that Buddha. And the people not knowing which Buddha, sir. They are smiling and praying but not knowing. But good people, sir. I am Muslim, I am saying, "I do not like these people, they are Buddhist," but this is bad, sir, and I am fool. They are good people. They are not cheating like the Kashmiris. They live simple life, sir. What are they eating? Much tea, sir. Very much tea. Tibetan tea. Morning, noon, night. This tea is tea and salt and soda. Very bad. But they are liking very much. Sometimes a little vegetables, sometimes a little meat, sometimes a little soup with noodles, tomatoes and cabbage. Thukpa they are calling it. Always thukpa thukpa thukpa. This is why I am thin, sir, I cannot eat this thukpa, I am having to go to market to eat samosa. Look at this family, sir. They are rich people. They have big house. They have fields. But they are not bad people. They say, "Ahmed is good. He works hard. He must have day free." Sometimes they are greedy, sometimes they are saying, "You must do this. You must get this," but this is not often. When I worked in Delhi everyone shouting, shouting, screaming, Money, money, money. Sometimes the Ladakhis they want money but not so much. They like family, they like talk, they like tea, they like simply sitting, sir, drinking tea and simply sitting. And they are working too, sir. The ground is very strong. Working, working, and then all winter sitting, sitting. And drinking, sir. I am Muslim, I do not drink. But these people are very drinking. They are drinking this chang. All winter drinking, drinking and playing cards. This chang is made of barley, sir. It is white. It is bad. But they are liking very much. When they are drinking, they are singing, singing, singing, and dancing, dancing, dancing. I do not like to sing. I do not like to dance. I am only liking woman and money. I am a poor man, sir, and my woman is in Delhi.'

Ahmed grins at me that evening. 'You are Christian. You are drinking. You are lucky. Next door in evening is best chang place.'

And the next evening I went. And I went nearly every evening I was in Leh — for the room, for the old Tibetan woman, regal and round-faced, who ran it, for the young Tibetans who when drunk would dance and sing the songs of Tibet and Lahul and Spiti, and for the chang itself. You drink it like lemonade, glass after glass, and suddenly . . . But it isn't heavy. It doesn't make you sick.

Sometimes the Ladakhi and Tibetan boys get rowdy. They start to dance in the small, dirty room with its pictures of Bodhisatvas and the Dalai Lama. They put their arms around each other, and sway and curl their arms out and swing their hips in the Ladakhi way. They knock over a table . . . Then the door swings open and the old woman stands there, regal and contemptuous. She raises one hand, like a Chinese Empress. Silence.

Yesterday she asked me to have a drink with her. She told me she was a Tibetan who lived in Dharamsala and came to Ladakh for the summer. She told me she had belonged to a rich aristocratic family in Kham. She said, 'Once we owned four hundred fields and three mountains.' She told me that her brother had been a head Rinpoche and that the Chinese had kept him in a cage and starved him. 'Only last year, after twenty years, did I hear that he was still alive.' She started to cry. 'After twenty years, the Rinpoche is still alive.' Voices came from the room outside: 'Mama, more chang! Now! We're thirsty!' She got up quietly, shrugged her shoulders, poured out some chang from a silver pitcher into a yellow plastic jug, and walked out.

I sit in the kitchen, watching the wife of the owner of the hotel make Tibetan tea in a huge long silver cylinder decorated with dragons and Buddhas. She is telling me it is the best

drink in the world, it is better than thukpa for you, you can
drink it at any time, in the morning, before sleeping, in the
middle of the night; it makes children's cheeks red, you go mad
for it when you are walking in the hills; Ladakhis, especially the
old ones like her mother and father-in-law, drink it all day and
that is why they are healthy and live long and last the long
winters, and the monks drink it all day too and that is why they
are fat and holy. I am nervous. My landlady turns to me. She has
finished. She pours a little into a chipped white cup. 'If you do
not love our tea you cannot love Ladakh.' I take the cup. She is
watching me very carefully. I take it. I like it. It is salty, subtle,
strong, delicious. I ask for another. She claps her hands.

I t is dawn. The muezzin has just been singing. All the dogs of
Leh are barking as they always bark at dawn, different bell-
like barks from the hills, from across the valley, from the river. I
have the 'Glass Room' in the hotel; it looks on to the garden.
The fat, already glowing sunflowers knock against my window
as I open it. The air is so fresh it makes me half-drunk, and my
hand is unsteady finding my shirt.

I sat later that day with the owner of my hotel. He had invited
me to drink Tibetan tea in his garden. We sat on ancient
deckchairs among sunflowers and giant tulips and cornflowers,
and watched the sunset on the peaks, the light moving slowly
from mountain to mountain.
  'When I was a child I was told that the Gods lived in the
mountains. And that if any man stood on the top of one of them
he would die.'
  I told him that I had been in Nepal a few years before, in

47

Pokhara; that I had been told that still the Nepalese government did not allow anyone to climb to the summit of Machepuchare, the 'Fish-tail mountain'.

'It is only a matter of time,' he said. 'Only a matter of time, and money. What can money not buy, my dear sir? When I was young there were many things that money could not buy. Now it can buy you anything, even the top of mountains.'

I said he seemed to be making a lot of money. He brightened up immediately. 'Yes, dear sir, I am getting rich. That makes me happy. I had a new baby last year. A daughter. She has still not been named. We will name her in the winter. The Bakula Rinpoche will choose a name for her and we will have a festival. My hotel is very good. It was my father's house, but he gave it to me when I got married. He is the old man that lives with us, who works in the garden. It is our custom for the father to give up his house when the son gets married.'

I asked him what other work he did. 'I do not work. I am happy. I am working in the drains department. This is no work. I get up at seven, I walk around Leh to see that all the sweepers are sweeping . . . And then I come home. Two hours a day, sometimes less. For five months of the year I run the hotel. But what work do I do? My wife does the work. I look.'

He laughed. He is a thin, handsome man, but weak-faced. He has had an ulcer, he tells me, since childhood. He twists his hands when he talks.

'Many things have changed,' he said. 'We have put in European toilets. I have bought my wife two European dresses. We listen to the English news sometimes. We have radios. There is a Leh radio station. Last year I bought a cassette. Rolling Stones, Bee Gees, Beatles, Hindi film songs. This makes me happy. Three thousand rupees. Expensive. But it makes me happy. Now this year I am going to buy a Sony walk set. Is that how you call it, "walk set"? I want to have a walk set for my job in the mornings. I like tape-recorders. I like trousers. I like foreigners. I like my hotel. I like making money. I am happy.'

But he didn't look happy.

'Can you tell me the names of the mountains?' I asked him. His face changed, and he said in a different, reverent voice, 'Kangri . . . Kangri-La . . . ' the ancient names.

His father, standing in a small patch of wheat at the end of the garden, turned and smiled at us. Namgyal and Rindchen, his two sons, ran round the corner, stood in front of us, giggled and began to sing, 'Baa, baa, black sheep, have you any wool?' rising to a great piping crescendo on 'YESSIR YESSIR TEEBAGSFUL.'

The owner turned to me and said, 'Everything is changing, and who can say whether it is for the good?'

All the mountains are dark now except for the summit of the highest, Kangri-La. It burns for a moment, fiercely, and then goes dark.

T he mother of the owner of my hotel comes into my room sometimes when I am working and sits by me, and watches me read or type.

This morning I awoke to see her looking at me through the window. She had some apples in her hand. She came in with them a moment later, small green apples, on an old silver tray, and waited until I had eaten one.

We sometimes wash our clothes together in the stream at the end of the garden. She beats hers so hard on the rocks that I wonder how they last. When we are washing, she talks.

'I have spent all my life in Leh. When I was young there were traders from Afghanistan and Russia in the market. You should have seen them! Very wild men!

'When I was young every family would send a child to be a Buddhist monk. Now every family wants their child to be a tourist guide. If I could have chosen my life I would have become a nun, a chomo. I would not have been a good chomo. I like to eat and sleep when I want.

'Why do you read so much? It is not good to read so much. And you have too many friends. Friends always want something. I have two friends only.'

I asked her once how old she was and she smiled coquettishly. (Three of her front teeth are missing.) 'How old do you think I am?' 'Twenty-five,' I said. She screamed with laughter. She told everyone, 'The Englishman thinks I am twenty-five.'

One of her grandchildren always sits with her as she works in the field or washes her pots and pans; she cooks her and her husband's meals, which they eat under a tree near the stream.

She sleeps anywhere. I have seen her settle down for the night on two old Indian trunks in the kitchen; I have even seen her asleep in the passage of the main house, in the afternoon, curled up like a great sheepdog.

I asked her once when we were washing by the river, 'Don't you have a special room for sleeping?'

She laughed. 'Sleeping is so boring, why should you have a special room for it?'

Of the children in the family that owns the hotel, Namgyal is the one I like best. There is a sober serious girl in pigtails. There is Wangchuk, eight years old, forever bandaging one of his brothers' cuts, or running errands or washing clothes on the rocks by the river. There is Rindchen, lazy, smiling, with sexy lidded eyes, who does nothing all day but play alone in the mud. But Namgyal, who is four, is the one I love; he is without any morality but self-interest; he screams when he is thwarted, really screams, so that it's hard to imagine how such a vast sound could come from someone so small, and beams, like an actress, when he is given what he wants; he knows exactly how to wheedle, seduce, command, flatter and manipulate. His mother is always kissing him; his grandfather carries him everywhere on his shoulder; his grandmother is always feeding him with apricots or playing with him on the verandah. He lives the life I have always wanted to live — idle, spoiled, imperious, and indulged.

He is aware of my affection and exploits it for what it is worth. He comes and sits at my desk and plays for hours with my typewriter, gazing at the small black letters with a kind of horrified fascination; he rummages in my clothes and books and picks out my knife and scratches the letters of his name with it, over and over again, in the crumbling wall. He watches me read or write through the window from the garden, until I look up, and then he giggles and says, 'I play, yes?' and clambers through the window and starts typing again, sucking the air through his teeth like a self-important bank clerk.

He and Wangchuk come to me most evenings to be taught English songs. They know only a few words of English, but their greatest ambition is to sing a few English songs. I have taught them the first verse of 'Cock Robin' so far. My mother used to sing it to me in the evenings when I was a child and it made me cry. They do not cry because they can't understand a word, and they sing it very badly and cheerfully, and always bring me as 'payment' a bowl of apricots and a sunflower.

In the old days the Ladakhis used to scent the streets by placing sticks of benzoin and juniper at each corner. Perhaps they still do in winter.

All over Western Tibet the hay that has been mown from the fields is piled up on the roofs of houses. It is piled in such a way that its weight comes only on the outside walls, and not on the ceilings of the rooms beneath. In Ladakh you notice that the piles at the edge of the roofs are tidily and regularly made; straw and fodder do not jut beyond the walls of the house, but keep an ordered richness all round. Even piling of straw on roofs is made a thing of beauty and proportion.

Every gompa, every temple, every house has its walls surrounded by a wide barrier of branches and twigs arranged and covered with a layer of earth, usually painted red but occasionally left plain. Often a white, uneven circle is painted on. The circle is the Buddhist symbol for enlightenment.

At this time of year many Ladakhi roofs are bright with drying apricots — circles and squares and lozenges of burning orange. I keep for dark days my glimpses of them from the inside of buses, from the tops of passes, or standing on the walls of a monastery: shouts of wild colour in a wilderness of ochre.

Today I found a spoon in the bazaar for an old friend in Oxford. The spoon is only a long copper handle with a roughly hammered end. All it has for decoration is a linked series of askew triangles indented, unevenly, on the handle. And yet it could be Egyptian or Mayan or Amerindian or Eskimo or the latest invention of an Italian designer; its simplicity is timeless.

I saw a silver trumpet in Spituk. It was coated in massy silver, decorated with dragons and peacocks and grotesque animals (one with the head of a lion, another with the harsh eyes and beak of a King Eagle), and worked in lapis and crystal, amethyst, turquoise, and three kinds of red coral. So much disciplined exuberance and fantasy . . . I held it up against the rock of the mountains and the light of the cloudless sky, and the tails of the lions and the wings of the silver eagles broke into flame.

On the desk as I write this, a pair of antique Ladakhi chopsticks. I bought them for the son of a friend, but when it came to it I could not part with them, and gave him an old bell instead. The chopsticks are small, made of old, scarred, yellowing, thukpa- and mok-mok-stained ivory, fitted into the back of the sheath of a silver dagger. Food and death, pleasure and wariness, happiness and a proper caution . . . a happy dance of opposites and paradoxes. If they were to be used in a Tantric ceremony, the most elaborate symbolism could be woven around them — the knife for cutting the strings of illusion, the chopsticks for eating the food of contemplation. Their handles are of rough silver and on each there is only one ornament — a fan-tailed, fire-breathing dragon, of such power that I expect each time I pick them up to burn my hands.

Helena, Hans and I were talking in Pamposh and Helena said, 'I have been here for three weeks and I have not seen anything ugly in Leh.'

But there is ugliness in Leh. There are the two great rotting green billboards outside the post office; there are the open lavatories in the bus station and along the wall of the Muslim cemetery on the way into town; there are the holes in front of Pamposh's, filled with potato peelings, slops, and newspaper; there are the mangy flea-ridden dogs nosing for food in the gutters; there are the sheep sprawled crumpled and bloody and stinking under the bridge; there are signs of poverty too — the wall eyes, the shaking hands of half-blind, stumbling old women with spectacles stuck together with sellotape, the old men with only a few black teeth left and open ulcers on their shins.

We met again that evening in Dreamland, the one half-good restaurant in town. I told them the three anti-Kashmiri expressions I had found in De Vigne. 'Many fools in a house will defile it, and many Kashmiris in a city will spoil it.' 'If you meet a snake do not put it to death, but do not spare a Kashmiri.' 'Do not admit a Kashmiri to your friendship, or you will hang a hatchet over your doorway.'

Hans laughed. 'Actually,' he said, 'they are not funny. Since 1947 Ladakh has been under the "rule" of the Kashmiris. That is what being part of the state of Jammu and Kashmir amounts to. The Kashmiris have all the power in this country — all the administrative power. Do you know, there isn't one Ladakh minister in the State Government in Srinagar? I could tell you the most hair-raising stories about the corruption, the diversion of funds from Ladakhi enterprises. For a long time the Ladakhis were patient. Many of them believed in the assurances that India made to them of a secure future, a progressive future in the Indian Republic. But nearly all Ladakhis are now angry. Angry at the Kashmiri officials who run almost every aspect of their lives and who have no sympathy for their religion and who think their country is a barren wasteland. Angry, too, that Ladakh is progressing very slowly, that there are few of the properly financed farming and irrigation schemes that are so urgently needed, angry at the lack of modern equipment, at the lack of work, at the Kashmiris who have the money to rent the shops up here for the summer season and fleece the tourists. There have been riots on and off for years, bad riots this year in January, and again in June, and there is a Protest Day scheduled later next month which could well turn violent. Many Ladakhis are secretly and illegally armed. Everyone knows that. Everyone knows too that the Ladakhi Scouts, who are here as part of the Indian Border Force, would not allow their people to be shot at by the Army, and would fight if the Army were called in.'

'The Ladakhis seem so friendly . . . do you really think they would fight?'

'Of course,' Hans said. 'How much passivity can they stand?'

'And could they win?'

'I doubt it. Their only hope is that Central Government will do something about the Kashmiris. And it just might. This is a very sensitive border area, after all. But it is also true that India wants to keep Kashmir sweet, and so might turn a blind eye to what is being done here. No one can know what will happen.'

There had been a power cut. The incessant noise of the powerhouse had suddenly subsided, and the restaurant was being lit with candles by the small Tibetan girl who ran it.

'The Kashmiris have almost totally pushed out Ladakhi as a language in schools,' Hans said. 'They only allow it to be taught up to fifth grade. And very little funds have been directed into keeping up the monasteries, or helping out the Buddhist philosophy school. The Ladakhis have already lost so much . . .'

We walked out of the restaurant and stood in the starlight. 'I hope this people will preserve its identity,' Hans said, 'but it is a Utopian hope. Besides, it is a hope I can afford; I will not have to pay for it.'

The Tibetans are everywhere in Leh. They come up for the brief summer tourist season, from June to September, from places as far away as Darjeeling or Mysore. They pay exorbitant rents for rooms with one bare light-bulb and a poster of Bruce Lee, or sleep in their own tattered tents in fields or by their open-air stalls. A thin Tibetan girl in faded French jeans runs Dreamland, working sixteen hours a day with her even younger brother, who at fourteen or fifteen already has the starved blank look of an opium addict; a chubby Tibetan woman of about forty, whom everyone calls 'Mama', runs 'The Restaurant', a wooden shack in the centre of town where I eat every day. The market, the long straggling open-air market, is almost entirely run by Tibetans, of every kind and age, fat old men and thin young girls learning nervously to smoke, young Casanovas with Brylcreamed hair, American tee-shirts ('I LOVE SNOOPY', 'PRINCETON UNIVERSITY', 'MAKE ME HAPPY'), sneakers, fat Japanese wristwatches and cassettes forever blaring out 'Saturday Night Fever' or the Stones, middle-aged women selling their beads and haggling in high voices at the same time. And they sit all day with their tough, tanned faces behind heaps of silver bells and scrolls, small ivory scent boxes, waving paper flags of Amitabha or Avalokiteshvara, Buddhas of endless light and compassion, blue and green and red jade necklaces, little piles of square and oblong and circular turquoises, haggling and talking and drinking Tibetan tea and appraising the foreigners that pass like punters eyeing horses in the paddock.

I have made friends with one of the Casanovas. He loves Bob Hope and Paul McCartney; he wants to live in California. 'I have heard the girls are very loving and happy' (closing his eyes and moaning gently). He dreams of doing nothing and driving a long red sports car, which he imagines to be the American Way of Life; he says, 'I will be your friend for ever if you teach me how to do disco'; he is handsome, dark, eighteen, but already he has crows-feet, and a strained look when he doesn't think he is being watched. 'I do not like this country . . . why should I like it? There are no films here, there are no good coffee-houses, there are no girls. What can I do with a Ladakhi girl? I can't even hold her hand. Ladakhi girls are not happy' (the moan again). 'I like cities, too, very tall cities . . . What kind of a life is this? I spend all day waiting to cheat some old German woman. Sometimes I wait for two days; three days for the right old German woman to smile at and sell my bells and necklaces to for fifteen times the price I bought them at. I smile a lot. This goes on for three months, and then I have to give the money to my family, to my father who is old, to my mother who is old, to my sister, who is still at school, to my brother, who is in Delhi studying, to my other brother who is in Delhi studying. And I have to spend the winter walking round the villages of Kulu and Spitu — the people are even dirtier than they are here — I have to spend all the winter getting frozen in Kulu trying to cheat the villagers there out of bells and bowls and spoons and turquoise necklaces so I can come and cheat the old German ladies here! No one lives like this in America, do they?'

'The Tibetans were always a tough people,' Hans said; 'they had to be to survive in their high cold world; and now, in exile, they continue to survive and adapt. Why shouldn't the boys wear sneakers and want to go to America? It's a sad dream but to them technology still seems miraculous . . . '

He added, 'But the old Tibet is still here: it is in some of the monks, some of the families; it is in the children, in the mountains, in the old women . . . Ladakh holds fragments of it in its old hand.'

56

'Have you met Loti? You must meet Loti. He is a Tibetan, just younger than you, very clever . . .'
I met Loti the next day. I was bathing in the river with some friends and he was with us. He didn't bathe but sat half-naked on a rock, watching us. He was very thin and intense-looking, and sat with his shoulders hunched forward.

'Look at you,' he said. 'You never get all the way in.'

'But it is so cold,' I said, 'and the water of the river is freezing.'

'Oh you Englishmen,' he said, 'I thought you were supposed to be the bravest people on earth.'

'And what are you doing sitting up there like a Buddha?'

He smiled, and we became friends.

'Come and have supper with me,' he said. 'I'll cook some thukpa and we'll talk! I have to go down to Srinagar tomorrow, so we must talk tonight, or I will not see you again!'

We sat in his small room and smoked a joint together.

'I did two things', he said, 'that shocked my world, and here I am sitting with you smoking a joint and talking to you in your own language. I left the monastery I joined very young, just after I came from Tibet to India. And I had a child by an American girl.'

Loti spoke for dramatic effect, so I looked suitably impressed.

'I was in a monastery in Benares. I liked it. There are many good things about the monastic life. The friendship, the laughter, even the discipline. It is good sometimes to have discipline. But I wanted to leave. I knew I had to leave. If I stayed in the monastery I would never see the world; I would never know what the world was like. I couldn't stay in the monastery. It was too safe for me, do you understand?'

I said I understood very well. I had spent most of my twenties in an Oxford college, after all.

'I didn't tell even my closest friends that I wanted to leave. When I left, I took hardly anything. I left all my clothes, my books, even my writing pen. I wanted no one to know. Even now I do not understand why I did that. Perhaps I was ashamed. For a Tibetan monk to leave his monastery is a very large thing.

'I went to my uncle. He is a lama. He is the head of another monastery. He is a good and kind man and he likes me. "Well," he said, "you have chosen the life of the world. You have chosen Samsara. Do not grieve at yourself for leaving the monastery; live with detachment and understanding." We Tibetans, you see, are a practical people . . .'

He took another long drag of the joint, throwing his head back and closing his eyes. When he opened his eyes again, they were mischievous and glittering.

'Soon after I left the monastery, I met the American girl. Isn't that funny, to leave a monastery and walk into the arms of an American girl? My generation of Tibetans has seen a lot of change, I can tell you.' He laughed drily.

'I met the girl in my village near Dharamsala. She was older than me. At first it was very sexy. I used just to go and spend the night with her. You look surprised . . . We Tibetans, you know, are very free about sex, especially where I come from, Kham . . . There is a tradition, you know, about sleeping with members of other families when the husband is away . . . I used to go on expeditions with friends. One would say, "So-and-so is away! Let us see if his wife will let me in," and he would crawl in through the bedroom window. Nearly always the wife said yes. Sometimes the husband did come back suddenly, of course, but he was very rarely angry. The most anyone got was a beating. Sometimes, of course, the husband had been doing exactly the same thing himself. Once I was with a friend. He went through the window to another friend's wife, and came out beaming. Then he went to the house of yet another friend, who was away. At that friend's window he met the husband of the first woman he had had that night. How we laughed!

'I was telling you about the American girl. After a while I went to my uncle and told him everything. He summoned us both. "Now if you are serious," he said, "you should live together and love each other for life. You should make a vow to each other." And I thought, I like this girl and it would make my mother very happy if I settled down, so why not? So we took a vow and settled down.' Loti took another long drag of the joint. 'But it was very difficult. Oh my god. She never talked. Never. All the time silent, silent. I love to talk. I love to laugh. Every time I made a joke, she would look at me very badly. What is wrong with the Americans? Don't they like to laugh? Then one day she says, "Your friends are useless," and after that when I go out drinking with my friends she comes and collects me, like a dog. None of my friends would dare to come back to my house with me, she was so angry. And she had no friends. That was the worst. She had no friends at all. Only me. So I had to be everything to her. That is very hard, to be everything for someone. And she wanted me to be everything — wonderful lover, wonderful husband, wonderful brother, wonderful friend. She was a Westerner, you see. She thought that if we lived together we would have absolute Nirvana, ecstasy all the time. We Easterners do not think that way. Yes, I wanted to marry her, but I did not expect endless joy; I just wanted to be with her more than with another woman, that is all. She used to scream at me, "You are selfish," "You are not romantic," and I would say, "Yes, I am not romantic but I do love you." Then she would cry and tear her hair! "You are a liar! You hate me!" And then I got mad and would leave the house and go out drinking. And then she made me cook. An Eastern man is not trained, you know. My mother had always done everything, cooking, washing. One day my wife said, "I am not cooking any more." So I had to learn. I learned fast, just to annoy her. I became a very good cook. Delicious. That made her angry. She thought she was going to humiliate me, you see. And I learned how to wash too. Very clean . . . '

Loti looked at me. 'You know what her big trouble was? She was very holy. She wanted to give up everything. Don't drink, don't swear, don't joke, don't have too much sex! Don't, don't, all the time. Some Westerners, you know, are worse than the holiest Rinpoche. They give up everything and are feeling so superior . . . Well, we had a child. She wanted to have a child, and so I said, Why not? We came closer over the child. I cooked for her and looked after her while she was pregnant. Then the child came. I insisted that the child slept with us. In Tibetan families the children always sleep with their parents. This is why they are happy, because they are always feeling close to them the bodies of their parents; they are always feeling the love of their parents. She bought a cot, from an Australian. I said, "What is this?" She said, "This is for the child to sleep in." I said, "No child of mine sleeps in a cot. It sleeps with us." We fought for many weeks but I won . . . And then the child was born, I was happy. Now she had the child to look after, she left me free. I could live again. After a while I said to her, "Why do you not go back to America for a few months, to teach? The child will get better food there. I will be in Ladakh for the summer and it is very high there, very uncomfortable." She cried a lot, but she agreed — I am so happy to be on my own. And I will go now to join her in November in Los Angeles.'

It was very hard to imagine Loti in Los Angeles.

'Does your wife write to you from America?'

'All the time.'

'What does she say?'

'She says she loves me and that she wants to come back here to India, to the Tibetan way of life. She says she hates America, that it is not her country any more. So *concrete*, she says America is. Money, money, money, sex, sex, sex. No spirit, no belief in other things. She says Reagan's face gives her a headache every time she looks at it. She says that her mother is very bossy and is always telling her what to do: the baby must sleep in a cot; the baby must not be breast-fed. She says she has no friends and that I am her only friend . . . '

Loti paused, and looked a little sad.

'Do you love her?' I asked him.

He blushed. 'I do not know. I never think . . .' And then he said, 'You see, we are for life. We took the vow. We are for life. We will stay with each other. Sometimes I think this is attachment, not love. Sometimes I think I am with her only because of her son. But, you know, when she was pregnant she got a little nicer. She used to have my friends in, she didn't mind if we drank, she stopped saying, "You smell disgusting. Your breath is like a distillery." She even drank a little herself. She may become a Tibetan yet. And you know something else — just before she left she said, "I want to see your mother, I want to know your mother." She had never before said anything to me about my family; she never before said she wanted to meet any of my family, and that made me sad. Because I love them and I want my son to grow up to love them. But at last she said it. She said, "I want to know your mother." Now I feel I can love her.'

Then he turned to me: 'I left Tibet when I was two years old. Then I left the monastery. Then I married an American girl. If I do not stay with my family, if I do not love and help my family, I will no longer be a Tibetan, I will have no home anywhere. It is not hard to love my family. They are brave people. They are kind. My mother I love very much. All Tibetans have a very deep bond to their mother. If even a modern Tibetan hears anyone speaking badly of their mother he will be very disgusted. I had a French friend once. He was very interested in Tibetan Buddhism. We have a vow, you know, to love and honour all things as our mother. We believe that all things have been our mothers in one or another incarnation. Well, the Frenchman said he could make every Buddhist vow but that one. "I can love every sentient being", he said, "*except* my mother." I was very shocked.'

L oti had said as we parted, 'Tomorrow I will see to it that you meet Jam Yang. I will be away in Srinagar, but he lives next door. I will tell him about you. If you come here in the evening, he will be here.'

'Who is Jam Yang?'

'He is my best friend. He is a Tibetan. He works for the same tourist agency as I do. He is a drunk. He is a tulku.'

'A tulku?'

'A tulku is an incarnation. At an early age, Jam Yang was "discovered" and sent to live for many years in the monastery of Karmapa in Sikkim. Then he left his monastery as I left mine. For the same reason: he wanted to see the world. But Jam Yang is sadder than I am. I think that the world hurts him more than it hurts me.'

I came back the next evening and Jam Yang was there, waiting for me, a little drunk already, sitting on the floor of his room with three full chang bottles and two carefully rolled joints by his side. There was nothing in the room but a bed and a large photograph of the Dalai Lama on the wall above it. He looked up as I came in, unsmilingly.

'Sit down,' he said. 'I am in a bad mood. I have had a bad day. Some stupid French people. I am going to sit quietly for a while.'

He closed his eyes and sat without stirring for about a quarter of an hour. I watched his sad, thin, handsome face relax slowly and his hands unclench in his lap. He was very different from Loti — darker, more turbulent, more lined. He could not have been more than twenty-six, but he looked older. 'I think that the world hurts him more than it hurts me,' Loti had said. And yet for all the depression in his face, there was something fierce in it also, something imperious, a pride in himself, a determination not to be defeated.

He opened his eyes. 'Loti said he liked you. I think I will like you. I am very direct.'

'I am direct also,' I said. 'I think I will like you too.'

He liked that, and smiled, a sudden, rich, child-like smile. We shook hands.

'I am sorry to have greeted you like that,' he said, 'but I have had a very difficult day. The new group that I have to lead is a very stupid one. I tried to explain to them the theory of reincarnation today. I tried to explain it very simply, very quietly. But they were cold. They said, "It is a very nice idea." At that, I got angry. It is not a *nice* idea, reincarnation. In many ways, it is a very frightening idea. Always to come back and back, always to have to come back until you have resolved the problems of your soul and achieved peace. Is that "nice"? Besides, I told them, it is not an *idea*. I believe it to be a fact. And then I told them a story, a true story, that shut them up.' Jam Yang started to laugh and slap his thighs. 'I know it is bad to say "that shut them up", but sometimes . . .

'Loti told you, I think, that I was once in Karmapa's monastery. Karmapa is a great and very powerful man. I do not want to talk about my days in the monastery, so I hope that you will not ask me about them. Perhaps I should never have left. What am I doing here, a tulku, taking people around Ladakh? And yet it is good money, and I can do something to open people's minds a little, and I must feed my family . . .

'I will tell you the story I told them. I don't think you will have heard it. When I was in Karmapa's monastery, it was announced that Karmapa had had a dream. A dream in which he was shown, in great detail, where a certain high lama was to be reborn. In the dream he was told that the rebirth was to take place in America. In America! We laughed a lot, in the monastery. In America! So the monastery sent three lamas to America. They travelled widely and at last found the place where the tulku was to be found. It was a small town in Arizona, I think. The lamas knocked at the door of the young tulku's house. Imagine it! In a small American town, three lamas knocking on the door of a house! Well, they knocked, and the tulku's mother opened the door. Patiently, and in broken English, they explained why they had come. At first she was very scornful. But when they told her details of her relationship with her husband, that no one else could have known, and a host of other small facts about the birth and upbringing of her son, she was completely convinced. She and her husband sold everything they had and came to live with their son in the monastery of Karmapa outside Gangtok. I knew the boy. He was very beautiful and gentle. He spoke many languages, fluent Tibetan too, which he learnt in a very short time. His mother, however, was a different story. She loved being the tulku's mother and was proud and overbearing with everyone; she thought that having brought such a special being into the world, she too deserved veneration. We did not want to hurt her, and so we were very respectful to her. I used to go to the pictures with her sometimes. She only liked comedies, and used to laugh like a man.'

'And were your group convinced? Did they all want to be converted immediately?'

He laughed. 'Of course not. Several of the men nodded, "Very interesting, very interesting indeed." One of the women said, "Even if her son was a tulku, or however you pronounce it, I still wouldn't have acted like her and given him up to the monks and the cold monastic life." At which I said, I'm afraid, "Madam, if you had been lucky enough to have a tulku for a child, you would also have been wise enough to know what to do with him." Which made her very angry.' Jam Yang laughed. 'I feel better now.'

'You cannot expect people to change their views of things so quickly,' I said.

'I do not expect change,' Jam Yang said. 'I do not expect transformation. And who am I, to know what a person should believe? Who am I, to say what a man should think or do? But I do, I suppose, expect respect. It is difficult to give to people if they do not make a movement of respect towards what you are saying.'

'Then isn't your job painful for you?'

'No. Today was a bad day. Perhaps it was my fault. I wanted the group to go too far, too fast. I didn't explain things properly, perhaps. So many of the groups I have led have been very respectful, fascinated, open. I feel that many Westerners are beginning to want to understand the East, and not just with their minds only, but with their hearts and spirits. It is very hard, I know, for them, and I must be more patient. But there is so much in this country, in its art, in its customs, in its attitudes to life, that can be of help to everyone; there is so much in the Tibetan way that is very strong and beautiful!'

He laughed again. 'I am speaking like a Westerner. I am selling my work to you. If I was a good Buddhist, I would be patient, I would know that people can open, if at all, only in their own time. Let's have a drink.'

We drank and smoked and talked. Jam Yang talked about his family, his son, his wife, all the difficulties he had in bringing up his child. 'I want him to have a modern education,' he said. 'Not like mine. I learnt nothing of any use. But I also do not want him to forget his tradition. I want him to learn the scriptures also. I want him to grow up a good Buddhist. It will be very hard to help him properly.' And he showed me photographs of his wife and son. When he looked at his son, his face melted. 'I miss him so much. I can hardly bear to be away from him for a week. Sometimes when I think the life I am leading is bad and stupid, and that I should never have left the monastery, I think of my son and then I think, "If I had stayed in the monastery I could never have had him, and I would have missed the greatest joy in my life." To bring up a child is a Dharma too, don't you think? It is so hard to do it well.

'Do you have children?' he asked me.

'No.'

'Do you have a wife?'

'No.'

'Then you must be very lonely.'

'I have friends. I have my work.'

'You talk like a monk.'

'I am far from being a monk.'

'What do you believe?' he asked suddenly.

'I do not know.'

'What do you mean?'

'What I say. I am in the dark. I am waiting.'

'What are you waiting for?'

'How can I know? If I knew what I was waiting for, I would make a move towards it.'

'Perhaps being here is your move towards it.'

'I hope so.'

As we parted, he hugged me and said, 'You smile a great deal and you listen well, but I see that somewhere you are sad. I see that nothing has satisfied you . . . '

I started to protest.

'No,' he said, 'nothing has satisfied you, not your work, not your friendships, not all your learning and travelling. And that is good. You are ready to learn something new. Your sadness has made you empty; your sadness has made you open!'

I said, 'Jam Yang, you are kind. But I do not feel open.'

Jam Yang smiled. 'You, my friend, are far more open than you know.'

The next day I took the bus to Rde-Zong. You have to leave the bus about three miles from the monastery. Then you walk up a slow-winding track.

Each gorge I walk through is so full of light that I wonder how the rocks sustain such an intensity of fire. A quiet breeze moves the leaves from green to gold. On the hills that surround me, snow has fallen, and it seems so good, that coldness, a reminder of the huge moon last night, flakes of moon on high hills. And something in this light too has been through an experience of 'moon' and 'cold': I have never seen sunlight so sharp, so precisely delicate, as this. There are so many blues in this one cloudless blue, and each invokes a different memory – of an afternoon in Santorini when I saw dolphins leap off-shore, of evenings in my Indian childhood sitting in the garden and watching the indigo deepen above the hills, of solitary walks in Oxford in the spring. So many blues, and so many distinct, separate radiances composed in this one radiance. Everything that has not been clear in my life falls away from me here; my imagination sheds naturally in this landscape everything that does not call to these rocks, and this light. And I feel that this purity is not my accomplishment, is none of my doing, and so I cannot be proud of it, or possess it. It *is*, as the rocks are, as the two stone-chats are, weaving in light above the stream.

Mind is as spacious as light in this country, as self-delighted, able to touch each object, each crag, each fern, each ragged patch of grass, with joy. It is hard not to shake writing that, not to fear that so much beauty and peace must be taken from me; but I will learn not to tremble. I will try to live this happiness without fear. It will be hard. I find that I am more afraid of this joy than I have ever been of misery. Misery I have learnt how to manage; joy breaks my feet up, takes away my old words and forms. What will be left of me when this light has peeled away all my skins? What words will this light leave me? And yet, even as I think and write those questions, they seem irrelevant. I have no choice but to be alive to this landscape and this light. I have no choice: I must let this light do to my spirit and my words what it has to. Having no choice, I find I walk very fast and lightly, hardly touching the ground at all.

I never get to the monastery. The beauty of the rocks in the afternoon and of the apricot trees and the streams holds me and will not let me leave. Just as it did not matter that evening in the mountains about Stok that Wangchuk and I would not get to the pass, so it does not matter now that I have not seen the monastery. I have felt, since the first days here, that I must leave everything to chance, that I must compose and will nothing in this country. To walk by a stream, watching the pebbles darken in the running water, is enough; to sit under the apricots is enough; to sit in a circle of great red rocks, watching them slowly begin to throb and dance as the silence of my mind deepens, is enough: I do not think I can contain or feel any more. Rde-Zong has given me all it could give. Twice as I walked, I found tears coming to my eyes. They were not my tears: I could not claim them; they were a clean response, that is all, to what was there — the great silent splendour that I was moving in, the sound of the stream, and the voices of the birds calling from rock to rock, ringing clearly off the rocks to rinse my mind of everything but calm.

I met Jam Yang again the next day, for the last time. He was going to Srinagar to join Loti.

'Jam Yang, you're scowling. You're angry again. What did the group do this time?'

He laughed. 'They are making me crazy, this group. I am a very bad Buddhist.'

'What happened?'

'We were in Shey monastery. One of the group started taking photographs of the monks. The monks do not mind. They think, if these people have come so far to be in Ladakh, why shouldn't they take photographs if that gives them pleasure? Besides, many of the monks are like children: they love to be photographed. Well, one of the women in the group got very angry at the man who was taking photographs. She called him an exploiter, a voyeur, a male chauvinist fool, and everything else you can imagine. I took her to one side and said to her, "Don't you think you might be angry because he is doing openly what you are doing secretly?" She looked at me as if I was mad. "What do you mean? I never take photographs." "I mean," I said, "that everyone here, including myself, is hoarding something, storing something of what we see and feel here. We are all, whether we like it or not, taking photographs, inward photographs . . . We are all guilty. As long as we do not perceive things purely we are guilty. And who perceives things purely, as they are, without desire or judgment, except the Enlightened? Only they are never 'taking photographs'; only they do not hoard and appropriate. Only they do not 'possess' in any way." That made her angry. She was angry at the thought that she herself might not already be perfect. "In a way," I went on, "the Kashmiris are better than all of us. They are honest. They are honest about their greed. They do not pretend to be holy or cultured or purified. They want money and they say so. Who is more guilty, the tourist who wants a little illegal tanka, or the Kashmiri who sells it to him or her for an extortionate price?" "Well," she said, "I do not want a tanka. I do not want anything." "Are you sure?" I said. "Only yesterday you said you were looking for something to fill your life. You told me in the bus that you were unhappy and that you were looking for a new direction to your life. Isn't that wanting something? Don't you secretly want Ladakh to give you a Great Experience? Don't you want Ladakh to transform you? Why have you come all this way if you do not want something, and feel that you can find it here? Maybe this wanting is more dangerous, more corrupt, than the simple desire for a bronze Bodhisatva, a piece of old flaking paint . . ." She walked away. She did not want to hear what I was saying.'

'But it is hard to hear what you are saying.'

'Not if you are seeking sincerely. Then you are ruthless with yourself!'

'It takes time to learn that ruthlessness. It takes time to dare that ruthlessness.'

'No, you are wrong. In my experience, it does not "take time". You have it, that sincerity, or you don't. Perhaps it is karmic, I don't know. The majority of people do not want to know that all their ways of knowing and judging are corrupt. And why should they? It is very uncomfortable. It leaves you with no choice but to leap beyond knowledge, beyond judgment . . .'

Jam Yang turned to me. 'You are a writer. You are taking photographs in words all the time. What do you do about that?'

'I try not to lie. I try to keep my lens clean. What more can I do?'

Jam Yang said, 'You must write and I must be a guide. It is our svaha, our nature. Perhaps next time we will be luckier, less condemned to our different vanities. I will talk less and you will carry no big black notebooks, full of illegible writing.'

'What will we do without our vanities?'

'We will drink. We will see visions. We will heal the sick and bring love and calm to the mad and evil. We will play cards all night and not need to sleep. We will walk on water in front of a hundred thousand cameras, to refute all materialists for ever.'

Superintendent of Police (Kashmiri): 'My dear sir, you have come to me to ask for a new visa. This I cannot grant. I am very sad. But I have one plan. It is a very good plan. It is always working, this plan.'

Hans: 'What is it? I would be very grateful.'

'If you write to Delhi, dear sir, for an extension of the visa, they will of course refuse you. But their refusal will take thirty days to get here. This is the beauty, dear sir, of being in Ladakh.'

'Thank you. I am most grateful.'

'I think I deserve something in return for this help. After all, I am being very helpful indeed.'

'But I am a poor American scholar.'

'But you have a tape recorder.'

'But I have sworn to give it to my mother on my return. She is crippled and blind, and very sick.'

'I am very sad about your mother. We Kashmiris are loving our mothers too very much. But, you see, I am also very lonely in Ladakh. I have one radio but that is not enough. I am still lonely; only a tape recorder can save me.'

We were driving in the jeep to Matho, about thirty miles from Leh. Hans reconstructed the conversation with the Superintendent, doing his voice and laughing.

'While we were out yesterday, the Superintendent sent his men over to search my house for the tape recorder, saying to my translator Wangchuk, "All that the Superintendent wants to do is to see the tape recorder." Wangchuk said, "If the Superintendent wants to see the tape recorder he can come to tea at four o'clock. I will personally show it to him." '

Everyone in the jeep laughs.

'What would Ladakh be without the corruption?' says Hans. Rindchen, the driver, says, 'Free.'

As we were standing at the gate of Matho, looking out across the valley, a fat little monk ran up to us and gave us a piece of yellow paper.

'Matho monastery, or Mangkto monastery, actually known as Thubten Shaling Chakor, was established in ancient times by the Sakya scholar Dorje Palsang . . . '

And so on.

But just standing there, looking out across the valley, across the scalloped fields, the patchwork of grass and barley, the poplars and streams of Matho village, gave me a stronger feeling than that text of what a monastery meant. Below me, horses and donkeys grazed together by streams or alone in the sunlight in the middle of thick grass fields; the yellow and red and green prayer flags on the roofs of houses shook in the morning breeze. We were at the heart of the monastery that was the king of these fields, and intercessor between all the worlds of Ladakh, between the fields and the sky, between the streams and the rock, between the earth and the mountains and the air. The monks were chanting in a chapel to our right, and through the open door, from the rich dark of the chapel, I could see two faces, of young Ladakhi monks, lit by sunlight, looking out at us.

'The monasteries', said Hans, 'are still the centre of Ladakhi life. They will all tell you, the monks, that they are poor, that they have no money . . . but the fact remains, they own most of the land, and the farmers still pay a proportion of their produce in tax. That means, of course, that there is usually not much money . . . many things are paid in kind, and it means too that resources aren't very flexible — everything is tied up in land . . . '

Hans smiled. 'The administrators of the monasteries, the Chakkzod, are often die-hard bastards, very conservative and unwilling to try anything new . . . but still, they keep the show going, the butter lamps burning — and look at all the hideous modern painting that is going on. There's a chapel here which I'll show you. The money must come from somewhere.'

We went into the older chapel where the monks were saying their morning prayers. The chapel was dark except for the almost blindingly bright rays of light that came from the high windows; after the bareness of the rocky land-scape, the poplar-silvers and ochres of the rock, the dark blaze of colour inside was almost frightening. Tankas hung from the pillars, square silk paintings of Buddhas and lamas, minutely detailed, some faded, some still with their original brilliance intact; yellow and red satin cloth in rollers wound round the pillars, and a small yellow parasol floated in the middle of the room. On all the walls, though you could only see them dimly in the gloom, there were paintings, paintings of the wrathful and the peaceful deities of Tibetan Buddhism, of Yamantaka and Avalokiteshvara, in sharp intense reds and whites and greens, their tender or terrible faces staring out at the onlooker as if from a dream.

Hans said, 'I never come into one of these places without being afraid for a moment.'

'And yet the colours are so warm,' I said. 'The colours of the wood, of the bowls at the altar, of the gold on the statue of the Buddha at the end, of the reds and browns of the paintings. They are warm colours, earth colours.'

One of the youngest monks came up to us and offered us a place on the rug next to him. Then he took out of a tuck in his robe a small cup and called to another monk to fill it with butter tea. We sat on the rug, in that blaze of colours, with the buzz of Tibetan chanting around us, for an hour, watching and listening.

'This is the strangest music I know. It's hardly music at all. Those long wind things . . . the way the drum rattles in the middle of a prayer . . . the long roll of cymbals that brings everything to a climax. It is hardly music at all. It is as if the rock were singing; it is as if the wind and the rain were singing. It is not music: it is sound, essential sound.'

I had never heard Hans so poetic. I looked at him. He smiled maliciously. He was mocking me. Then he said, 'We must go and see the Oracle room.'

'What's that?'

'Come out and I'll tell you.' We walked out into the sunlight, putting on our shoes again in the doorway, stumbling a little in the light.

'Ever since Matho began as a monastery,' Hans said, 'it has had two protectors, two Oracles. Originally they were brothers who lived at a place called Kawa Karpo in Kham, the eastern part of Tibet. They attached themselves to the scholar Dorje Palsang. When he came to Ladakh they followed him. They liked his sacrificial cakes. Since they were very strong and violent, the only place they could be settled was in the upper part of the valley. That's how they got here. The Oracles are chosen about every five years. The names of the monks are put into a bowl, which is whirled round until two names fall out. The day for selection is the fifteenth day of the tenth month, approximately every five years.'

'Do they go into "training" then?'

'Yes. They have to stay in a one-year meditation retreat, perform sacrificial cake offerings to the Protectors. During the retreat they have special meditations, keep scrupulously clean, bathe once every week, and receive baths of scented water from the Head of Meditation in the monastery. As they end their retreat, they go into a trance and are entered by the Protectors, who are known as Rongtsen Karmar.'

'I love the bit about keeping very clean and bathing once a week.'

'After that they go through very detailed ceremonies day after day — prophesying, answering questions, blessing the coming harvest, etc., etc. They run up and down the walls too, very fast, and never fall. They cut themselves and bleed and don't have any scars the next day. So we're told. On the fifteenth day the Oracles go about with a mask that has no openings for their eyes. They are supposed to be able to see through the eyes of the wrathful deities which are drawn on their chests and backs. On the last day the two Oracles ride to the original shrine of Rongtsen Karmar about two miles away. When they reach the shrine they examine the grains in a vase that is kept there. This foretells, apparently, whether or not the crops will be good for the coming year. Then the Protectors leave the bodies of the Oracles. Where do you imagine they go?'

'Into the rocks?'

'Better . . . much better . . . into the juniper shrubs.'

The ceremony wasn't till January, Hans said, and the monks who would be the Oracles were already in secret retreat, and so we couldn't meet them. But we could go to the small room where their clothes and masks were stored.

Hans led the way, up a stone staircase, through long low-lying musty corridors. Eventually we came to a largish covered courtyard where the head of a dzo was pinned to the wall. 'Turn right,' Hans said. We went through a low ancient wooden door, into the Room of the Oracles.

It was about fifteen feet square, airless, with only one small window and a thick smell of ancient clothes and butter lamps. The floor was covered with grain. Near the window there was an altar with a large corn-cob in the middle of a heap of grain, with two red ribbons around it. Hans pointed to two tattered five-foot silk screens. 'Behind there are hidden the statues of the two Oracles. They are taken out only once a year. They are too sacred to be seen on other occasions. They stay there, behind the screen, gathering power.' On the walls around us, hung on long iron rails, were the clothes of the Oracles, very ancient and torn silks, some so faded that you could not imagine what their original colour had been. There were masks everywhere — grinning and terrible masks, with wild popping eyes and slavering tongues, red and green cheeks and crowns of skulls.

Hans said, 'The power of this room goes back to a cult older than Buddhism, some original fertility cult of which we know nothing. A few years ago a monk came in, saw the filth of this room and said that it had to be cleaned up, that all the grain had to be swept up and thrown away. It was. All the monk's fields failed. He became ill. Then he came back and said, "Put all the grain back on the floor, or all the fields in the village will be barren." You see, traditionally some grain of the first crop of every field in the district has to be scattered here, or there will be no harvest.'

I met Hans next day looking drawn and distracted in the bazaar of Leh.

'I've just had one of the strangest afternoons of my life.'

We went and sat in Pamposh's. There was an Italian couple in the corner, in their late twenties, I suppose, one with green hair, the other with red, twanging a guitar and singing old Beatles songs.

'Oh god,' Hans said, 'I don't think I can take this. Let's move.'

We walked slowly up to the river.

'I've just been to interview an Oracle. Wangchuk told me about her. He came too. She lives in Skara, about ten miles away . . . She's sixty-seven; she looks about two thousand. This air makes them all so wrinkled. She had a hard, cold face and piercing black eyes. She talked incessantly, in a high-pitched screech. We sat in the small, windowless main room of her house. Everything smelt of incense and rancid butter. She told me that she had her first crisis at twenty-nine. It was then that she suddenly understood she had to be a nun and Oracle. "I was as if dead for nine days. I left my body and went to Rde-Zong, where I met three monks who sat in a dark corner and stared at me. Then I met a God. He said, 'Fewer and fewer people believe in spirits. You must go back to earth and live your life so that people can be brought to believe in them again.' At first it was very hard. The spirit would possess me suddenly, I did not know what to do, it would come at strange moments. Now I can tell when it is coming, I feel a tickling along my arms and I can control it." '

Hans stopped. We had reached a small old mill by the river.

74

It was just a wooden shack with a turning wheel inside. We went in.

'She said one moving thing,' Hans said. 'When I asked her, "What happens after death?" she looked at me quietly and answered, "I do not know." Usually when I ask that question here I get a very confident answer.'

'Does she remember anything when she is in a trance?'

'She remembers nothing. She is not the Oracle, she says; the Oracle comes and possesses her. When the Oracle is in her, she says, there is nothing left of herself.'

'The Lhasa Oracle', Hans said, 'once received a letter from the Tibetan Government with the following message: "Somebody who has been born in a sheep-year is very sick. What should be done with him? Please give a clear answer." The Oracle Priest replied, "If possible, buy new ones. If not, then get them repaired and you will be able to use them still for some time." This was the right answer: "Somebody born in a sheep-year" referred to a pair of bellows which were kept in the government office in Lhasa and had recently become worn out.

'Usually, Oracles begin their "career" earlier than the Oracle of Skara, at the beginning of puberty. The first fits occur "spontaneously", and often to the great alarm of the persons who experience them, since only a few Tibetans and Ladakhis seem to want to become professional Oracles because of the mental and physical strain it imposes on them. These fits are not ordinary cases of epilepsy: the Ladakhis are well able to differentiate between an epileptic and those cases when a man or woman is supposed to be "possessed".

'The ceremony for finding the identity of the spirit that possesses the Oracle is very odd. Somebody ties together the thumbs and forefingers of both hands of the layman or priest conducting the inquiry. Another string is tied round both feet, and the hair on the crown of his head is also tied into a tuft. The spirit is asked to remain in the "patient's" body and to answer all questions concerning its identity clearly . . . until the strings are untied. A God or "Dharmapala" will often reveal his identity of his own accord. If a person has been possessed by another kind of roaming spirit, or a low-ranking demon, a further ceremony is undergone to drive it away, or it is sometimes made to avow Buddhism and placed in the hand of other "gods".'

'Do the Ladakhis believe in Oracles?' I asked.

'Some of the more "educated", Westernised Ladakhis pretend that they don't. But they still go to consult them. We're going to visit the Oracle of Sabu tomorrow. See for yourself.'

That night I asked my landlord what he thought about Oracles.

He looked at me sharply to see whether I was mocking him, saw that I wasn't, and said, 'They do good things. This I am telling you. My mother had a big lump on the side of her neck. The Sabu Oracle cured that. She touched my mother on the head and the next day the lump was gone. Once, Namgyal my son was ill. I took him to another Oracle. She said some prayers over him. In a week he was good again.'

'Perhaps he would have got good anyway.'

He shrugged his shoulders and said nothing. Then he laughed: 'You know, I am very famous in Leh.'

'What for?'

'I can tell the future from dreams.'

He came into my room and sat down on my bed.

'I will tell you very simple things. You will be able to tell the future. You will become very famous man in England and you will please send me money every year.' He was laughing. 'Yes, you will become very famous, like me. It is very simple. If someone comes to you and says, "I have been wearing a gold cloth in a dream," you can say, "You will get a big honour." If someone comes to you and says, "I have been crossing a river or climbing a mountain or riding a dragon," you can say, "This is very good sign. You will make good spiritual things." If someone comes to you and says, "I have seen a sun rising in my dream without any clouds and I have heard the sound of drums and trumpets," you can say, "Soon you will be getting some money," and this will make him very happy and he will give you money. If someone comes to you and says, "I have been without a hat in my dream and looking into a mirror," you can say, "You will suffer." '

I did not dream I was hatless or looking into a mirror or riding a dragon. I slept deeply, woke early and refreshed, and caught the morning bus to Sabu with Hans and Helena. It was Sunday and the bus was empty except for us and three peasant women.

Hans said, 'I went to Sabu last Sunday too, did I tell you? There was this old woman sitting next to me in the Oracle's room. Suddenly, she got up and started screaming, "I'm an Oracle too!" She ran up and down the room. "I'm an Oracle too! The Rinpoche says I am a great Oracle! You fools! You understand nothing!" Two young men grabbed her and led her out. She reappeared at the window and screamed, "One day you will understand! I am the real Oracle! I am the real Oracle!" Wangchuk was with me, and I turned to him and asked him if this sort of thing happened often. He shrugged his shoulders and said, "Of course." '

Sabu is a small spreadeagled village set among fields and rushing streams, about ten miles away from Leh. By the time we arrived the sun was up, in a mostly cloudless sky, firing the corn on both sides of the road. We got out of the bus and had to stand for a moment shading our eyes before we could walk on. Some village children came out of houses to our left and ran round us screaming, 'One pen one pen one rupee one rupee,' but as soon as they saw that we weren't giving anything, they ran away.

Helena said, 'They aren't serious beggars. It's only a game.'

'They aren't serious beggars yet,' said Hans. 'How long will it be before they learn?'

Hans knew the way to the Oracle's house and led us there, past a stream, a few houses, one-storeyed, with small gashes in the walls for windows. I don't know what I expected, but I was disappointed when we reached the house. It could not have been more ordinary — a small, rather bedraggled group of sunflowers outside the door, a concrete porch, brown walls with the same small windows as the rest of the village. Only the seven or eight prayer flags on the roof revealed that there was anything special about this house, and even they seemed worn and tired. Two small children were playing in the dirt near the sunflowers.

Hans said, 'You look disappointed. You haven't seen anything yet.'

I could hear chanting. We went into a low gloomy corridor, took off our shoes, and were beckoned into a room on our right.

There were about sixty people in that small green-walled room — sixty people of all kinds and ages. And they were all kneeling. Old women with their dusty peraks, old men in their dirty red robes, young children, a Kashmiri official in his Sunday best, two aristocratic-looking young Ladakhis in American jeans and white shirts, open to the waist. They were all kneeling, even the Muslim Kashmiri, and praying, and looking at the Oracle in the corner. We were the only Europeans. No one seemed to notice us.

We had hardly sat down on the cold stone floor before it started. The figure in blue and green and orange brocade in the corner, the Oracle, started shaking and screaming and moaning. The helmet that she wore was so large and wide-rimmed that I could not at first see her face, but slowly I made out two fierce eyes, a slit of a mouth. The Oracle was shaking and trembling and clapping her hands and writhing and banging the floor and moaning. She seemed so frail, so small, when you looked at her, half-hidden in her rainbow brocade, and yet the force that came from her was extraordinary. She was screaming, 'Come closer! Come closer!' At the end of every phrase, she would spit on the floor and break into mocking laughter.

The crowd around us started praying louder and louder. Some of the old women also started moaning subduedly. Two stone-faced young women stood by the Oracle, watching everything. Her daughters, probably. Slowly, a queue of kneelers formed in front of the shaking figure. An old woman with a cyst above her left eye walked on her knees towards the Oracle. Suddenly, with a scream, the Oracle lunged forward, tore open the woman's blouse, and buried her moaning head between her breasts. I felt myself go faint, and the old woman screamed. She did not move, however, and the Oracle kept her head between her breasts. I thought for one moment that she was sucking her blood, and I wanted to leave. One of the stone-faced girls came forward after about fifteen seconds, and held out a small silver bowl before the Oracle. She raised her head, cackled, and spat a bluish-green liquid into it.

'What is that?' I asked Hans.

'They say it is the evil forces. The Oracle sucks all the evil from the woman's body.'

Everyone around me was, by now, moaning and swaying. One after another, people shambled on their knees towards the Oracle for the same process to be repeated. She would stare hard, scream with laughter or abuse, and lunge forward. Sometimes after she had buried her head in a patient's chest she would blow on the place she had sucked through a long silver tube. Everyone looked scared. The Kashmiri took off his watch and tie, loosened his collar, and bared his chest, but kept his eyes tightly shut; the two young Ladakhis tried to be cavalier, but when their turn came clenched their hands tightly together and trembled; one small boy who was held out by his mother to the Oracle, almost like a child-sacrifice, writhed and sobbed in such terror that I could not watch.

Everything the Oracle did was violent — her movements were wild and jerky, the way she shook her head, the way she lunged forward . . . Once she hit an old woman so hard that the old woman started to cry silently. One young boy she beat about the head, screaming, 'You are a liar! You are a liar! You are evil!' She seized one old man by the collar and shook him so hard I thought she wanted to kill him. She cackled and screamed as she shook him, and when she had finished, spat into his face.

Helena said, 'I want to go. I can't take this.'

'You can't go yet,' said Hans, 'The ceremony isn't finished. Besides, Andrew wants to ask her something.'

'I don't. I want to go too.'

But Hans was insistent, grabbed me by the sleeve, and pushed me forward. I was trembling. I was now a foot away from the Oracle. She was sucking the chest of an old woman who was moaning. She reared up her head, glared at me, and spat into a bowl by my knee.

'What do you want?' she screamed.

I could not answer.

'He wants to ask you a question,' said Hans.

She cackled. 'What question?', shaking her hands in the air. 'What question?' She stared at me, and spat again, contemptuously, into the bowl.

'He is a foreigner. He does not believe. He has come to test me. He is a fool . . . I will not answer any of his questions,' she screamed, her voice rising higher and higher, her hands moving more and more wildly in the air.

Then I found my voice. I said, 'I believe in the power of the Buddha. I come in good faith. I am not here to test you.'

She cackled and went silent. Then she said, in a softer voice, 'If I answered your question, what could you do about it? You could not do the rituals I would tell you to do. You couldn't say the prayers. You have no lamas in your country.'

I said, 'There *are* lamas in my country. I will find one. I will say the prayers.'

She cackled again. Then she said, 'Ask your question. I will reply simply. You will not have to say any prayers or find any priest. I will give you something simple to do.'

'I have a friend,' I said, 'who has suffered many deaths in her family. She is very unhappy and tells me often that she wants to die . . .'

I did not finish. The Oracle screamed, 'Hold out your hand!' I did so. She scattered some rice into it. 'Throw these into the four corners of your friend's house!' I thanked her. She screamed again, 'Hold out your hand!' She reached down to her right and fetched up a dirty white scarf. 'Give this to your friend. Tell her to wear it always. It will give her protection. She is in danger. She needs protection.' Then she screamed again, something I did not understand, and waved me away.

I went back to my place in the corner shaking, but I was determined not to leave now. I had to stay now until the end of the ceremony. Slowly, the line of swaying and moaning kneelers thinned. When the last old woman had been 'healed', the Oracle screamed loudly, a long high-pitched scream, clapped her hands, and turned abruptly to the wall. There, in the corner, was a small altar I had not noticed before, with a bell and vajra on it, and two silver bowls. She grabbed the bell and vajra, turned back to us, and started praying loudly, ringing the bell with one hand and waving the vajra in the air with the other. Now everyone who had been 'healed' started to move towards her again, this time not for healing, but for blessing. The Oracle touched some with her forehead; some she touched with the vajra on their necks or backs. Many of the people were openly crying by now. When everyone had been blessed, the Oracle screamed again and turned to the altar. From her robe she fetched up a drum and started shaking it. She trembled, she screamed, she cackled, she swayed, and all the time she shook the drum, louder and louder, faster and faster. Suddenly she screamed again, the last long scream; the whole room froze; she reared up, almost stood up, and then fell backwards, into the arms of the two stone-faced young women. She lay in their arms shaking and moaning, and then fell forward again, to beat the floor with her hands. Then, quite suddenly, she sat up, sat back, and folded her hands. The trance was over.

I looked at her. The transformation was complete. For nearly an hour she had been hysterical and commanding, even terrifying. Now, in a small exhausted heap in the corner, there was only an old woman smiling weakly and wiping the sweat from her forehead with a white rag. She was speaking to one of the young girls in a low voice, quite unlike the screech of the Oracle. I went up to her and thanked her. She smiled dimly up at me, not recognising me. One of the young women shook a wooden box in front of me. I put five rupees in it.

Outside, in the stark noon sunlight, we all felt shaky. Hans said he wanted to walk off on his own for a while. Helena and I walked down in silence to the stream we had passed on the way, and sat down by some rocks. Further upstream two boys were bathing naked and splashing each other.

'I was frightened,' Helena said. 'Were you?'

'Yes.'

'I do not believe in spirits and yet I could not deny the power that woman had. Did you feel it?'

'Yes.'

The two boys had seen us and were making whooping noises, leaping up and down and splashing each other. 'One pen! One pen! One rupee!' Their wet naked bodies glistened. I had some

apples in my bag and held up two. I threw them to the boys.
They caught them and stood munching and laughing on a rock.

'Will you give your friend the scarf?' Helena asked.

'I'd like to, but she'd think I was mad. She thinks I was mad
to come to Ladakh in the first place. If I returned with a dirty
white scarf and a few grains of rice and said they would save her
life, she'd never speak to me again.'

'What will you do with them, then?'

'I'll hide them in her house when she's not looking.'

Helena and I talked evasively for the rest of the afternoon.
Neither of us was prepared to go more deeply into what we had
experienced in the Oracle's presence. Helena's face was pale as
she talked, and her eyes strained.

Back in Leh, I realised that it was the Oracle's violence that
had frightened me, her flashing, brutal violence, far more than
any power she may have had. In her savage wit and energy
she had revived old fears within me, of my grandmother and
mother, buried male fears of a female cruelty that no reason
could restrain, of a female dark and crazy wisdom that no
concern for ordinary justice could keep from its work of destruction. I realised too that witnessing the Oracle's violence,
and now exploring the range of fears it had awoken in me, was
an extraordinary opportunity — an opportunity for a clarity that
included violence and did not seek refuge from it, that could
contain without judgment a knowledge of what that violence
was, and what the distress it caused me revealed to me of what I
had left unhealed and unexamined in myself. For years, out of a
dread of confronting the fearful in myself, I had wanted to
repress the violence that I knew came from my mother and
grandmother; by repressing that violence I was also repressing
the wisdom that was hidden in its fire. I understood, too, that
part of my love for Eastern philosophy had been a desire to have
done with that inner violence once and for all, to live beyond it
in a harmless serenity. But no true transformation can be
achieved by a neurotic refusal of a whole side of the psyche; I
could not progress, I saw, until I no longer used my love for the
East as a way of pretending to myself that I was not violent and
not destructive. I began to understand that night, for the first
time, the inner usefulness, the psychological value, of the
Terrible Deities painted for meditation purposes on the walls of

the gompas. I saw that in their frank portrayal of the horror of anger, desire, greed, and lust for power, they did not merely terrify the onlooker, they gave him an opportunity to confront those parts of his energies which he was repressing, to confront, understand and master them, to turn them, as the Oracle had turned her hysteria, into a power to heal.

'We must get up early tomorrow,' Helena announced. 'The bus for the Tak-Tak dance festival starts at eight.' I woke up about six, shaved in cold water, and walked across Leh to Hans's and Helena's hotel. Then we got talking so hard that we had to run to catch the bus. And what a bus! Ladakhi buses are ancient relics from the plains, so old and battered that the bird-cage we came up in to Leh from Srinagar seems a Pullman in comparison. They have nothing spectacular about them, these buses, nothing like the painted dragons, tigers and wall-eyed elephants of Afghan lorries; they are distinguished only by their age and uncomfortableness. And the people in them. Once a very benign-looking old lama with ancient spectacles mended with sellotape kicked me so hard in the shins that I could hardly walk for a morning; and once too I made the mistake of assuming that the stooping old woman behind me should be allowed on the bus before me — for some reason she thought I was trying to steal her seat, screamed, and dug me fiercely in the ribs.

We had been told that the bus for Tak-Tak would leave at eight. Nothing happened until nine, when a young Kashmiri driver got into his seat at the front, yawning, rubbing the sleep from his eyes, and smiling around at everyone, satisfied, evidently, that he had caused the most discomfort possible. Once he'd got in the Kashmiri just sat there, stretching and picking his teeth and talking desultorily to a few friends. He had the biggest wristwatch that I have ever seen, a huge painted lollipop of a watch, and he took it off at least eight or nine times to show it around.

Slowly, you learn the first, and perhaps most important,

lesson that riding on a Ladakhi bus has to teach you — to give in, to surrender. There is no point in being impatient, gritting your teeth, praying that the bus will go, cursing the driver operatically, wishing you were back in England or America or even South India (where the buses do, occasionally, go on time), exchanging bitter conspiratorial asides with fellow-Europeans — you just have to give in, to accept everything without hope or reserve. There is nothing else you can do without going crazy. And once you have given in, you begin to enjoy it all. And on an early morning in Ladakh with a bus full of people going to a dance festival, there is so much to enjoy, even if you are wedged, as I was, between an old woman whose bony shoulders were digging deep into my stomach, and a Kashmiri official whose daughter was sitting on his shoulder and hitting me happily over the head with her plastic doll. There are the old men in their cleanest red gowns and pointed wool shoes, each with his hair washed, oiled and tied back, a turquoise or small seed-pearl in one ear; there are the children, scrubbed and cheeky, sitting on the wheat-bags at the front, eating apricots and throwing the kernels at each other or at the driver; there are the Ladakhi women, above all, whom festival days find at their most regal, with their cloaks of dragon brocade, their peraks of turquoise over their heads, their oreillettes of black wool, their dark lustrous hair, often with a wool pigtail woven into it to make it stretch down to their waists, their earrings, those scalloped bunches of seed-pearls from India or China that are so prized here, and hang so brilliantly against the dark red-brown Ladakhi skin.

Even the smell of the bus, a smell of sweat and oil and dust and old clothes, is oddly comforting, like the smell of certain attics, or the cupboards of childhood.

At last, at about ten, the Kashmiri deigned to start. He put on his wristwatch, turned round, smiled at all of us, spat out of the window three times (was this some sort of ritual?) and began. The bus wheezed and clattered. Helena and Hans and I cheered. The Ladakhis thought this was funny and started to cheer too, cheer and stamp. Then all the people on top of the bus (in Ladakh people do not just ride in buses, they also ride on them) start to stamp and bang and cheer too. I thought the bus would come apart. The Kashmiri looked very happy, as if all this was just what he had planned, and drove especially slowly, to torment us further. I thought about the people on the roof — how would they avoid being decapitated by the low-lying electric wires that spanned the road? Undoubtedly there must be a Bodhisatva of Buses, a special protector for all who ride on these battered old death-traps. Which Bodhisatva it is in particular and what His mantra is I must remember to ask a head lama when I meet one.

A boy stands stroking the flanks of a horse by a stream; two old men lean on their hoes in a field, surrounded by stacks of freshly cut wheat; two girls walk bent double along the road under a vast bundle of sticks; an old woman stands outside her house, her thin grey hair blowing in the wind, staring at nothing; a group of ragged red-cheeked children chase each other round a stupa and then chase after the bus, laughing and throwing sticks at it. Each image seems to exist in an eternal present, lit by that clear afternoon light of Ladakh, so like the light of certain dreams.

The courtyard of the monastery of Tak-Tak would have been too small to contain the crowds that came, and so the dances were held under a large tattered canvas tent in a field above the monastery. The Dalai Lama's rain-maker was there, with his lank pepper-coloured hair done up in a bun; lamas from many of the nearby monasteries were there, in their different hats and robes; the whole of Tak-Tak village was there. The children sat nearest to the clearing of the stage in small mischievous cabals, chattering and scrapping. I sat with them near the orchestra, a group of six elderly impassive lamas in faded and tattered robes, whose drums and cymbals accompanied the movements of the dancers.

At first it was the crowd that interested me, not the slow, monotonous turnings of the dancers and their great painted masks, with their fixed grimaces and lurid colours. I longed for the comic interludes, the moment when two of the youngest monks dressed as skeletons with hay in their hair would run on to harangue the crowd, or turn somersaults and kick and chase each other. Slowly, however, I was drawn into the sacred rhythm of the dances, their strange and unfamiliar time. I understood that what was being danced with such slowness on the stage in front of me was the inner drama of all the spectators; that it was the psyche itself, in its different dignities and powers, whose progress towards transformation was being charted and displayed; that the external forces, the Buddhas and Bodhisatvas the dancers were representing, were no different from the inner forces of the psyche, that psyche in which the dances lived and whose life contained all the dances within it. I ceased being the half-bored spectator; I entered the dance; I allowed it to begin to enact itself within me, in its own rhythms.

In the last long movement of the dance, a monk with the mask of a deer, symbolising Awareness, danced round an effigy of clay laid on the ground, the effigy of a corpse, of the Ego, ugly and splashed with all the paints of desire, red and green and blue and yellow. The afternoon light fell in a dark fierce gold on all the spectators, on the fields and hills around, on the mask of the dancer, and the slowly turning blade of his sword, the Sword of Discrimination, as he turned it in the air above the prone effigy, to the steadily mounting crash of cymbals and drums. Then, as these reached their height of intensity, the dancer fell to his knees and raised his sword, and with four quick, savage cuts quartered the body of the Ego. The drumming stopped. There was a silence, the loudest, most charged silence I have ever heard. The Deer-Dancer swayed above the body of the dismembered Ego, swaying backwards and forwards, opening out his arms, miming an enormous laughter that embraced the world.

' I am Perec. Georges Perec. I am in despair. Otherwise, I am thirty-five years old, unmarried, and rather cheerful. Witness the following smile.'

And he smiled broadly, revealing a set of yellow smoker's teeth. 'Every morning I practise that smile. I want it to get broader and more vivid. I dream of having one day a smile as large as my face.

'I sell antique furniture. Only five months a year, or I would die of wealth. The rest of the year I travel. I like primitive people on the verge of extinction; I feel at home with them. I smile more broadly than ever when I am with the doomed. I hate women and cats. I'm being very brave and loquacious. Who are you?'

I told him what I could. He was small, furrowed. He sat forward intensely when he talked, hunching his shoulders. What a repertory of accompanying noises he had! Sucking his teeth, snorting, speaking suddenly high, suddenly low.

I asked him if he had visited French India, and he talked about Pondicherry with a kind of rapture. 'The bread in Pondicherry! The wonderful bread! O mon dieu! Not even the Parisians eat such delicious bread! But the ashram! Quels cons! Quels pigeons blancs . . . ils emmerdent tout, tout! How can anyone believe anything? There should be asylums for people who believe things. Do you know Cioran? You should. He believes in nothing. I love him. Every morning I say to myself, "Je songe à un Eleusis des coeurs détrompés, à un mystère net, sans dieux et sans les véhémences de l'illusion." I dream of an Eleusis of undeceived hearts, of a clean mystery, without gods and the vehement enthusiasms of illusion. It is as good in English, no? You should try saying it in the morning. It is very relaxing.

'I like you. I am going to show you my most prized possession. You are very lucky. I will not even show it to my mother. She is Jewish. She would cover her eyes and say, "Georges, Georges, what have I done?",' and he did an imitation of her standing up and shaking and covering her eyes, and then ran out of the room, returning with something wrapped up in a green shawl.

'You will never guess what it is! It is −' he unwrapped it with a flourish − 'a skull! A Tibetan skull, decorated! Three hundred

and fifty rupees, worth every anna . . . Look at the delicacy of
the workmanship! Look at the row of tiny grinning skulls
around the top. O crâne, comme je t'aime . . . Look at the eyes,
how dead they are, little burnt-out grapes! Look at the nostrils!
Like an angry pig's! Marvellous! This is what I love up here, all
those sweet smiling people, and underneath . . . this, this sense
of the horror and grotesque comedy of life and death. A good
phrase, no? The horror and grotesque . . . I shall write it to
Cioran. I hope he doesn't die this summer. Like all true depres-
sives, he survives everyone. Ha ha. Survives everyone. Forget all
those bland blancmange Buddhas! When you've seen one you've
seen them all! All those good-boy Buddhas sitting there as if
they needed a good shit . . . Pardonnez-moi . . . I am French, I
am despairing, I like the Tantric figures, Death fucking life and
making her scream, je les adore, his pot belly decorated with
skulls! I love the look of agony on the faces of the women
fucking Death! So subtle! Do not lecture me on how Buddhist
Tantra is not sexual. I have read all the books. J'ai lu tous les
livres.

'Non, mon cher' (he leaned forward and stared wildly into
my eyes), 'no, the really interesting thing about this Tibetan
business is not the calm, la Sérénité . . . My mother, for god's
sake, believes in that, poor idiot. It is their belief in the crazy
wisdom, la folle sagesse . . . This is what I want, this crazy
wisdom! Look at the monks! They are angels of depravity!
Haven't you guessed? And all those Ashramites imagining that
holiness is white, is sweat, is reading the Holy Texts under the
trees by streams. They are raving, mon cher. Holiness does not
exist except in the imagination of schoolboys. Holiness is a
head-prefect's dream. Holiness is a fantasy of Mummy's Boy
who wants Mummy back, transfigured and perfect (doesn't
matter if she has to change clothes and become the Buddha).
The crazy old Buddha! I love him! He knows the whole thing is
meaningless, toute l'affaire, and he is dancing on the bones,
mon cher, he is peeing into the faces of the world!

'And shall I tell you what is best about this Buddhism? Not
renunciation, not all the bits about fighting demons . . . No,
it's all in the bit where Milarepa comes back and finds his
mother's rotting corpse. Remember? What does he do? He uses
it as a pillow for seven days of meditation! Quel style! And he

goes into ecstasy. I love to think about death, I have three skulls in my collection so far, and it's expanding. And now this beautiful Tibetan skull — I feel sexy just looking at it, I may say, very sexy. I have my skulls in my bedroom in Paris. Girls love them. It makes their nipples hard. You don't believe me?

' "The will to believe is a lyric leprosy that contaminates the soul." Ha! Cioran says that. "In every moment there is a prophet asleep . . . and when that prophet wakes there's a little more evil in the world . . . everyone is waiting for his moment to propose something . . . it doesn't matter what . . . he has a voice, that's enough. He has to say something with it." Ha! And who wouldn't be a prophet if they could get up the belief? That's what's hard. Each absolute, my friend, is no more than a panic of the senses! Making a discipline is the frivolous and funereal debauch of the spirit! If you destroyed in man his mad hunger to believe and his monstrous faculty of hope, who knows!' He paused dramatically, rolling his eyes. 'Human life might . . . *begin*.'

Perec ran into my room before breakfast. 'I am coming to say goodbye! I am leaving! Until next year! Who knows? I might be dead if I'm lucky!

'I am coming to say goodbye and I want to give you two palindromes and four quotations! You are too trusting, my friend! I want to protect you from the evils of trust.'

He sat down on my bed, out of breath. 'Here are the two palindromes! Take them down! ÉLU PAR CETTE CRAPULE. What perfection! Last summer I wrote forty pages of palindromes! The second one, perhaps my masterpiece — ÉSOPE RESTE ICI ET SE REPOSE.'

He sighed a little at his own mastery. He threw open the windows as if he wanted the morning light to flood the room in his praise. His hands were trembling.

'And now for the four quotations! I have written them out on lavatory paper! What other paper should one use? Learn them and they will protect you from hepatitis, snake-bites, Buddhism and women! "Sick with hope we go on waiting; life is waiting to become hypostasis." Ha! Wonderful! Numero uno! Numero due: "We only begin to live at the end of philosophy . . . when we have understood its terrible pointlessness, that it was useless to run to her and that she was of no help." O quel désespoir pur, c'est magnifique! And now for you, my dear poet, a special quotation: "SALVATION IS THE DEATH OF SONG!" Listen carefully: "Salvation is the death of song!" Do you understand? Don't be saved, go on singing! You have to remain, my dear, ill with all the illnesses, sad with all the sadnesses, otherwise how will you write? Eh? Eh? And now for the last . . . this is for all travellers in ancient worlds! It is from Cioran! It is wonderfully depressing! You will need it! It will protect you! Are you ready? "All men who look after past ruins imagine for themselves that they can avoid the ruins to come, that it is in their power to begin again something radically new. They make a solemn vow and promise to themselves to get out of this mediocre abyss destiny has plunged them into." Ah, how I love "mediocre abyss". But nothing comes. Everything goes on being the same. We only see around us degraded inspirations and ardours . . . I have never known one new life that was not illusory and compromised at its root.'

He stood flexing his biceps (very small) in the light. He said, 'I am going. We will never meet again. Be careful. You are very enthusiastic, you are a great fool, you will be eaten alive if you don't watch out. I wish you all the melancholy wisdoms and a relatively early death! Ha! Yes!' and ran out into the morning laughing and slapping his thighs. 'All the melancholy wisdoms and a relatively early death! What rhythm! What style!'

The last time I saw Perec was when I was going by bus to Alchi. The bus shuddered past a small bus stop near a stream. There were two monks squatting in the dust, and Perec standing apart from them, staring into the distance. I leant out of the bus window and shouted to him. He turned and looked at me, sadly, and raised one hand.

That morning he had put this under my door: 'The world does not exist. What we see around us and what we call the world are constructions of our desires and instincts. When these fade, the world fades. All that is left, unhappily, is us. And that only for a while. That "short time" cannot be called life.'

An old man was singing in the bus, clapping his hands to keep time.

Alone in Alchi for five days.

First day. It is six in the evening. I have been watching two birds on the other side of the river, chasing each other from ledge to ledge in the vast ochre rock-face. Sometimes the birds fall a hundred feet, and I am afraid for them, but they always reappear and vanish into a small opening in the rock, and appear again, flashing red and dark blue in the twilight.

An hour ago I looked up and saw that the vast bald hill opposite was not dead. It was moving, swarming with life. For a moment, I thought it was the rock itself that was alive. Then I saw the goats, the colour of the rock, moving against it.

It is seven. I turn to look down at the Indus for the last time. There is a small white curved beach. A quiet purplish light is falling on it. Not a rock, not a grain of sand, not one short grass darkening in the wind, can be changed. Everything exists in its own perfection.

Second day.

Why do people talk about the 'solidity', the 'still majesty', of mountains? Nothing is more theatrical, more unstable. Each shift of light changes them. You look up; they seem immeasurably distant, about to vanish over the horizon. You look up again; the light has brought them so close you think you could breathe on them.

Six. Sitting on the rocks by the river. The mountain opposite is a drawing on ricepaper. I have only to stretch out one hand to tear it.

Third day.

I sat on a pile of stones, and slowly my breath grew quiet and my mind emptied. Below me, the river. Above, the great ochre face of the rock overhanging the river.

I can hear the songs of harvesters carried down to the river on the wind, and sometimes the high call of a bird.

In the new transparence of my mind, I find that everything — the roar of the river, the bird-call, the harvesters singing — is the same sound, the same ringing sound, only in different registers, different intensities. Even the rocks are ringing to this sound, even the small stones I can see dully shining at the edge of the water; even the tuft of moss and sheep droppings to my right. My breath is that sound also, and my heartbeat, and the brush and creak of my body as I stir.

I am frightened that I shall not be able to survive so much feeling. Each bird-call is a knife through me; each twist in the rock brings me almost to tears. I am afraid of dying and yet I know that dying is not possible if I am part of all this ringing energy. But how to calm my mind with that knowledge? For a long moment, it happens. The fear passes. The river runs and roars through me; in the late evening light, the rocks slow their dance, golden, and darken.

Fourth day.

To take this river, these rocks, this light, these mountains changing in the light, 'for granted', and to revel in them — I am learning that slowly here. I am learning not to fling names at things. Even when I write or think simply rock, river, light, mountain, I begin to see through the word to the thing, to be alone with the thing, the rock, this light on my hands, without fear or need to speak.

Things exist in the unnameable. Sometimes I am free, or

freed by this landscape, to see them as they are and not wish to name them. Sometimes, as the rocks glow in the late sun, or the river flashes suddenly between boulders, or two birds hide in a burst of light above me, I understand that all names fall short of the shining of things. And that understanding, while it lasts, is peace.

Fifth day.
It is good the river will not stop roaring and lunging through its dark gorges, whatever happens to the village, or the monastery. The things that ignore us save us in the end. Their presence awakens silence in us; they refresh our courage with the purity of their detachment.

And yet I have learnt from these days here that I need more than this good silence and solitude; I need more than this rock, this light, these birds. I need to be taught how to work with what I have begun to know here; I need to find a man or woman who has learnt the language whose first, simplest, words I am stammering.

I have never admitted this so clearly to myself before. As I do, something I have kept imprisoned within me for years breaks free, I find, to my astonishment, I am no longer afraid of happiness, I feel, I do not know why, that it will be a master, clearer and more powerful than any of the griefs I have known.

I returned to Leh. The day after, Hans, Helena and I went to Thikse monastery.

Thikse is not far from Leh, perhaps twenty-five miles, and we got a ride in an army lorry, with three Australians and five bored soldiers. God, how bored the soldiers get here with no women and only one film a week! The sergeant buttonholed me: 'Ladakh very important strategic. Yes. But very boring place, dear sir. My dear boys are going mad very often. Fighting, swearing, very bad things. They are lonely, they go mad up here, I am very sad for this. In the winter the madness is very bad. Nothing but snow and wind. It is bad. I say to my men, "You must not go out except with a friend, or you will go mad." And if they go out alone they go mad.' He leant forward, put a pudgy ringed hand on my knee. 'And I? Sometimes I am mad also. Dear sir, my wife is very loving. She is good and fat. She lives in Madras. And my daughter also. And my son also. What to do?'

And then Thikse. We clambered out of the lorry in a flurry of handshakes. Hans said for the fifth time, 'Thikse is an imitation of the Potala in Lhasa.'

H elena said, 'I don't feel like walking up.'
        I said, 'I don't either. I've been before and today I just want to sit here and look up at it.'

Scandalised, Hans strode off up the hill in large, melodramatic, German strides.

Helena and I laughed, sat on a rock, and said nothing. We were sitting out in the full sun, in the waste of shining rock and sand that surrounds Thikse and stretches for miles towards Hemis. I remember Helena's hands on the rock, glowing, as if lit from within. She wore a simple red and white dress that made her suddenly seem very young.

We looked up at the monastery. As we watched it, it seemed to both of us that it was alive. It was as if everything that was happening in front of us, every prayer flag that shook, every monk who walked out slowly on to his balcony, scratching on ear or picking his teeth, every dog that wandered aimlessly between the shadows and rocks and crumbling black and white buildings, were part of one vast, luminous, transparent, living organism. We were not looking at a monastery as a collection of buildings built over different centuries at different heights, an imitation of the Potala; we were looking at a living creature, a creature of light and rock and air; it breathed and moved to its own laws; nothing that we saw seemed accidental. When a monk bent down to water his geraniums, and a dog a hundred feet below him started to trot slowly up the path, it was as if the two of them were connected, in a slow, strange, and yet absolutely simple rhythm; when the wind suddenly shook all the fringes of the windows, the green and red and orange silk, it was as if the walls and the rock they stood on were alive also, shaking in the sun-washed wind. The monastery had a few trees around it, a few burnt, scraggy trees, but all the birds of Thikse, hundreds of them, were not in the trees but crowded into the high right-hand corner of the monastery, where the vast statue of the Buddha of the future, the Maitreya Buddha, stood in silence in its brick-red box of a building. When the birds sang the walls sang too, and the paths, and the four or five fat monks on their balconies, and the dogs nosing from rock to rock; and the sound of this singing filled all the corners of the desert and its silence, and was its essential sound, the sound that sustained all that ramshackle splendour of rock and stone and light.

We were walking home from Thikse in the late afternoon. Twilight lay on everything — the stubby young poplars, the fields, the stream that ran alongside the road, the river, wide and brown and turbulent, in the valley beyond it. Several army lorries stopped for us. We waved them on, because we wanted to walk.

'I love Ladakh and I love many of the Ladakhis I have met,' Hans said, 'but so what? What use is my love to the Ladakhis? They have given me so much, but what have I given them? What could I give them, except money?'

Another lorry passed. This one did not stop; it was already full, of young Ladakhi workers going home from the Irrigation Project Works on the road to Hemis. They looked drained and dusty, but waved to us, and we waved back, as un-ironically as we could manage.

'I'm going to get a lot from my time here, many memories, friends, perhaps even the book that will finally get me tenure . . . what are the Ladakhis going to get? The very fact that I am here at all, asking them questions, taping their replies, means that their world is ending.' Hans stopped. 'The worst is that we know that, but they don't, or the majority of them don't. They are so trusting, these people. Sometimes it makes you sick, how trusting they are.'

We walked on in silence, watching the darkening on the road and the sunset begin on the mountains.

I said, 'All we can do is to bear witness to our love of the country and its people as clearly and intelligently as possible.'

Hans clapped ironically. 'Bravo! But that's only another kind of exploitation, isn't it? I mean, if you "bear witness" eloquently, and, as you say, "clearly", who else will get the reward but you? And your readers, of course, a little . . . but aren't you inviting them to a rather corrupt party? "Another moving study of a doomed culture", "Another poetic rendering of the East".'

'I know that what we are doing here is ambiguous,' I said. 'I know that it would be better for us and for the Ladakhis if we were doctors or engineers or even picture-restorers. Much better. What I cannot accept is that what we are doing is of no value whatever. If Ladakh has to die, then some living fragment of its life may survive in what we feel and what we write.'

Hans replied, 'I say the same to myself every day, as I brush my teeth and listen to the tapes of the day before.'

I met Nawang Tsering that evening. Hans had often spoken about him with admiration, and told me that he was the foremost Ladakhi scholar of his generation (Nawang is thirty).

I found at once that he was different from any of the other Ladakhis I had met. He was more restless, uneasy, and anxious; he fidgeted with his hands when he talked, plucking his palms with his nails; his eyes were pinched and had dark bags under them; his fine-boned melancholic face was sallow with nervous strain. He could not sit still. Each time he sat down, he stood up again and walked round the room.

The three of us talked, and then Hans said he was tired and wanted to go to bed. I asked Nawang if he would like to walk a little.

'Why not?' he said. 'I never sleep well anyway.'

As we were walking downriver to my hotel, I told him what Hans and I had been talking about that afternoon. Did Nawang think it was true that we could do very little?

'Yes, it is true. And not just for you foreigners. For me too. I can do little for my people. They believe it is good to have more money, more radios, more medicines. And they are right. We have lived backwardly, we have lived away from the world. Now we must join the world. But they do not know what all these things will cost. I know. I have been in Benares for five years; I have seen what Westernisation has cost India, how much sadness it has brought, how much suffering, how much cheapness of the spirit, how much ugliness. And yet I cannot say, "Ladakh must not be Westernised." How can I say that? My people are poor, they have eye infections, skin infections; they need good agricultural equipment. They need so many things . . .' And then he said, 'Hans told me you were a writer.'

'Yes, I am.'

'You can help us.'

'How?'

'You can write about us.'

'How can that help? Everything that I write will be false in some way. Everything I write will appropriate you in some way, falsify in some sense what you are. The more I come to know and love Ladakh, the less I feel I can say anything of what I have found here without betraying it. And even if I did write a book on Ladakh, who do you imagine would read it? Professors, poets, travellers . . . not the people you would need to read it if anything was to be changed for Ladakh and for the Ladakhi people. Not the politicians. Not the heads of government.'

'You are right,' Nawang said. 'But our situation is even more desperate than you imagine. I think that it is almost certain that we will be destroyed as a culture, and that nothing, now, can save us from that destruction. Our only chance of being remembered at all may be through being "appropriated" and "consumed", as you say, by the West, by some Westerners who have come to visit our country and have been moved by what they have found there. I am not asking for rescue, or for the sudden political and spiritual transformation of my people. It is too late to ask for that. I am asking that something of us be saved from oblivion. You must write about us. You will get many things wrong, and you will only be able to give a limited and subjective picture of us; but if you can do that with craft and love, you will have helped us a little, and you will have given to those of us, like me, who are fighting to preserve something of our culture against probably impossible odds, a sense that we are not living our lives in vain; that we have friends in the world who recognise what it is we stand for.'

He had spoken with great sad passion. Then he turned to me and said, 'Are you interested in folk songs?'

I smiled.

'Why are you smiling?' he asked.

'During the last three years, I have translated several books of folk songs from various languages. My new book . . .'

'So, you are interested. That is good. We can work together. We can start tomorrow. We shall have to start tomorrow because I have to go to Delhi the day after to visit my brother. We can work all day tomorrow.'

'Nawang, what are you talking about?'

'I am talking about translating together some Ladakhi folk songs. Very few translations have ever been done of our songs, and the few that have been are very bad. And there are many, many of them. And many of them are beautiful. And you are here and I am here. So why don't we work together? We can begin tomorrow, and I can send you the rest when you are back in England.'

'Can you sing?'

'Yes.'

'Will you sing me the songs as we work on them?'

'Yes.'

'Then we can work together.'

We worked all the next day and late into the night, sitting in the hotel garden.

Nawang said, 'Our folk tradition is dying, as everything else of our past is dying. When I was a child, people would sing often, with their friends, on ordinary as well as special occasions. Everyone knew how to sing, even if they didn't sing very well. Now people listen to the radio. There are still some wonderful singers in Ladakh, dedicated singers. My cousin is one. He sings on the radio sometimes . . . but the tradition of singing among the people is dying out. Sometimes in the villages where there are few radios, people still sing. But in Leh . . .

'So much of our history, of our identity, is in our songs. There are songs to the Kings, there are songs to the great monasteries and gurus of Ladakh, there are harvest songs . . . if they are lost and the dances that go with them are lost, how will we remember what we were, how will we find the strength to remain ourselves? I say that to the friends of my age and they think I am mad. They say, "You are always talking of the past; we are interested in the future." But what future will there be if we do not remember and honour our past?

'For a long time I believed that the old culture could be revived, and kept alive. When I first understood that there was little hope of that, I suffered very much. I was in despair; I wanted to give up everything. I even thought of becoming a monk. Now I know that I must work harder, as hard as possible, to preserve what little I can, in whatever way I can. If we translate fifty songs together and publish those translations, we will not, it is true, have accomplished much. We will have accomplished hardly anything. A few poets in England and America may read our work and say, "These are beautiful." That will not do much to halt the dying of my culture. But it will be a gesture against that death.'

And he began to sing. He sang well, and his voice filled the garden.

'In the old days
In the old days of Shey
Everyone wore brocade of dragons

'And danced like peacocks

'In the old days
In the old days of Shey

Everyone wore shawls of silk
And belts of pure sheepswool

'And danced like peacocks.'

'This song refers to the time', Nawang said, 'when the Kings
of Ladakh lived at Shey. You must have seen the ruins of the
castle of Shey by the gompa. It is one of the saddest sights of
Ladakh — those great walls against the sky. "Brocade of dragons" is Chinese brocade, the brocade that used to be sold in the
market of Leh, and came from Yarkand or Khotan. Now what
can you buy? Kashmiri cloth, jeans, old cotton clothes, a few
simple Ladakhi costumes, but very little of the old cloth. The
time is coming soon when anyone who sings this song will not
know what the song is referring to, what the old dancers looked
like, with their silk shawls and belts of sheepswool. Or if they
do know it will only be a kind of museum knowledge, or
because troupes of dancers have been supported by tourist
agencies.'
    He began to sing again.

'I had a dream last night
I had a beautiful dream
I had a dream
In which all my hopes were fulfilled

'I saw a great iron bridge
Being built over the sea
I saw a garland of jewels
Floating on the water

'Taking up your sleeves my friends
Turn gently to the right
Winding your woollen shawls
Turn gently to the left

'May the young men of the village
Grow strong as tigers
May the men of Tsangra village
Live free and strong as tigers

'May the young women of the village
Grow like corn in summer

May the women of Tsangra village
Grow shining in the sun like corn.

'It is hard not to feel bitter, singing that song now. How can I
sing the first verse without anger at what is being done to my
people? What dreams for their future could I have that had any
hope of being fulfilled? The great iron bridge built over the sea
is the Buddhist faith, and the sea is the sea of Samsara . . . will
Buddhism last in these mountains? Can the young men grow
like tigers under Kashmiri domination? Will the young women
grow like shining corn when their innocence is gone?'

We sat silently. Nawang's sadness was too deep and too clear
to be touched by anything but silence.

Then Nawang pointed across to the mountains that were
shining in the afternoon light, and said, 'There are many songs
to the light in Ladakh. The light is our real King. Without that
light, day after day, I think I would have despaired long ago.'

'It is the light', I said, 'that has amazed me most in Ladakh
and brought me most joy. It is unlike any other light I have seen
— more absolute, more intense, more pure. There are some
mornings when I am almost frightened of it, frightened of
living another day under its scrutiny.'

'Sometimes,' Nawang said, 'we say that the Light is the Eye
of the Buddha, that penetrates all masks and reveals the true
nature of things.' And he sang:

'In the dark blue sky
There are thousands of stars
In the dark blue sky
There are thousands of stars.

'When Venus rises
I am happy
When Venus rises
Silver breaks over the palace

'On the high mountain ice
There are thousands of lions
When the Sun the Father of lions rises
Gold breaks over the palace

'On the high lake
There are thousands of geese
When the Sun the Mother of geese rises
Gold breaks over the palace.

'The light', Nawang said, 'is one thing the Kashmiris cannot
take from us.' He paused. 'There is another song about the
light, which I must sing you. It is a religious song. It is called
"The song of Basgo village". Have you seen Basgo?'
'Yes,' I said, 'many times!'
'And so you have walked round the ruined castle there?'
'Yes.'
'The castle is in the song. But in the song none of its stones
has fallen.

'The sun rises in the East
How warm it is
The sun's rays break from the three directions
How warm and beautiful the sun is

'The land is holy in the sun
The sun strikes the roof of the palace
The great copper Buddha
Burns in the sun

'On the heights of the mountains
Sits the Lama in meditation
On the top of Basgo Hill
Sits the Lama in the sun.'

'That is a beautiful song,' I said.
'It is more than beautiful,' said Nawang. 'It expresses a whole
world that is almost gone, a whole philosophy of living that has
almos¹ vanished from Ladakh. "The land is holy in the sun."
What modern song could say that?'
The garden we were sitting in looked across the valley to
Spituk monastery; we could see Spituk gompa on its crag, lit up
by the sun.
'Is there a song about Spituk monastery?'
'There are many.'
'Sing me the one you like most.'

Nawang stood up, faced the monastery, and folded his hands in prayer. Then he sang:

'Look the sun is rising
It lights up the monastery
It lights up Spituk monastery
Its crag of glittering rock

'Near the monastery of Spituk
There is a tree of white sandal
May it last for a thousand years

'On the heights above the village
Sit the gods of the village
On the hill of Spituk
The Protector God sits forever
May the God always protect the village
May the young men of the village live long and well

'In the new courtyard of the monastery
The Head Lamas are sitting
They are protecting the villagers
They are driving away all evil
May the lamas give their blessing always
To the people of Spituk
May all the young of Spituk live long and well

'In the new rooms of the monastery
There are thousands of monks
In the throne of the main room
The Rinpoche sits in splendour
He preaches the Dharma to the villagers
He teaches his world how to live

'In the kitchen of the monastery
The village heads are gathered
Drinking chang and joking
This is the tradition of our country
What a beautiful tradition.'

'I love that song,' I said, 'because it does not end with the splendour and wisdom of the Rinpoche teaching his world how to live. It ends with the village heads in the kitchen "drinking chang and joking".'

'That is very Ladakhi,' Nawang smiled, 'that feeling for the happiness of ordinary life. Do you know, there are no unhappy love songs in our folk literature?'

'Why? All the other folk literatures I know well are full of the misery of passion.'

'Buddhism teaches the transience of all things, a certain calm detachment from others and from oneself. We are taught not to take ourselves too seriously, and we are taught to believe that there is little ultimate truth in grief or misery. The real wisdom is joy. The real wisdom is happiness. The true wisdom is that of the Buddha, who is always shown at peace with all things. There is no tragedy in Ladakhi literature, no concept of tragedy, in fact. There is a Ladakhi saying, "The greatest courage is the courage to be happy." It takes a great courage when you are suffering to see beyond your suffering to the clear relations between things, to the laws that cause and govern your suffering; it takes great courage to be ruthless with one's griefs.'

Nawang was smiling as he talked, but his eyes were sad. Then he said, 'It is especially hard now, I find, to have the courage to be happy. So many of the facts seem to be against it. And yet without this strong inner happiness, how will one work? How will one survive at all the years that are coming?'

We had been talking and translating all day. The moon was rising over the mountains.

'Let us get some chang,' I said. 'We'll be like old Chinese philosophers, drinking under the moon and talking of poetry.'

'Yes,' Nawang smiled, and called Rindchen to bring us some.

'Even our chang songs, you know, can be spiritual. We make no separations in Ladakh between the ordinary and the holy. Every action can be holy; every good pleasure can be dedicated to the Buddha. Why shouldn't drinking with your friends be holy?'

And, pouring a glass of chang for me, and blessing it, Nawang sang:

'The monastery is like a huge bird
No words can describe its splendour
May it last forever

'On its right is a shining glacier
It is an offering to the Buddha
May it last forever

'To its left there glitters a lake
It is an offering to the Buddha
May it last forever

'In front of the monastery
Stands a beautiful sandal tree
May it last forever.

'That is the most spiritual of the chang songs, and it is one of the finest songs of Ladakh. We believe that the whole landscape is an offering to the Buddha, that the whole world has Buddha-awareness — even this flower, this stone. A glacier is specially sacred because it looks like a great white scarf tied across the rocks on the mountain, and white is the colour of purity for us, of purity and enlightenment. The lake too is sacred. Have you seen the seven bowls of water that are usually placed before the image of the Buddha in the monastery? They symbolise the gift of all the senses and appetites to the Buddha. There are many sacred lakes in Tibet, such as Mansarovar. A lake in the mountains is like a vast bowl of shining water offered to the Buddha. The smallest lake and the smallest stream are sacred, because they flash in the sunlight some part of the Buddha-awareness, of that pure light that is Supreme Understanding. To an Enlightened man, or a man on the path to Enlightenment, the whole world becomes a revelation of his own inner nature, of the inner nature of all things.'

'Do you have a guru?' I asked him.

'Yes. Nearly every Ladakhi has a guru of some kind. Do you?'

'No. I have never found anyone I could trust enough to give myself to in that way. I have met some clever and good men, but no one I felt was Enlightened. Not that I have any real idea of what Enlightened means.'

'How could you until you meet it? And you will not meet it until you are ready to.'

'Then I may have to wait a long time.'

'You may have to wait many, many lives.'

By now, the moon had risen to the heart of the sky. We sat drinking chang, saying very little, watching the night shadows shift on the mountains, listening to all the voices of the night, the laughter from the alleys, the dogs barking in distant fields.

'Nawang, thank you,' I said. 'I have felt closer to this country and this world through your singing and through your company than I have felt before.'

'I will sing one last song for you,' Nawang said. 'It is a religious song. It is a song of devotion to the Guru. When I go to see my guru, I sing it to myself as I walk to meet him. The song is addressed to the Great Guru of Tibet, Padmasambhava, the Indian master who brought Tantrism to these mountains:

'In the Upper Valley
Is a three-peaked snowy mountain
It is not a mountain
It is the throne of my guru
Of my Guru Padmasambhava

'In the Upper Valley
The great sun rises
It is not the sun
It is the hat of my guru
Of my Guru Padmasambhava

'In the Upper Valley
The moon rises white as conchshell
It is not the moon
It is the face of my guru
It is the face of Guru Padmasambhava

'In the Upper Valley
Corn and water laugh in the sun
This is not an earthly valley
It is the valley of Amitabha Buddha
It is the valley of the Blessed

'On the high peaks of the valley
Lamas are talking of the Dharma
It is not they who are talking
It is my Guru who is talking
It is the sacred voice of Padmasambhava.

'There is a Ladakhi saying,' Nawang said, ' "When you have
met the Guru everything shines with his wisdom and his
beauty; you see him in everything; you feel him in everything
that happens to you." '
He stood up. 'It is late. I must go now or I'll miss my plane in
the morning. I get back in two months. Will you be gone?'
'Yes.'
'I will send the rest of the songs to England.'
'It will be sad not to hear them on your voice. It will be sad
not to hear them in this garden.'
'Then you will have to come back.'

I n Tak-Tak again with Helena and Hans.
The willow grove where we sat a fortnight ago after the
dances is deserted now. The trunks of the poplars are stark white
in the afternoon sunlight, the ground is littered with newspaper, and empty chang bottles. I feel as sad as I did as a child,
when the circus in Delhi folded its tent and vanished, leaving a
bald wilderness behind it. After the ice-skaters dancing to
'Stranger in Paradise', the Siamese twins and the Great Wheel—
nothing, an empty compound, this empty grove with the
newspaper blowing about it.
Helena and I sat down. Slowly the images of that afternoon
returned. The old woman waving her bottle of chang at us; the
group of young women in their scrubbed shining satins, giggling at us as we offered them a packet of Swiss cheeses; the two
young boys chasing each other between the trees, trying to trip
each other up; the heap of green and red apples on dark blue
cloth by the gate. I remembered too how the Siamese twins in
that Delhi circus twenty years ago had lain, in a tent decorated

with six-armed gods and goddesses, and wheezed darkly, their naked bodies sweating in the lamp-light.

Helena said, 'Look at the mountains. It is the same light as before.'

There is a mani to the left of the fields of Tak-Tak. A mani is a wall with a long flat top where prayer-stones are left, open to the wind and rain and snow. There are many all over Ladakh, outside monasteries, villages, along the road from Leh to Choglamsar, in fields, in scrub wasteland, in the cleft of mountian passes. Many of them were built by the prisoners of war of a Ladakhi King in the seventeenth century; the King had wanted them to do something useful which would bring them merit.

The mani outside Tak-Tak is not especially large or long. The plaster along its sides is crumbling; there are clumps of coarse grass all along its top; sparrows perch on the stone slabs, shitting serenely on the Buddhas and sacred invocations.

So many stones . . . large, small, chipped, whole, red and ochre and grey . . . and so many different things carved on them: heads of Bodhisatvas, long quotations from the sutras, the great mantra of Avalokiteshvara again and again. Three centuries of prayers — for a good rebirth or a good marriage, for a child, or a quick and not too painful death. No names; no signs, to show who gave them or made them.

No one has arranged the stones, either: they are just thrown together haphazardly, as if they had been deposited by a strong wind, or in the wake of a mountain glacier. It is better so. The Ladakhis pray naturally, on the sides of roads, in buses, selling vegetables, standing wiping the sweat from their faces in the middle of a field. They need no special pomp. It is only the shape of the wall that gives the stones any order, and that not for much longer. Not only the plaster is crumbling.

For as long as the stones are there and the wall is standing, the wind that blows down the valley from the mountains will carry those prayers and blessings from field to field, mountain to mountain. The Ladakhis believe that the wind speaks the prayers silently as it blows over them, and speaks them, over and over again, along the streams, in the hair of the growing wheat, in the empty alleys between the houses at night, where the dogs sleep.

W e drive back. The stars are out, the road to Leh is deserted. Everyone in the jeep is shivering with the night cold. On our left, the Indus winds in the moonlight.

Rindchen says he wants more money. His wife is sick, his sister is sick, his son is sick. He needs a lot more money for the day because we kept him late and because he needs the money for medicine. We are too tired to disagree with him. He knows that we know he is cheating us, and smiles happily.

Suddenly, Hans shouts, 'Stop the jeep.' We have just turned the corner that brings Stakna monastery into view. There it is in front of us, half a mile away, standing on its rock in the Indus, its walls white in the moonlight, the river flashing and roaring around it.

Helena, Hans and I clamber out of the jeep. Rindchen looks at us and shrugs his shoulders. We walk down to the river and stand among the rocks at its edge.

'Look at the sky over there!' Helena pointed. It was purple and orange, the last blaze of sunset, just to the left of the monastery.

Pointing to Stakna, Hans said, 'It will be there in fifty years, but what will it mean?'

A hundred yards away there is the beginning of a vast concrete pipe that will carry badly needed water from the Indus to the fields around Leh. It has been 'nearly finished' for years. Its white walls gleam dully.

Rindchen chain-smokes and chatters away. He is happy. He has an old French couple arriving by plane tomorrow from Srinagar. They came last year too, and paid him a lot of money.

I met Helena at Pamposh's the next morning. Hans was working on some last interviews, she said, and would not join us that day.

'I dreamt of my husband last night. He died almost two years ago exactly. I dreamt that he was with us here in Ladakh. You, he and I were walking in the late afternoon in the hills near Lamayuru. He was carrying a dark leather book under one arm. It looked very old. From time to time he would stop to show you a passage from the book, and from the expressions on both of your faces, it must have been a work of great beauty. I asked him, "What book are you reading together?" but he did not answer. Perhaps he had not heard me. A little later, he left us, and went down to a stream on the right. He bent down and laid the book tenderly in the stream. "Why are you doing that?" you asked. He did not answer for a long time, and I thought, "He is dead; he cannot answer," but then he said, "None of us needs those words any more." He walked on ahead, alone. We all walked alone. The valley where we were walking narrowed and filled with an even light. We were walking separately, but I felt that we were each part of the same mind, a mind that contained also the rocks around us, and the stream that now began to shine with the same light. I found myself talking to myself with your voice; once I looked down at my hands, and saw that, in that moment, they were my husband's hands. And it was not frightening at all, this mingling with each other and with the rocks and water around us, and with the light; it was very calm, and natural.'

Something of the radiance of Helena's dream penetrated everything we saw and did that day, and we spoke little, walking in the morning up-river to Sankar to sit among the gentians and sunflowers of the monastery garden, and then in the early afternoon across the valley to Spituk.

In the main shrine-room of the monastery, in the corner, around a large white marble circle that had been raised slightly on a platform, seven monks were sitting. They were holding silver instruments in their hands, silver funnels that tapered to a point, and by their sides were heaps of what looked at first like glass beads, green, yellow, blue heaps, small iridescent mountains that shone in the candlelight.

'What are they doing?'

'They are making a mandala. The white marble circle is the Emptiness, Sunyata, from which all form comes, and in which all form is inherent. Through the small silver funnels the monks will place, in an ancient pattern, the stone colours heaped by their sides. When the mandala is ready it will be blessed by the Rinpoche of Spituk, the Bakula Rinpoche, and then all the colour will be scraped from it again, and only the white marble circle remain.'

'And this happens every year?'

'Every year. It is one of the most sacred rituals of the year. It falls always near harvest. As the fields ripen, the mandala is prepared. Ladakh turns gold in the sun, and the mandala, the sacred diagram of Reality, is revealed. Through the making of the mandala, the whole of Ladakh is charged with a sacred power. The mandala is always present; Reality is a mandala, of which each of us is the centre. So when the Rinpoche blesses this mandala, he is blessing the whole of this world through it.'

The monks had seen us, and were waving to us to come closer, to come and sit by them. Two chipped white cups were filled with Tibetan tea for us; and two lumps of tsampa placed by each cup. When we sat down, the youngest monk, who was sitting next to Helena, took her lump of tsampa, and made a small Buddha in meditation out of it, with long arms and a pot belly. He lifted it solemnly into the air. Everyone laughed. 'Eat it!' he said. 'Be happy.'

The monks worked in bursts, each in his own rhythm. They talked or chanted as they worked. Sometimes one of them would yawn and leave the circle to lie down for a quarter of an hour on one of the benches. When the youngest monk was tired, he sat

111

in the lap of the old monk next to him, and leant against him, pretending to sleep, but opening his eyes slyly from time to time to see if we were watching.

After an hour we thought we should leave. The monks said, 'Don't leave us. Stay a little longer!' The youngest monk took one of Helena's hands in both of his and said, 'Now you cannot go.'

We stayed all afternoon. When at last it was almost time to finish work for that day, the old monk said to us, 'Now each of you must make part of the mandala.' Helena and I looked at each other. It was such a delicate operation, trickling the stone dust through those silver funnels . . . The monk smiled. 'Do not worry. I will help you.'

First Helena and then I added a small heap of dark blue stone dust to a long line enclosing two large triangles in the diagram.

'Blue is the colour of Akshobhya Buddha,' Helena said, 'one of the Dhyani Buddhas, the Buddhas of meditation. He rules the East, and he brings the wisdom of emptiness, the wisdom that is "like a mirror".'

On her last morning, after I had said goodbye to Hans in Leh, Helena and I went to Likir and met by chance the Rinpoche of Phyang. We were visiting the upper rooms of the monastery, and an old monk suddenly appeared, and ushered us into the Rinpoche's room. Tankas freshly cleaned for the Dalai Lama's visit last year shone on the green and red walls; a long Tibetan carpet of blue and red dragons was unrolled before three large cushions on which three priests were sitting, the Rinpoche, a large exuberant Chinese-looking man, in the middle. No one said anything. We smiled at each other and bowed to each other. The three priests beckoned us to sit down. We sat on cushions near them. One window was open, and the sun fell in warm quiet squares on the walls. We could hear the laughter of young monks from the courtyard below, birdsong, and the noise of a stream.

And no one said anything. None of us was uneasy or embarrassed. Helena sat quietly and closed her eyes. There were two small brass lamps burning on a red lacquer table in front of the Rinpoche, and their flames were tall and unshaken. I stared at them, and at the delicate hands of the Rinpoche moving in ritual circles above them. He saw me watching him and smiled.

Two young monks brought in a large brass pot of tea and started making a fire to heat it. They sat in the corner of the room, working silently, almost invisibly. Soon the sound of crackling wood mingled with the mantras and the laughter of the young monks and the stream.

At first I could not understand why I was so exhilarated. And then I realised: the wood the monks had used for the fire was eucalyptus; the sweet harsh smell that was filling the room was the smell of the Nilgiri Hills, where I had been at school as a child, the smell that the fresh wind had carried across the hills and blown through the cold dormitories in the morning. And as I sat silently smiling and drinking the hot Tibetan tea that was poured for me, images of my childhood that had been hidden from me for years returned: the face of the old fat woman who had looked after us at school; the upturned head of a deer in the garden of the school, standing in grass and spiky frosted lavender; a clump of wild yellow gorse lit up by the sun and a girl running round it with burning red hair; the smell of the laundered sheets at the Lodge my parents stayed at nearby when they came to see me; a friend whom I never saw again standing waving to me from a hill, a book in his hand flashing in the sun. For years that part of my childhood had been lost to me, buried under England; drinking that tea, in that silence, in the thick of that fragrance, I had found it again and felt I could never again lose it. The images that came to me so intensely came from a quiet light and returned to it; they were mine and not mine; I did not own them or want to possess them; they burned and faded and I was not afraid of their fading, because I had seen and known them again, because I felt that, at last, after so many years, the road between me and them had been opened again and they would return.

W e left the Rinpoche and walked down the hill to the jeep. Helena laughed. 'My tea had a hair in it. Do you think I should have kept it? I could have taken it back to Wiesbaden and cured everyone . . .

'Why do I want to laugh and sing in these gloomy rooms plastered with gods I don't believe in, with those fat old men in robes sitting and drinking tea and doing nothing? And I have to go so soon. It's always like that, isn't it? Never enough time. And perhaps it is a mercy, never having quite enough time to have to change . . . But I *have* changed. It's too late.' She stood in the middle of the road. 'It's too late.'

A gaggle of young monks ran round the corner and started to leap around us. They dragged us round the corner to where the other monks were bathing, in a large yellow pond.

Twenty naked monks of all ages were leaping up and down in the water, giggling and splashing each other, and diving, and filling their cheeks with water. Two old fat ones, long past swimming, sat on the banks, looking on benignly, seated on two rocks that were surrounded as if by a Persian carpet by all the robes of the monks in the water, drying in the sun. As soon as they saw us, all the monks started shouting, 'Come in! Take your clothes off and come in! The water is warm! Come in!' Soon they were all chanting and clapping their hands. 'Come in! Come in!'

❧ 3 ☙

To the Rinpoche

Helena and Hans left at four this morning for Srinagar. I woke at seven, felt lonely in Leh without them, and went to the bus-stand to take a bus back to Lamayuru.

A man and an old woman sat next to me on the bus. They were poor, and dirty. The man had a worn purple rag around his head, and his shoes were held together by string. At first, I did not notice that the old woman was ill. She leant against the man with her eyes closed, her right hand resting on his neck. Then she began to moan, softly at first, then more and more insistently. The man stroked her forehead sadly.

'She is my mother,' the man said to me. 'We came to Leh yesterday to see the doctor. She was burnt the night before last.' He rolled up her left sleeve and showed me the bandage the doctor had wound round her wrist and a part of the large festering burn above it. 'The doctor said she would be better today.'

The bus started. The moans of the old woman got louder. Every time the bus jolted and shook her whole body trembled in pain. She started to cry. Her son held her closer and dabbed her eyes with his sleeve.

There was a French girl, a medical student from Paris, on the bus. We had met and talked in Leh. I called out to the conductor to stop the bus and walked up to where she was sitting.

'Louise, we need your help. There is an old woman at the back of the bus who is very ill and in pain. Could you have her sit next to you and give her something?'

The man helped his mother up the bus. Louise put her arms around her and the woman lay against her. Louise found some tranquillisers in her bag and gave them to the woman. At first she would not take them, but Louise's calm voice persuaded her and she slept a little. The son sat on his own staring out at the

117

road. His mouth was moving in prayer. From time to time, Louise took out her scarf and wiped the woman's forehead.

Just before Lamayuru, the bus stopped. The man and his mother got up. The mother tried to smile at us and raised one hand in a wave. Then she tottered slightly and her son caught her. The two of them stared up at us helplessly from the side of the road. She seemed to be shivering from cold, although it was the middle of the day. The son took a black shawl out of a bag and wrapped it around her shoulders.

When we got to Lamayuru I asked Louise, 'Was she very ill?'

'She was dying. She won't live out tonight.'

'Did she say anything to you?'

'She said she knew she was dying and that she wanted to die in her own house.'

The monastery seemed heartless in its pomp and bustle. I tried to drink some cold cabbage soup in the kitchen but kept thinking of the old woman and couldn't finish it. I tried to sleep in the afternoon, but I had only to close my eyes to see her eyes staring up at me from the side of the road. There was a fat German woman meditating on the bed next to mine. After she had finished, she began to play a long wooden flute and sing. I asked her as gently as I could to stop singing as I was trying to sleep. She looked furious and said, 'Everyone is so tired around here! Where is all the good energy these days? When I first came to India there was so much good energy!'

I left my bed and walked into the afternoon. The sound of the woman's idiotic flute followed me down the valley.

Looking back at the monastery, I found it hard not to hate it a little. I wanted the hills to be bare again. I wanted there to be nothing but rock and water and the mountains in the changing light. I wanted to see Lamayuru as Naropa, its founder, must have seen it, before it had a name, before it had walls and fields and prayer flags and Spanish men with 'Viva Madrid' sweaters taking flash photos of its frescoes.

118

And then I turned a corner into another valley. There was not a sign of human habitation in the valley — not even the crumbling remains of a chorten or a prayer flag.

My mind changed, emptied. I walked more and more slowly, more and more rhythmically. I felt my breathing grow even and my blood clear. I walked higher up the valley.

The rocks around me were the strangest I had seen in Ladakh. Vast fluted cathedrals of rock, cathedrals that might have been designed by Dali, loud with birds of all kinds. I saw an oriole high on one of the spires of gold rock, and all around me small gnarled rose-bushes, some with the last roses of summer still on them, shook in the breeze.

A stream glittered ahead. I walked faster, so that I would have time to bathe in it before I had to return. I took off all my clothes and lay in the freezing brilliant water, shouting at the cold. I turned on my side so that the water could run down my back and jabbed my elbow on a stone sticking out slightly from its bed of pebbles. It was the most delicate fossil I have ever seen — a primeval fern, each small filigree unfolding fixed and preserved for as long as the stone would last. I took it as an omen of hope.

That night in the monastery I dreamed I was in Benares. I arrived by an evening train. The station was deserted. None of the lights was on in the city and there was no one in the streets. A few ghostly, thin dogs wandered in the dirt. I walked slowly through the deserted city and at last came to a hotel. There was an old man asleep at the counter. I woke him and asked him if I could have a room. He looked at me tiredly, rubbing his eyes, and said, gesturing to an open door, 'No one comes at this time of year but there is a bed in there.'

Then I found myself sitting on the ground near the river. I couldn't see anything at first but I could smell the burning of the bodies. As I sat in the dark, I remembered my childhood home in Hyderabad that had been near a cemetery and the smell of burning that the wind sometimes carried into our garden, and I saw for a moment the large red and yellow flowers of the garden, lightly powdered with ash. My mother was sitting in a deck chair reading, in a white dress. I wanted to cry out, 'Come in! Come in quickly!' but she couldn't hear me . . .

A man sat down next to me. He was younger than me, perhaps twenty-five. His hair was white, whether from a strange ageing process or ash, I couldn't say. He had small, narrowed, yellowish eyes.

'Why are you here?' I asked him.

He said nothing.

I asked him again, 'What is your name? Don't you want to talk? What do you think of this place?', my voice rising higher and higher.

He leant towards me and breathed over my face. 'Why are you here? Why are you here?' he repeated in my voice, vacantly. 'Why are you here?'

The dream shifted: I was lying in my room in the hotel. From the street below I could hear sadhus singing — on and on, monotonously, in the chill moonlight. I looked up and saw on the ceiling a large square of darkness, a square of pulsing darkness, as if a pit of black snakes were writhing and tumbling over each other. I wanted to look away but could not. I went on staring at the square. It cleared, slowly. At its heart, a small, ragged patch of light appeared.

'Have you met the Rinpoche?'
I said I hadn't.

'You haven't met the Rinpoche? How long have you been here?'

I said I had been in Ladakh six weeks.

'My god, what have you been doing? The Rinpoche *is* Ladakh.'

'Which Rinpoche? There are several.'

'Thuksey Rinpoche, of course. The Bakula is mostly a politician. The Rinpoche of Hemis is too young. I've never met the Rinpoche of Phyang but reports say he's a bit of a playboy. Perhaps they are wrong. But Thuksey Rinpoche . . .'

Dilip Chatterji looked at me pityingly. Dilip's bald brahmin head gleamed in the afternoon light in the Tibetan restaurant. His plump Sindi wife sat at his side chewing a piece of mutton.

'Dilip — don't be such a bully! Dilip is such a bully!' She giggled and nudged closer to him. It was amusing to see this thin dignified sixty-year-old brahmin blush a little.

I had met Dilip only an hour before. We had been the only three people in the restaurant in the middle afternoon and I had sat down with them. Dilip, in his Gandhi clothes, had asked me, in a perfect English accent, 'Where do you come from?' I said I was an Englishman from Oxford.

Dilip nearly fainted with joy. 'My god! How amazing! Sit down! Sit down immediately! I was at St Paul's! Yes, and at London University! Engineering! Lived in Connaught Square! A rich aunt, you see . . . the Chatterjis wanted all their children given the British Treatment! Some hated it! I loved it! I was a very good cricketer. You know, only last month I won the Bombay Squash competition. But I mustn't boast. Sit down immediately! I get so very bored in India. I am an industrialist, god only knows why. I'm going to retire soon. I'm developing a plan of solar heating. But anyway . . . no. I get so very very bored in India. No one to talk to . . .'

'You have me to talk to,' Moneesha giggled. 'But I am so stupid, I know.' She had finished chewing and sat back against the wall, content.

'You know what I want to talk about?' Dilip asked. 'No? Can you guess? I want to talk about Indian philosophy. Are you interested?'

'It is my deepest interest.'

Dilip looked at me. 'Really? When I was at school in England everyone thought Indian philosophy complete rubbish. I remember one of my masters at St Paul's saying, "Chatterji, I hope you are not going to grow up to contemplate your navel? That would be a sad, sad waste, Chatterji." I can hear his voice now. Ask an Englishman then about Indian philosophy and he'd say, "It's complete balls. A lot of fat-bellied men sitting in the dirt doing nothing." I didn't care at all then about Indian things. All I wanted to do was to play cricket. But cricket is a very philosophical game, isn't it? So much patience . . .'

Moneesha yawned. 'You say you need patience. What about me? I have to sit on the sidelines and watch. My god, Dilip, the boredom I have endured for your sake. The cricket matches, the squash matches. Thank goodness I'm so plump I can't play any games.' She yawned happily again.

Dilip ignored her. 'No, when I came back to India at twenty-five I really knew very little about India. I felt lonely, strange, as foreign as an Englishman. I took up yoga, yes, but only to get fit for cricket. Imagine taking up yoga to get fit for cricket! And I was an engineer, you see. Still am. Built most of the dams in India. Most of the hydro-electric things too. Rather famous actually . . . Being an engineer I only read Engineering things. I was completely rationalistic. Moneesha says I am still a fiend of rationalism. But slowly I became aware of everything I had been ignoring about my own country. I saw that Western values, Western government, Western materialism, could not help India — India must find its own spirit, its own identity . . . and so I began to read. I read the Gita, I read the Upanishads, I began to read the Buddhist classics. I talked to sadhus, holy men of all kinds . . .'

'Those bloody holy men,' Moneesha said. 'My god, Dilip, how many of them I had to feed. Remember the sadhu from Bangalore who stayed four months! You said he was very austere. But he ate more than my whole family put together. And he slept all afternoon. And your yoga teacher. You said he was very holy too. He was always trying to get the ayah into bed.'

Dilip looked at her with weary patience. 'My wife is a cynic. All Sindis are cynics . . . they care only for money . . . Don't get me wrong. I do not believe India will save the world or anything. I'm more disillusioned than you could imagine by India and the Indians. The Indian middle class . . . you cannot believe their greed and stupidity. Last week a business colleague in Bombay spent one hundred thousand rupees in covering a hotel roof with flowers for a reception for his daughter, and in an area of Bombay where millions are starving. I did not go. In all this chaos what else is there to do but turn one's mind to God? And try and preserve something of one's heritage?'

'I wish I could turn my mind to God,' Moneesha giggled. 'I am very superficial. I like to eat and sleep and talk. Dilip says I'm hopeless. But he always gets me to read his books. And he takes my advice on all business matters. In fact I'm going to start a business and leave him to his yoga.'

Dilip looked up at the ceiling.

'What have you been doing in Ladakh?' I asked Dilip.

'I have always been interested in Buddhism. I have travelled in Nepal. I lived in Sikkim for a while. You know, I once went to a ball in the Palace of Sikkim.'

'Not that story again, Dilip, please.'

'Anyway . . . This is the second visit to Ladakh. I came last year and I fell in love with the place. It is the strangest place in India. And I love to walk . . .'

'What an understatement! Do you know, my husband has dragged me up most of those mountains? Why didn't I marry a film star instead of a yogi?'

'As I was saying, I love to walk. I love to be alone . . .'

'He loves to have me carrying all the things behind him . . .'

'I love to walk and be alone in the mountains. It clears my mind.'

'It may clear *his* mind. It makes me sick. I have lost ten pounds already.'

Dilip looked at me, suddenly. 'You say you are interested in religious things. I am sure you are. It is strange and wonderful how many foreigners are interested in Indian philosophy now. It is wonderful for us Indians because it shows us that we are not fools, that we have something to give to the world.'

'Give to the world,' Moneesha said. 'My dear, these gurus make fortunes! Think of Sai Baba! Think of Rajneesh! Sometimes just to annoy Dilip I say that when I have become a multi-millionairess I will give it all up and become a Holy Mother and become even richer!' Moneesha thought this very funny and went off into a peal of high-pitched giggles. 'Imagine me a Holy Mother!'

'You'd have to be a silent Holy Mother,' Dilip said.

'My husband is so cruel, don't you think?' She giggled, snuggling closer to him. He blushed happily again.

'You must come with us tomorrow,' Dilip said, 'and meet Thuksey Rinpoche. I met him when I came last year. He is the

Guardian of the Rinpoche of Hemis, Drukchen Rinpoche. He is an old man, an old Tibetan. He used to be head of several of the highest meditation abbeys in Tibet — of the Kargyupa sect, you know, the sect that Milarepa founded, I think . . . I saw him a few days ago. He said that I must go back and see him while he is at Shey. He's taking the prayers there for a fortnight. We will go tomorrow night.'

'Dilip is always going on about one holy man or another . . . but this man is something,' Moneesha said. 'He is a very beautiful old man. I like that. And he is kind. He does not look at me as if I were a leper or something. I think he rather likes me. He sees my soul. Dilip says I have no soul. But the Rinpoche sees my soul.'

'For god's sake, Moneesha . . . No, you must come with us tomorrow. I insist. Do you know what the Ladakhis call the Rinpoche? Thuksey Rinpoche. It means "The Rinpoche whose heart is a sun".'

D ilip and I met later that evening. Moneesha stayed at home to eat sweets and wash her hair. 'My wife', Dilip said, 'is a very remarkable but tiring woman.'

Dilip had changed into a long simple white dhoti and with his thin gold spectacles could have been a younger brother of Gandhi. He walked very briskly, very fast.

'My god, Dilip, do you always walk as fast as this?'

'Yes. I am frightened that if I slow down I will die.'

All afternoon I had been thinking about what Dilip had said about the Rinpoche. We were walking in the hills beyond Leh, by the row of small crumbling white stupas. An old man was sitting in the shade of one of them, spinning.

'What is it about the Rinpoche that impresses you, Dilip?'

'Contrary to what Moneesha told you, I am impressed by very few people. I have met everyone in India. All the politicians, all the leaders of industry. And most of them bore or disgust me. And I have met many so-called holy men who have not moved me at all. Either they have seemed venal or they have said idiotic things or they have been surrounded by adoring Westerners in a way that made me ashamed of them and suspicious. But the Rinpoche seems to me different. Perhaps I am fooling myself. Perhaps it is Ladakh, these mountains, this air, that makes me think so . . . '

'What is it in him that makes him seem different?'

'He makes you feel immediately at home with him. He does not want anything from you. He is tender to all the people around him . . . You feel you have been seen by him. Oh god, why do you ask me to describe him? You have to meet him. I am no good with words anyway.'

We walked on.

'Moneesha says I am a snob. That if I had met the Dalai Lama I would love him because he is a King and an Incarnation. That I like the Rinpoche so much because he is so grand, because he is old, because he is a Tibetan. Moneesha says all this is just spiritual snobbery.'

'Is it?'

'Who can be sure of anything?'

Dilip and I walked up to the top of the hill. The sun had set and the first stars were appearing over the mountains. Below us, the stupas seemed to shrink into themselves and into the dark shadows of the hillside.

At last, Dilip sat down.

'I have wasted my life. I have built dams, run companies, made roads. I have done all that and sometimes I am quite proud of it, for a moment. But what is that really? Many men could have done that. I was lucky, I was privileged, I was ambitious, I had the right contacts . . . and I had the capacity to make decisions and work hard. But none of it has given me any lasting satisfaction. When I say this to Moneesha she laughs at me and says, "The trouble with you is that you want everything. You want to be a millionaire and a saint, a businessman and a yogi, an industrialist and an artist and a philosopher. You are just greedy, Dilip. And your search for God is just another greed. God is a company, Dilip, you haven't yet taken over." She is not stupid, my wife. She has a matter-of-fact approach to everything. Perhaps she is right. I have left it so late, this search. I am embarrassed even to call it a search. What right do I have to say I am searching for anything? I follow no guru, no philosophy.

125

The yoga I do every day is mostly for vanity and to annoy Moneesha. "Don't get up, Dilip. It's five o'clock." '

He stopped, and looked at me.

'It must be a great thing to be a poet.'

'Poets are just as vain as businessmen, just as cut off in many ways from the life of the spirit, by vanity, by ambition, by the hunger to see things their way. To be absorbed by language, by art, can be as selfish as making money, and as cruel. I am tired of the way I have lived, enclosed in my words, my past, my griefs, my relationships. It is very small to live like that, very trivial.'

We sat gloomily watching the night deepen over Leh.

'Moneesha says that all this soul-baring is just an excuse to talk about ourselves. All this talk about getting rid of the Ego is just another chance for the Ego to go on about itself . . . Once I was sitting with an old sadhu in our home outside Pune and Moneesha came in. "What are you talking about?" "We are talking about the soul." "Oh my god, what are you talking about that for?" The sadhu got angry and gave her a stern lecture on how sometimes certain kinds of talk could lead the spirit to greater understanding, and that anyway she should listen to her husband. Moneesha said, "If I listened to my husband I would fall ill with boredom. What does he know anyway, my husband? He is just a man. Men can go on talking about business, or politics, or God . . . we have to keep the house together. That is much more serious." '

Dilip laughed. 'I think that is why the Rinpoche likes Moneesha so much. And he does. He always holds her hand the longest. And makes her sit next to him. And smiles at her continually. Because he sees that she is not vain. Because she is close to things, as he is. Because she is funny. They must get very tired, these holy men, of earnest, intense "searchers", of all the talk about the Ego and Compassion and whether there is a soul or not . . . Once Moneesha told the Rinpoche all about her relatives and how they were trying to cheat her and each other and he laughed until the tears poured down his cheeks.'

Next evening, Dilip and Moneesha and I took a jeep to Shey monastery, about twelve miles from Leh, where the Rinpoche was taking evening prayers.

Dilip said, 'Don't expect anything. It would be fatal to expect anything.'

On the journey there Dilip was in a grave philosophical mood. 'My dear, I am tired of everything except philosophy. As a young man, I thought it was all crazy, something for layabouts and old men. I loved Nehru, you see, and he thought the whole thing bunk, although he couldn't say so or he'd have been murdered.'

Moneesha was sitting in the back eating toffees. 'Dilip is always saying I think of nothing but money. Actually I am very spiritual. In my way I am a Bhakta, you know. I am very much in love with Krishna, especially the young Krishna. But I am lazy. I will need many incarnations to get there. But I am lazy and patient. So what's the hurry?' She finished one toffee and began another.

'Actually, sometimes,' Moneesha went on in the dark, 'I think I am very religious; I want to go on a pilgrimage; I want to wear orange robes. And then I think, Moneesha, Moneesha, look at yourself! You are being stupid. You couldn't leave the house. Who would see that the servants didn't cheat? Who would feed the dog? Who would amuse Dilip?'

Dilip went on, 'I wasted so much of my life on useless things. Committees, reports, dinners . . . Oh, my god. But I was a patriot, you see. I thought by doing all that rubbish I'd help India to a great future. Look what has happened. Poverty, hypocrisy, corruption everywhere. Hardly anyone of talent or integrity in industry or government . . . To have given your life for *that*. It makes me want to spit. And now it is too late to begin again. I think about God, but what do I know about Him? What hope do I have now? My brain is tired, my body is tired.'

Moneesha put one of her fat ringed hands comfortingly on his neck. 'Dilip, what rubbish; last month in the squash championship you beat men of thirty! You made them run like rabbits!'

Dilip looked out of the window. 'And what is going to happen to Ladakh? Will it become shoddy and ramshackle like the rest of India? Will the road we are going along now be lined with cinema advertisements and shanty towns? The people are so good, but I suppose they are stupid like everyone else and want radios and comforts.'

'Dilip, you like comforts,' Moneesha said reprovingly, patting his neck.

'I suppose I like comforts,' said Dilip grimly. 'I suppose I like them.'

We rounded the corner into Shey. There were two white horses on the side of the road. The headlights of the jeep made their eyes glitter. The first stars were coming out.

Dilip said, 'I may not see the Rinpoche again. He is not a well man. I am not a well man. Who knows what the future holds for any of us? What did he say to us last time, Moneesha? That life was a candle in an open doorway and at any moment it can be blown out? Didn't he say that, Moneesha?'

Moneesha was eating again.

'If you think you're going to die, Dilip, you're mad! Look at the way you skipped up those mountains! The Tibetan guide said that you were a real Tibetan! He said you were as strong as a yak!'

Dilip smiled slightly, and put his hand on her hand.

E vening prayers had already started. As we walked up the long winding hill in the early starlight, we would hear the monks chanting. A conch sounded. 'That means: listen to the Buddha,' Dilip said. Then a drum was beaten, its short rapid taps shocking the evening air. 'That means: this is the Law! This is the Law!' A bell rang. Dilip said, 'It is the Rinpoche who rings the bell. It means: awaken to the Knowledge that leads to Reality.' Moneesha tapped Dilip's shoulder impatiently. 'For god's sake stop lecturing and hurry up! I'm freezing!'

We stood in the huge wooden doorway, turned and looked out across the valley. The two white horses had stayed where we had first seen them, their tails swaying slightly in the night wind. The moon had risen and all the small twisting streams of the valley were flashing in the moonlight. To our left, in a large bowl of desert, a handful of stupas shone softly. A lorry passed on the road below. We listened to the sound until it vanished and then went up the half-ruined stairs of the monastery, lightly powdered with starlight, to the main room, where the chanting was coming from.

The door to the main room was half open. At first all I could see was light, thick golden light, shot through with incense and chanting. In that cold dark evening, the intensity of that light hurt my eyes. I could hardly look at it.

I cannot remember how we entered the room or what happened as we entered it. All I remember is sitting down on a mat by the side of the door and looking around me for the first time.

Dilip was sitting on one side; Moneesha on the other. We were in a huge room whose walls were covered with dark red and gold frescoes. I could dimly distinguish the faces of several Buddhas, but the light was too uncertain for me to tell which they were. In that light, the room seemed a hallucination of red and gold.

Around us the monks were chanting. A young monk in front of me leant forward and gestured up the room. I turned. There, at the end of a long double row of monks, sitting on a small throne, in a glowing red and gold robe, surrounded by the flickering of a hundred butter lamps, was Thuksey Rinpoche. He had a drum in his right hand and a bell in his left and was sounding them together. He saw us looking up at him, bent his head, and smiled. I saw that there were no other visitors to the monastery that evening but us, not even local people. The Rinpoche was alone with his monks and we were alone with him.

The Rinpoche did not look at us again. He did not look at the monks either, that evening. He seemed to be staring impassively beyond them, beyond the monastery, beyond the trembling red and gold walls of the gompa, concentrated and calm, performing all the movements of the ritual as if in trance.

Dilip leant over to me and whispered, 'The Rinpoche is a Khampa. He comes from the Tibetan region of Kham. The Khampas are very wild, great fighters. The Tibetans say that the Khampas make the best killers and the greatest saints . . .

Look at those huge shoulders of his, those hands, that head . . .
It's the head of a lion, isn't it? A kind lion, but a lion . . . Last
year he drew a map of Tibet for me and put his birthplace on it.
He said, "It is my only sadness that I will never see Tibet
again." '

Looking at the Rinpoche at the end of the room, in that light,
it was hard to imagine him being saddened by anything.

It was near the end of the ritual. Slowly, the Rinpoche began
to sing. Om mani padme hum, the old mantra of Avalokiteshvara, the Buddha of Compassion, the great Mantra of
Tibet, the mantra I had seen carved on hillsides, on the
stones in the mani. 'Praise to the Jewel at the heart of the Lotus.'
He sang it again and again, slowly, quietly, with a dark tender
gravity, rising and falling. And the monks sang it with him
also. Again and again, he would pick up the vajra by his side,
the Sceptre, symbol of the Unified Consciousness, of the Mind
that has gone beyond Duality, and turn it in the air, writing
with it on the light circle after circle. Once he took up a handful
of rice with his left hand, threw it into the air, looked up to see it
shine briefly in the light, and then fall.

'The Rinpoche will see you now.'
We had been standing outside in the starlight, on the
crumbling stone steps, watching the clouds cross and recross the
moon. Moneesha said that in Sind people told each other's
fortunes by the shape of the clouds crossing the moon. 'Don't
worry,' she beamed, 'I have just seen a horse and a dragon. Both
very propitious.' Then she and Dilip quarrelled about the
moonlight. Moneesha said it reminded her of the moonlight in
Sind. Dilip said, 'Nonsense. Sindi moonlight is much thinner.'
'Thinner! There is nothing thin about Sind or the Sindis.'

'The Rinpoche will see you now,' the young bright-faced
monk repeated, taking me by the arm. We walked up to the
upper part of the monastery, Dilip and Moneesha still arguing.

'What do you know about moonlight anyway, Dilip? You can't see anything.'

'I have better eyesight than you.'

'Only a woman and a poet can really understand moonlight.' Dilip growled.

Shey monastery is virtually in ruins. In fact, the only parts of it that have not completely fallen down are the room in which prayers are held, and sections of the upper storey, the long smoky kitchen, the room with the famous large statue of the Buddha of the Future, the Maitreya Buddha, and the small bare room which the Rinpoche had taken over for his personal use in the fortnight he would be there.

The young monk knocked twice. A noise like a soft growl came from inside. We entered. It was a bare room, bare walls with a small slit for a window, two long mattresses covered with red cloth, a lacquer table and a threadbare blue and green carpet, decorated with dragons.

The Rinpoche was sitting on one of the mattresses, sipping tea noisily, in the full unflattering glare of a paraffin lamp. No greater contrast could be imagined than that between this relaxed worn man and the man I had seen only a quarter of an hour before in the shrine below. There had been something forbidding in the calm, the majesty of the man who presided over and guided the evening ritual; there was nothing forbidding at all in the face that looked up at us, with its deeply set brown eyes, its thin white goatee beard, its soft unlined golden skin. The Rinpoche's cloak had fallen while he was drinking — he swung it round his shoulders again, smiled broadly, and gestured to us to sit. We went up to him in turn, presented our white scarves, as is the custom, and he returned them to us, putting them around our necks with a deep haaah sound, a noise I would often hear him make of welcome and blessing. I found myself shaking slightly as I bowed to him. He patted me gently on the head, as if to reassure me.

We sat silently and he looked at each of us in turn. I noticed for the first time what I would notice often with him — his gift of silence. He always spoke softly and slowly when he did speak, in a deep, sonorous but gentle voice; but often he would not speak at all, he would sit, as he was sitting now, with his hands folded casually in his lap, looking at everyone in the room in turn, with a relaxed and playful but charged intensity. In all the time I spent with him, I never saw him greet anyone perfunctorily. As he looked into my eyes that first time, I found myself smiling back at him. I had no conscious idea why I was smiling at him. I felt I must look ridiculous, sitting there and smiling with such intimacy to an old man I had never met before, but I did not care. Suddenly, he roared with laughter, opened his arms wide, and said in his deep, beautifully accented Tibetan, 'I am so glad you all have come.' We all laughed too, a little nervously.

A young monk, Nawang Tsering, had come into the room. He sat at the Rinpoche's feet and would be our translator.

'Where are you from?' the Rinpoche asked me.

'I am from England.'

'Why have you come to Ladakh?'

'Since I was a child I have been interested in Tibet. I was born in India. I met a young Frenchman in Delhi who told me about Ladakh; I had a friend at Oxford who first instructed me in Tibetan Buddhism. I have come to see the living tradition of Tibet. I have come to try and understand something of the essence of Tibetan Buddhism.'

The Rinpoche thought for a moment, looked down at his hands, and said nothing. Then he looked at me very directly and said, 'You have come to know something of the Buddha? Is this true?'

'Yes.'

'Good. You have come to the right place, and at the right time. You are lucky! You must learn everything you can.'

We sat in silence. Then I asked the Rinpoche a question:

'Your Holiness, I have been in Ladakh several weeks now. Already I feel it is a good place and that it is in danger — of losing its identity, of losing its heart. What can any of those of us who come to Ladakh do for her?'

The Rinpoche did not answer at once. I came to know that he never answered questions immediately. He brooded on them and on the person who had asked them. When he answered, he would always lean forward slightly, as if listening to the inner spirit of his hearer, to a rhythm far beneath the words that were being exchanged. His answers, even to the most perfunctory question, were nearly always long and elaborate, studded with beautiful turns of phrase, sudden startling images.

'Ladakh is very poor and sad at this time. Ladakh is ringed with dangers. The heart of this country, its soul and its life-blood, is Buddhism, a Buddhism that has been in these mountains for two thousand years. And this heart is threatened. The monasteries are falling down, the monks are losing discipline. You cannot help Ladakh except by loving her, by understanding her heart. And if you love her you will learn that Ladakh will be dead if its heart, Buddhism, is not kept alive. Our monasteries must be restored, our monks must learn again the beauty and nobility of the Dharma, schools, many schools, must be built to help the people retain their old beliefs and make them new in a changing world. Without Buddhism, Ladakh will be helpless, an old ox, blinded and stumbling about in the dark on sharp rocks.'

Dilip said he had seen the paintings in the monasteries and that many of them were crumbling off the walls.

'That is not a problem,' said the Rinpoche. 'We have many new painters.'

'But many of the old paintings are masterpieces. And most of the new painters are not as good as the old ones.'

'It is more important that the tradition of religious art should be kept alive in the hearts of the people than that Ladakh should become a museum.'

Then the Rinpoche added, 'Schools are more important than paintings. The future is more important than the past. Why preserve the paintings if there will be no one left in the country to understand their meaning?'

Then he looked at us and said, 'Would you like to come and see my school?'

Although it was late, and dark, and we knew that the driver of the jeep would be getting restless, we decided yes, we would go and see the Rinpoche's school. He seemed very pleased.

We walked down the monastery's hill and then to the left a few hundred yards in the starlit dark, into that large bowl of desert I had seen from the gompa steps. There, near a clump of moonlit willows, was the school.

There were only two half-finished rooms, two stark concrete rooms with slits for windows. In the moonlight the rooms looked forlorn. It was hard to imagine any children learning in them.

We walked round the building dutifully. The Rinpoche kept clapping his hands. To him, evidently, the school was already built, and huge, and full of students all practising the Dharma and learning Tibetan and mathematics.

Nawang Tsering whispered to me, 'The Rinpoche is an optimist in all things. Actually, there is no money. This is all the building that has been done in two years. It is difficult to believe it can ever be finished. And how will anything be done without schools?'

The Rinpoche was striding around the building, pointing out the sturdiness of the walls, the solid beauty of the design, the rooms where, one could tell, he already saw generations of schoolchildren reciting their mantras and beginning to learn the techniques of Tibetan debate.

'It is true,' the Rinpoche said, 'that we have no money. It is true that the Government is not helping us. It is not stopping us from doing anything, but it is not helping us either. But I do not give up hope. This land is a Buddhist land. Buddhism will never die out in these mountains.'

He laughed. 'And if we cannot build a school we will teach out in the open. We will teach in caves or under trees by the river. Isn't that how the Buddha taught his disciples?'

Nawang Tsering said, 'None of us can understand why the Rinpoche is always so hopeful about anything. Perhaps it is because he has already lost so much. He has no attachments and so there is nothing to grieve him.'

I was standing in one of the rooms, looking at the moon through the high glassless window. Nawang came up to me and put his hand on my shoulder.

'Do you know what the moon means in Buddhism?'
'No.'
'The moon is the symbol of Enlightened Consciousness. The

134

Buddha was born on the full moon and entered into Nirvana on the full moon.'

'The moon is full today.'

'Yes. We are very lucky to be all together on this full moon.'

Then Nawang said, 'The Rinpoche is taking special prayers tomorrow. Prayers for Avalokiteshvara, the Buddha of Compassion. Many people will come from all over Ladakh. You must come too.'

The Rinpoche was walking out of the door of the room. He turned in the doorway, his face and shoulders shining in the moonlight and he looked at me, smiled, and nodded twice without saying anything.

In fact I didn't go to Shey the next day. I felt nervous, abashed almost, at the intensity of that first meeting with the Rinpoche. I wanted to keep my distance from him a little longer.

Next afternoon, I went with Dilip to Stakna monastery. Moneesha stayed at home to wash her hair and haggled for presents for her family in the market. 'You boys go and do something together,' she had said, waving us impatiently out of the khaki bungalow. 'I want to be alone and think about serious things.'

In the jeep Dilip and I talked about the Rinpoche.

'What did you think of him?'

'I was moved and impressed.'

'Why?'

'He was so simple.'

Dilip laughed.

'You are afraid, too, aren't you?'

'Yes.'

'I was afraid when I first met him. I couldn't go back and see him for several days afterwards. Men like him are frightening. They are so clear they make you feel dirty. For the last twenty years I have been wanting to meet a man like him — and when I did, the first thing I wanted to do was to leave, to leave Ladakh immediately, and never to see him again. I thought I wanted to find a Master; when I did, I felt threatened. I had thought, in a rather idle kind of way, that I wanted to change my life; when I was offered the chance I suddenly did not want to give up anything. For a while, I hated him. What right had he to show me to myself? What right had this old Tibetan to make me feel ridiculous, vain, helpless, false? I even felt his power could be evil, that he was some kind of black magician juggling for my soul. I tried with all my good old English training in scepticism and irony to keep him at a distance — but it didn't work, it couldn't work.'

'What happened?'

'Eventually, I went to see him. I was full of all sorts of strange, angry thoughts and questions before I went in. When I was in his room, I could not say anything. In all my life, I have never been at a loss for words. That morning I could not say anything, I could hardly move. He looked at me and said, "Would you like to stay here today?" I said, "Yes", and I spent the whole day with him, in silence in his room watching him with all the people who came and went, all the monks and villagers and Westerners, saying and doing nothing but just being with him. That day I realised who I had met . . . He blessed me before I left that evening, and I realised that he had accepted me.'

'Have you become a Buddhist?'

'Labels do not interest me. I have found a man in whose good power and spirit I believe and that gives me strength. In the East we believe that the connection between Master and Pupil is stronger and more important than any doctrinal beliefs, that truth is a living intensity transmitted from person to person, a living experience, not a set of practices or even philosophical positions. I revere Buddhism; I meditate in Buddhist ways; but I would not call myself a Buddhist or a Hindu. I am a man searching to understand myself, before it is too late, after a rather spoiled and ignorant life. That is all.'

And then Dilip turned to me. 'You must let me tell you something. I have known you only three days but I feel very close to you. You could be my son. I have a son your age and you would like each other. If you have felt something from the Rinpoche, follow it, follow your feeling as bravely as you can.

Find the humility to open to him without fear. He can help you understand something if you let him. Forgive me if I am preaching at you, but we do not have much time together. Moneesha and I have to go tomorrow. For so long, I believed only in what I could see and touch and know with a narrow, sharp, hard part of my mind; I was a sceptic, a materialist, an engineer, a cynic — and I am grateful I was those things, I needed and need the toughness of mind they have given me, the clarity and the power of judgment. Do not imagine that the spiritual life requires only abandon; it demands the highest kind of intelligence also, the clearest powers of discrimination and judgment. I do not feel I have abandoned my old life; I feel I have built on its foundations, begun to bring it to ripeness. Of course, I may be fooling myself, and you may only be listening to the hopeful drivel of a frightened old man. That is for you to judge and for life to reveal.'

We had reached Stakna. We walked up the long winding gravel path to the monastery.

The greatest painting in Ladakh is in Stakna monastery. It is in the main shrine-room, on the right. You need a torch to see it, and it is peeling off the walls. In a decade, it may be gone altogether.

It is a portrait of a great teacher of the seventeenth century, a Rinpoche from Bhutan, sitting in the lotus position in a circle of light. His eyes are half-shut, his left hand is raised in blessing. The painting is life-size.

There is nothing idealised about the portrait. This is a real man in a real place, not a Mythical Hero, not a God. The lama's beard is scraggy, his hands are strong peasant's hands; the lines on his face bear witness to the stress and turmoil of decades of self-discipline, all the long struggle towards self-mastery. His square shoulders stoop slightly.

The nearness of the large square altar and the narrowness of the room prevent you from standing too far away from the painting. The Rinpoche stares at you; you stare back at him. He smiles at you; you are half-compelled to smile back at him. He is bending forward slightly, as if he finds any distance between you and him intolerable.

There is only one painting I have seen that matches this in spiritual intensity — and that is the 'Resurrection' of Piero della Francesca in San Sepolcro. But the Rinpoche of Stakna has none of the eerie majesty of Piero's Christ, none of his 'sacred terror'. All the colours in the Ladakhi painting are warm and intimate — deep reds, glowing greens, the earth-brown orange of the robe. The Rinpoche is not a risen God but a man who by great labour has mastered himself. You feel reverence, but no final distance, no ultimate, sacred separateness: the Rinpoche is the highest part of yourself, come at last to its expression.

'There are no Gods in Buddhism,' Dilip said. 'All the so-called "Gods" and "Bodhisatvas" of the Mahayana pantheon are inner principles, energies of spiritual growth that are in every man. When the Buddha was dying he said, "I am not a God. I am only a man who has learnt how to cross the Sea of Being and shown you the way. Go and work out your salvation with diligence." Everyone and everything is Buddha, contains the Buddha principle. What did the Rinpoche say to me last year? He said, "It is not a question of becoming, it is a question of *uncovering* what you really are, of letting yourself be yourself, of letting everything that is not yourself fall away." '

'But what remains when everything falls away?'

'Nothing. Emptiness. Sunyata. There is no real Self. There is no final Identity, no God, no soul, no Absolute. Only Sunyata. There are two ways of saying Sunyata, the Rinpoche said. You can say it harshly, and you can say it gently. You can say it so that it sounds like the iron hand of death beating on the door, or like waves fanning out and whispering on the sea-shore. When you say it the first way you tremble slightly because you understand that to know Emptiness is the end of the Ego you have cherished and you are afraid; when you say it gently you are happy because in the experience of Emptiness is spaciousness and freedom, is Nirvana. To be freed from a false perception of the Self is the end of Buddhism; to realise that there is Nothing and No one is also to understand that one is in everything and in everyone, that there is no death, no fear, no pain, no separation.'

'Have you felt what you are talking about?'

'In moments. Enough to know that it is not nonsense. Not enough to live in constant awareness of its truth.'

I looked up at the painting again and noticed something I had not noticed before — that the circle of light around the Rinpoche was painted roughly, in great whirling brush-strokes. The Rinpoche that had seemed so solid, so real, so characterful before now seemed an apparition, a figure conjured out of the depths of Dilip's and my meditation. For a moment, in the torchlight, even the flickering dark stone walls seemed weightless.

Moneesha was lying back on the bed. 'All these great experiences, all this high philosophy . . . They only make people vainer, crazier, less human. Remember that sadhu with one eye, Dilip? You thought he was a miracle of wisdom. He was the most arrogant old idiot I have ever met and since I have met a lot of old Indian politicians, that is saying something. I told him one day I was depressed. He said, with his ghastly leery little smile, "You must say I AM GOD I AM GOD with great feeling," and I didn't feel a thing. I just gave myself a headache.'

'You cannot deny the Great Experiences though,' Dilip said.

'No, of course I don't deny them. It's just that I refuse to give them the importance you give them. It's more important to live well than to have mystic revelations all the time. It is more important to comfort a boring old woman or give to the poor than to see God in a tree-trunk or a grain of sand.'

'And yet you are always saying how much you love the Rinpoche.'

'Yes, I love him. Most of all because he never goes on about his perceptions, his visions, his experiences. He's beyond all that. He's spent his nine years in solitary meditation — I should think he's fed up with all those mystic things, all the vanishings and Nirvanas and apparitions and whatnot. He's an attentive, simple, tender, funny old man and that is why I love him. He's too busy attending to the world around him to have time to tell everyone about his *experiences*. And even if he had time he wouldn't want to. You are looking; he has found what he has been looking for. That is the difference, and that is why you are always worrying, talking, analysing, comparing. It's enough to drive anyone to chocolates — all this chatter about the Buddha and Nirvana from a lot of neurotics obsessed with their own sensibilities and reactions! You should scrub latrines or something, do something useful.'

She looked at us and burst out laughing. 'God, you two are so serious! You think I'm attacking you! And you are the ones who are supposed to believe that you don't exist, that all this is just a dream, Maya, Sunyata! My, my — what self-important No-bodies you are! Have a toffee! Don't just stand there looking stricken!'

And then she said, 'It is you who make so much of the Rinpoche, who make him so grand, so wonderful. Really he is just a good old man. And that, of course, is what is so wonderful about him. A good old man with powers of all kinds, probably, but entirely unenchanted by himself or any image of himself your adoring eyes show to him.'

She turned to me. 'You won't let Dilip preach at you too much, will you? He is a great fool. All talk, talk, talk and big words and Self-Searching. Why can't he be simple? Why can't he just take things as they are? Why can't he be wise and ordinary?'

'Because he is still looking for wisdom,' Dilip said. 'Because he is afraid that he will die without knowing anything worth knowing.'

'Oh my god, listen to him! What does it matter if you do die ignorant? What's so important about you?'

'This goes on every day,' Dilip said to me. 'I asked the Rinpoche about my wife's spiritual state last year. He said she was very good for me, because she knew me too well to take me seriously. I told him that her scepticism and mockery upset and humiliated me and often discouraged me. "Good," he said. "Very good. It will make you more honest." I was very angry.'

That evening Dilip and I walked to where we had walked the evening before — the hill above Leh. All the stars were out.

'To think that I have to go back to Bombay,' Dilip said, 'and to what . . . the office, the relations . . . all that squalor. But we always have to go back to where we come from, don't we? Last year I thought of staying here. I didn't tell Moneesha — she would have laughed at me, or worse, hated me. I thought seriously of giving up my job, my life, even Moneesha and coming here. I could have gone into a monastery and studied under the Rinpoche. Why didn't I? Was it cowardice? Or was it that I just couldn't believe in myself doing something so radical, that I couldn't believe that I wasn't play-acting somewhere even in that? It would be dreadful to renounce and then realise that you had staged your renunciation also, staged it with the same selfishness as you had staged everything else!'

'Were you changed when you returned?'

'I would love to say: I became more aware, more caring, more intelligent. If I am to speak honestly, though, that isn't really so. For a while having been here and having met the Rinpoche made me completely disconsolate. I couldn't bear the company of anyone, hardly even Moneesha. I wandered about like an ill old dog. I was irritable, bitter, easily bored. And of course I felt guilty. I felt I had been given so much and could make nothing of it . . . and then slowly I changed. I became more resigned. Instead of hankering, or moaning, or criticising myself, I began to meditate. Nothing grand, nothing very sustained. Really I am no example to anyone. I began my search too late. I came to philosophy, tired and saddened by disappointment, with most of my youthful energy exhausted. To have met a man like the Rinpoche is much, very much, but it is only the beginning of another search, a deeper practice — and I feel too worn-out to embark on this longer voyage. Perhaps I will find the courage. I doubt it.'

He paused. 'There is only one mercy in believing in reincarnation. Some Westerners imagine that it is a tender doctrine.

Not so. To come back again and again, not to die — what a frightening thought! Never to be able to sign off all this longing and searching . . . to be caught perpetually in Samsara . . . There is one mercy, though. One may have another chance to approach Reality, another opportunity to learn. I asked the Rinpoche about that. He said, "Why do you want to wait for another life? If you have been given a car and petrol do you wait ten years before driving it and walk everywhere?" Moneesha and I are going in the early morning. Please do not come and see us off. Write to us some time. I wish you luck and courage.'

He spoke with such kindness and earnestness that I was touched. We shook hands and Dilip walked down the hill. At the bottom he turned, waved, and walked on.

I stayed on the hill to watch the stars and listen to the streams talking from their beds of rock. I thought: 'Tomorrow I shall go and see the Rinpoche. I will put him off no longer.'

That night I had this dream: I was sitting in the drawing room of a house I had once lived in in North America. I was alone. The great sliding windows of the room were drawn because it was winter. I could see the lawn covered with snow and shags of snow in the pines outside.

I was alone and unhappy. I felt I could never leave that room. I noticed that everything in the room was older than I remembered it. The desk was coated in dust; each of the four china birds on the mantelpiece was broken in some way. A wing was missing, or a beak. In all the corners of the room there were piles of magazines and books, some of them open, haphazardly, as a depressive might open them. The arm of the gramophone was on the floor.

The autumn I had spent in that house two years before had been full of distress, and in the dream I lived through that sadness again. A friend had had a breakdown that summer, and was in Philadelphia, where I could not see him or reach him. In my dream I could hear him talking in another room, laughing and then sobbing, on and on, and then talking clearly, but in a high-pitched idiot's voice. 'This is your work. This is your best poem. I hope you are satisfied. Do I shout at the right pitch? Do I say what I am supposed to say?'

I closed my eyes. I felt my whole body cave in, as if I was dying, as if I were made of a dark sand that was trickling away.

Then I opened them again. Everything in the room had been cleared away — there was no gramophone, no books, no dirty khaki carpet, no broken china birds. The room was empty. I was sitting on the floor. There was no voice in another room, laughing and sobbing and accusing. I looked out of the window, and where the garden had been, the lawn of snow and the pines, there was an expanse of water, stretching to the horizon, glittering in an even, white light.

D ilip and Moneesha left, as planned. I did not wake up in time to see them off. When I opened my door to go to breakfast that morning I found this letter:

I am so happy we met and talked in Ladakh. Perhaps we will meet again, perhaps not. Reading tonight in the *Songs of Milarepa* I found these two quotations —

Cool mountain water
Heals the body's ills
But only grouse and mountain birds can reach it
Beasts of the valley have no chance to drink it.

The wonderful jewel beneath the Ocean
Is a marvel granting all desires
But it belongs to the Dragon of Happiness
Men of the earth cannot obtain it.

I am not a mountain bird. I am an old horse trying to climb the sheer sides of the rock, out of breath and easily tired. As for the Dragon of Happiness — I have never even seen it. I hope you do.

My love to the Rinpoche. Learn from him. Love Dilip.

Dilip had drawn a dragon in the left-hand corner. It had vast, flapping, scaly wings and a fiery jewel in the middle of its forehead. Its face, however, was very benign. For a moment, I could not place where I had seen it before, and then I realised; it was the face of the Cheshire Cat. Dilip's English education had not been wasted.

I caught the early morning bus to Shey. I was afraid. What if Dilip and I had invented the Rinpoche? What if we hadn't? Both alternatives were distressing. Disappointment would be safest; I would at least still have the refuge of irony. But to have come so far . . . and yet if the Rinpoche was what Dilip and I felt him to be, then what would I have to do? I would have to do something. I could not just look, learn a little, record what I learnt, and leave. That would be bleak, that would be corrupt. Yet what could I do? What should I do? I had no idea. I almost got off the bus at Choglamsar, the Tibetan village five miles outside Leh. Why not see the village, go back to Leh, and return to Kashmir tomorrow, and leave all this craziness for good? Yet I knew I couldn't do that. I had come that far, I had to go further. I had to attempt to understand what had drawn me to the Rinpoche, and why, for all my fear and desire to leave, I was nevertheless smiling to myself at the thought of seeing him again.

The first time I had walked up to the monastery, it had been in moonlight. The whole plain of Shey had been dark, except for the silver of the small streams and the glow of the stupas in the night. Now I was walking up in full morning sunlight. The fields had not yet been harvested and so were thick and glossy with grain and swaying in a light warm wind. The stupas that had looked so ghostly at night, even when we had walked close to them, now shone solidly, cakes of dazzling bread the warmth of the sun had made rise. On some of them green and red and yellow prayer flags were flapping in the wind, trembling flames of pure colour against the ochres and reds of the rocks and the pale sun-struck blue of the sky. The first time I had come to Shey there had only been the three of us, Dilip, Moneesha and I; now I was being jostled on the narrow path by half of Ladakh — old men and women with wrinkled brown faces, black teeth, and creaking prayer wheels, young girls in their Sunday satin and brocade, young fathers with clean red robes and flowers in their ear. The father of the owner of the hotel was walking with me and saying, 'So you have come to see the Rinpoche. We are all going to see the Rinpoche. It is good to pray with him. We will pray to the Buddha of Compassion. We will pray and drink tea and talk and we will catch the last bus home. It is festival. It is Summer Festival,' pushing apricots and apples into my hands, into the pockets of my Indian shirt, into the small brown canvas bag I always carried with me. We paused on the top. He took out an old flask filled with stream water and passed it to me. I drank, tasting the rock and the light.

We walked up the steps to the main shrine. There, too, everything had changed. The first time that I had seen it, it had been empty except for two short lines of monks, the Rinpoche, and a handful of flickering lamps; it had been hard to make out anything more than a few dream-like faces of Buddhas on the walls. Everything, that evening, had seemed ghostly and hieratic, a trance of ritual I could be moved by but not enter. Now, the room was flooded with morning light. From all sides, the brilliant reds and greens of Buddhas in meditation shone at me and I could see plainly their quiet faces, raised hands, haloes of green and red and yellow light. On the far walls huge whirling mandalas flanked two large wooden structures, full of holes for

145

books, whose silk bindings shone in the gleam of a thousand butter lamps and the sunlight from open windows in the roof. And this time, too, the building was full, so full I could hardly find a place to sit down, full of Ladakhis, at least three hundred of them, mothers and small children, old men, young men, the whole of Shey and its surrounding villages, talking and praying and singing and whirling prayer wheels and walking up and down greeting each other. And at the centre of all this brilliant, noisy, exuberant life was the Rinpoche, seated cross-legged on a small throne. When I came in, he had raised one hand to sound the drum and the other to ring the bell. I stood in the doorway a moment to watch him. Light poured from the roof on to his head and shoulders. He was shining, a paterfamilias radiant at the heart of his family. After he had sounded the drum and bell, an old woman stumbled out of the crowd to his left and bowed to him. He leant forward the whole length of his seat and took her head into his hands. She stood up and was about to give him a white scarf. He took the scarf out of her hands gently and put it around her neck.

I came for the day, but I stayed the week.
    As I sat all day on the cold stone floor of the gompa, drinking tea and talking and praying and meditating and watching the Rinpoche, I thought again and again of what Dilip had told me of his first visit to Benares.

'I was terrified,' Dilip had said. 'Yes, I, an Indian, was terrified the first time I went to Benares. So much noise! So much life! I thought it disgusting, irreligious. I was used to St Paul's Cathedral, you see. Ladies in dark hats, the soft drone of cultured voices. "Now let us pray," and "Here beginneth the first lesson." And at school Religion had been rows of boys in starched collars and the Headmaster droning on about Team Spirit and Service and the Professions. To go to Benares after that . . . I wanted to run. But I didn't run. I stayed. And slowly

I understood. I understood that India has not cut off God from life; that to the Indians God is in everything, is expressed in everything, in cleaning your teeth, in selling sweets, in taking a tonga ride, as much as in meditation, or bathing in the Ganges.'

He had turned to me: 'The highest love of God, the Indians believe, is not to love God as the Father or the Lover or the Friend — but as the child. To be tender with him, as Krishna's nurse was with Krishna . . . It is the hardest thing. It is easy to abase ourselves before God; what is hard is to forget our guilt, to abandon our self-hatred, and to come to Him smiling . . . '

Everything Dilip had said about Benares seemed to speak to me, there, in that large crowded room in Ladakh. The noise, the chatter, the dogs, the old women singing — it had all frightened me at first. I felt absurd in my dirty dungarees and brown Kashmiri shirt, absurd and inhibited. Slowly I relaxed, gave up my sense of baffled and half-ironic detachment and began to delight in everything — in the faces of the old nuns, sitting towards the door with their hands always folded in prayer, in the movements, the sly unctuous movements of the dogs, in the way the monks poured the tea, in the turquoise and pearl earrings of the young women, swaying slightly above their shoulders as they prayed, in the noise, all the elements of it, the chanting, the singing, the talking, the muffled cries of the young children, the creak of the great monastery doors, swinging to and fro. I began to experience a little of what it might be like to live all one's life as a meditation, to feel every action spacious and delightful, every gesture part of a prayer that had no beginning and no end, that was older and fresher than any ritual, however elaborate and beautiful. Nothing that happened in that room was more important than anything else — a man getting up and stretching in the light from the doorway was as compelling as a roll on the Rinpoche's drums; an old woman sitting half asleep with her grandchild on her lap seemed as complete an image of tenderness and protection as one of the Buddhas on the walls in his circle of green or red fire; a dog's bark was as vivid a reminder of the Law, of the Wheel of Life, of all the poignant transience of things as the low chanting of the monks and the ringing of the sacred bell; a girl suddenly running into the room from the outside light seemed, in her youth and ragged laughter, as sacred as the Rinpoche, was part of him, in fact, part of the meditation that was being woven from his hands, his gestures, his looks, his smiles.

One day I met a young German on the bus and invited him to join me that morning in Shey. He crouched with me between two old Ladakhi women, and watched everything with distaste.

'But they are not serious,' he said. 'Look at them — look at that woman over there! She is talking to her friend. She is not praying. And look at the monks . . . that monk over there is half asleep,' pointing to an old bald monk whom I'd often seen on the verge of dozing off.

'In fact what we are watching, my friend' (he always called me 'my friend'), 'is a scene of social oppression. The Rinpoche is the Boss-Man, the Ladakhis are the hirelings, and this is the party at the end of the year that all the slaves are invited to, to keep them happy.'

The trumpets started again. The two old women we were sitting between took up their rosaries and began singing loudly, swaying, touching shoulders. An old man had come up to the Rinpoche with a bag of apples and was presenting it to him.

'How can you sit here in all this mediaeval rubbish!' the German said. 'What possible use can all this be to you?'

'It gives me joy,' I said.

He looked at me scornfully.

By the time I met the Rinpoche again, on the evening of the fifth day, I had observed him closely. I had watched him hour after hour, day after day, sitting at the heart of his monastery and his people.

In the evenings back at Leh I tried to write down something of what I had seen in him and felt about him. They are glimpses, no more. They probably say more about me than about him. But I must try to say something about him, knowing that whatever I say will be inadequate.

'Like his people, the Rinpoche worships with genial relaxation. He acknowledges everyone's presence; no one comes up to him to bow to him or ask for his blessing who is not seen, talked to . . . He is playful. He laughs when a dog barks in the shadows, jokes with some of the old men and women who ask his advice, makes every movement and every gesture as if he had all the time he wanted.'

'There is an exaltation in his playfulness. It is a continual outpouring of deep humour, of friendship. Like the Rinpoche in the painting in Stakna, this man wants no barriers between him and others, no distance. Humour is the bridge between him and his people, who are in awe of him.'

'I mustn't describe him as *too* playful. There are times when I catch a glimpse of the man who spent ten years in a cave in solitary meditation. When, in the ritual, he sounds the bell and holds the vajra in the other hand, his face has an expression of extraordinary remoteness. For those moments, he is no longer the tender and welcoming Father, the Good Father; he is something stranger, more uncanny, further away from anything or anyone I have ever known. There is a fierceness in the way he holds the sacred sceptre and tings the bell and sounds the drum that could be frightening if afterwards he did not relax immediately, look around the room, as if to see if everyone is still with him, still safe.'

'The more I understand the ritual and his gestures, the more I become aware that the Rinpoche's relaxation comes from a state of nearly continual meditation.'

'He sits on a throne, yes, but it is not a high throne. He is surrounded on all sides by his people. There is nothing self-advertising or rhetorical about the way he sits or acts. He is their spiritual leader, their symbol of perfection, their Father; he assumes all the responsibility of their love with a naturalness so complete it seems pure of vanity.'

'Today a dog barked in the middle of the most exalted part of the ritual. The Rinpoche looked up and smiled. He motioned to one of the young monks to give the dog some food.'

'This afternoon a group of elderly Germans came in when we

149

were praying. They talked loudly, strode round the Gompa, took close-ups of Ladakhis, asked the monks to smile and move and show their sacred books . . . I was furious and ashamed of them. The Rinpoche waved to a young monk to greet them, offer them each an apple, and invited them to sit near him. They sat near the Rinpoche for an hour, quiet and absorbed.'

'This morning, two children started crawling towards the Rinpoche on the open floor to his left; the monks who saw broke into laughter. The mother of the children bustled out of the crowd, picked them up and instead of returning to her seat, took them up to the Rinpoche. As he saw them he smiled broadly, bent forward so far I was afraid he would fall off his seat, and put both hands on their cheeks.'

'How can I write this without sounding mad? But I shall write it nevertheless. For many hours in those days I felt that everything that was happening was happening inside the Rinpoche's mind. He was not directing what was happening and not controlling it, but I felt that his mind was vast and contained all that was there — the Buddhas, the dogs, the old women, the chanting, the singing, my thoughts and meditations, everything. And that vastness did not seem alien to me, nor frightening, but natural, the most natural thing, in fact, I had ever experienced. His was, I felt, not a personal mind at all and not a mind with any design, any desire to possess or order or dominate – but a mind-at-dance, a mind as vast as the sky . . .'

'What would the German say reading what I have written? He would say: "This man is mad or naive. Has he not seen politicians kissing babies? Does he not know that incessant smiling benevolence is one of the hoariest tricks of the ecclesiastical trade? How can he be so taken in? The answer, I'm afraid, is banal: this man is in search of the Good Father and has found him. He has found him in an old man from a culture so strange to him that he cannot understand it and so is relieved of the burden of irony, of criticism, of detached judgment. He can therefore indulge his fantasy to the full, elaborate it to the most absurd (and possibly dangerous) lengths. The Rinpoche is not only the Good Father; he is also an idealised portrait of the writer himself . . . In this old man from another, unknowable world the writer has found the perfect way to aggrandise himself, advertise his own spirituality . . ." None of the German's objections surprises me. There is something in all of them. But hearing them in the end I can only laugh — not smugly, with more than a little fear in my laughter. If the Rinpoche *is* real, and my joy at him is real, what then?'

I t is evening. Most of the people have caught one of the last buses home. The monastery is nearly deserted. Down in the main shrine-room a few dogs are sleeping in the corners, their worn heads lit by the butter lamps. The Buddhas on the walls have returned to their mystery — their faces veiled by the dark, only a hand here, a foot there, catching the light of the lamps. An old monk is sweeping the huge room clean — a pile of apple peel, apricot stones, paper, bits of thread; one broken shoe sits in the middle of the room where only three hours ago there would have been the long brazen necks of trumpets and sacred books bound with red and yellow silk.

I had been waiting an hour. Nawang Tsering said to me after the day's prayers that the Rinpoche would see me when he had finished his business. I had not minded waiting, walking up and down the monastery walls, round the Great White Stupa to the left of the main building, watching all the subtle stages of the valley's folding into night. Slowly, the lights in the farms below were coming on, small fiery signs in a gathering dark-ness. It has always been the happiest part of the day for me, the moment when the lamps are lit. Standing on Shey, I remem-bered all the other places where I had been delighted by the first lighting of the lamps — in childhood at my grandmother's house in Coimbatore, the white curtains dissolving in the light, an old servant moving in the shadows, only his face illuminated; in Venice, ten years ago, on a brilliant frosty winter evening, standing on the Accademia Bridge, alone, with only the steadily darkening water for company; in Oxford a hundred times, with the day's work over.

Nawang Tsering walked down the steps, looking insubstan-tial in the thickening moonlight. In that light, the deep red of his robe was almost black. 'The Rinpoche can see you now.'

We walked up to the Rinpoche's room without saying anything. We knocked. Again that low dark half-growl came from within, and we entered.

The Rinpoche was alone, seated cross-legged on his red mattress. In front of him, in two small china bowls, covered with a small white cloth, some food had been placed. He was drinking tea. He looked tired. There were three candles in the room and a weak paraffin lamp. Only the Rinpoche was completely in the light — the rest of the room looked ghostly, soaked in darkness.

The Rinpoche motioned to me to sit down on one of the mattresses to his left. Nawang Tsering sat on the floor between us.

The Rinpoche looked at me and said, 'You have come a long way. I think you would like to receive teachings. Is this true?'

'Yes.'

He looked at me again and then looked away. He closed his eyes. He seemed to be concentrating hard. And then he began to talk, slowly and sonorously, his deep voice building paragraph after paragraph in a kind of low unbroken chant. Nawang and I waited quietly until he had finished. I had caught some of it but not all. Nawang translated.

'Many people say they want to receive teachings and all they are saying is: I want a little more knowledge so that I can impress people. What is the use of that? Many people say they want to learn about Buddhism, but their way of learning is an escape from the truth and not an approach to it. So it is important that you understand that what is most necessary is the true motivation, the true approach. If you do not have that, everything that you learn will be of no use to you.'

He paused, with his eyes still closed. 'To come to the Teachings in the right spirit you must know and feel many things. You must understand, not merely in your mind but in your heart and spirit the impermanence and transience of all phenomena. You must understand that all things are suffering — that love without awareness is suffering, that desire without awareness is suffering. You must have understood the nature of suffering so deeply that you see that all the world is in pain, that all Being is suffering. The Buddha said that the world is on fire.

Even these words will burn you if you do not hear them with the right purity. You must understand the nature of suffering and want with your whole being to escape suffering, to transcend it, to leave the world of fire and enter Nirvana, to overcome the torment of desire and live in calm and love.'

He put his hands to his forehead. 'In the Hinayana they say that the end of discipline is to escape suffering. This is not what we say in Tibet, in the Mahayana. We cannot bear to escape ourselves while we see that the rest of creation is in pain; we could not endure to be free while the rest of the world is still in prison. And so you must not only want to attain Nirvana for yourself, you must also want with all your heart that the whole of Being should attain Nirvana, should enter into bliss. And if you truly love all things, you will renounce your own salvation for the joy of continually working for the liberation of others. This is the ideal of the Bodhisatva. The heart of the Bodhisatva is so great that it cannot be content until the whole of creation, even the small insects and the blades of grass, have entered into Nirvana. This ideal of the Bodhisatva is the great ideal of Tibet.'

He was silent. The word 'Tibet' seemed to make him sad. I watched the shadows the candles were casting on the walls.

'To be a Bodhisatva is to be free from all delusions of selfhood, to have finally realised that all things arise contingently and have no separate absolute existence, to be free of the falsity of the notion of Personality. The Bodhisatva does not act for his own benefit; he acts in full awareness of emptiness, of the emptiness of all things, in full awareness of the emptiness of all his actions, in full awareness, even, of the emptiness of his compassion. And yet his whole being is compassion. Everything he does is dedicated to others, every action, every thought, every ecstasy, every meditation — given effortlessly, dedicated without regard for the "Self" that gives.

'This is the true motivation,' he said, after a pause, looking suddenly fragile and exhausted. 'This is the true feeling — to love all things so much that you wish to bring them into Nirvana, to love all created things so much that you want to become perfect, so that you can be of help to them. You should meditate on this. It is the beginning.'

We sat in silence. The Rinpoche sat looking down at his hands, folded in his lap. Nawang said, 'We should go now. The

Rinpoche is tired. Come back tomorrow.' I got up, and bowed to the Rinpoche. He reached out his hands and touched mine.

Nawang came out with me into the courtyard. The moon had risen. All the stars were out. He took my arm and said, 'Now you must eat something. Come with me,' and we went together into the kitchen, a long smoky room, where an old monk ladled some soup for us into two brass pots. It tasted salty and good. The old monk nodded and smiled, his hands and face blackened with soot from the fire in the middle of the room.

'What is the Rinpoche like to work for?' I asked Nawang.

'To work for!' Nawang laughed. 'You make it sound like a business. I do not work for the Rinpoche. I serve him.'

'Are you happy?'

'You ask strange questions. Yes, I am happy. I don't think much about whether I am happy or not. It is hard, you know, being his interpreter. I have to sit there for hours. So often I have to translate the same things . . . Now I know very well how his mind works. I know what he will say and how he will say it. Sometimes, though, he catches me out. He will add a little elaborate phrase and then look up at me and laugh, as if to say, "There, you see! Wake up!" '

'But you are more than his interpreter, aren't you? You are with him most of the day.'

'Yes, I do almost everything for him. He is old and weak now. You wouldn't believe it, looking at how hard he works. He never seems to be tired of meeting people and talking to people. Look at today — after working all day, leading prayers and healing people, he still finds time to talk to you. That is like him. His whole life is lived for others. But sometimes he gets very tired. I see him sometimes late at night and he can hardly move, he is so tired. I wake him in the morning, bathe him. Sometimes I have to escort him to the toilet when he feels too weak to walk there on his own.'

Nawang finished his soup noisily and asked for more. The pot was empty. The monk vanished into the shadows to find us two

154

old loaves of bread and a bowl of cabbage.

'Sometimes I am very tired in the mornings,' Nawang said. 'These monasteries are cold in the morning . . . but the Rinpoche hardly ever angers or annoys me. In our tradition it would be a very bad sin to be angry with a Rinpoche, and anyway it would be hard to be angry with him.'

'I cannot imagine being angry with a man as gentle as him.'

'Yes, he is gentle,' Nawang said. 'But that is only one part of him. Perhaps you will always only see one part of him. After all, you do not see him as I see him, day in, day out, in the morning, in the afternoon, in the evening. The Rinpoche can be very fierce when he wants. With you and with everyone who comes to learn he is gentle, but with his own monks, sometimes he is as terrifying as those Gods you see on the walls of our monasteries, with their haloes of flame and their knives and their bowls of blood and their terrible stares. His anger always has a reason but never a *personal* one. Never in all the time I have known him have I seen him angry for a personal slight or a personal misfortune. He is angry, as those Gods on our walls are angry, to dissolve pride and destroy ignorance.'

Nawang laughed. 'It's all very well, to know why he is angry . . . but sometimes he scares me very much. The walls shake. You know, in our tradition, we believe the Teacher can do anything to us for our own good, even in exceptional cases kill us or send us to our death. Sometimes when the Rinpoche is angry with me I feel he will kill me! Once I was given a present, a book, and some money, and I kept them back secretly. The Rinpoche called me to him and said, "Go and get the book you were given." I brought it to him. He said, "You are a monk. You are trying to live beyond greed. You do not keep presents." I was only ten years old and the look in his eyes terrified me. I said I was sorry and cried. Immediately, he found three apples in a bowl by his side and gave them to me. That is what his anger is like. It is always accompanied by a gesture of love.

'You mustn't think I never have "small" thoughts about him. The Rinpoche is not at all practical, and sometimes, as his aide, that annoys me. We can be in a railway station, for instance, going up to Darjeeling, say, for the winter — and the Rinpoche will still be talking animatedly with a group of people as the train is about to pull out. He cannot bear not to communicate with people. This is beautiful but sometimes annoying too. And then he is sometimes very dreamy. I think it is hard for him to be here in Ladakh, to be continually in front of the public. He is happiest in the winter when he can be in retreat, seeing only a few monks. He does not really enjoy organising anything. The Abbot, Kempo, does most of that. Have you seen Kempo yet? He looks like an old cook. He is completely modest. He and the Rinpoche have been friends for forty years. The Rinpoche, you know, has an old-fashioned slow mind, very rich, very majestic — but sometimes I get impatient with him. I want him to hurry up and say quickly what he has to say. But he comes from a world in which people had much time to talk, to be with each other. That is good, I know. But I am a modern Tibetan. I was educated in Benares. I like modern films and modern books. Sometimes the Rinpoche mocks me and calls me "film-star", because of my black glasses and my wristwatch and my love of films.'

The old monk was gesturing to us to leave him alone to sleep. Nawang said, 'Come with me. You can sleep on a spare cot in my room. You won't get back to Leh tonight.'

We lay in the dark and talked.

'What powers does the Rinpoche have?'

'I don't know and if I did I wouldn't tell you. Buddhists do not believe in boasting about powers. The Buddha, you know, once defrocked a monk because he did a miracle. Did you know that? And why? Because the real miracle is a change of heart.'

'I know that, Nawang, don't preach at me. I'm not asking vulgarly.'

'Well, I really don't know. Perhaps he can levitate. Perhaps he can foretell the future. Does it matter?'

'No.'

'The most important thing is to live in the present, isn't it, without fantasy or illusion. Isn't that true?'

'Yes.'

'I have been preaching again.'

'Yes.'

'The Rinpoche would be very pleased. He is always saying I should talk more.'

'Nawang, how could you talk more? You have talked for two hours without stopping.'

156

'The Rinpoche is a very funny man.'

We woke before dawn, washed in icy water, went down to the prayer room for early morning prayers. The Rinpoche was amused that I had stayed the night. After prayers he waved me to him and said, 'So you have decided to stay with us?'

'I wish I could.'

'You can stay as long as you like. Come when you like and go when you want.'

I bowed my head to thank him and my glasses fell off into his hands. He laughed and laughed and waved my glasses in the air, and then put them with a great air of conspiracy into his yellow silk shirt.

'I am going to keep them for myself,' he said.

'You can keep them, of course. But I wish', I said, 'you would give me back your eyes instead. You can keep mine as long as you like.'

He put my glasses back on with his own hands.

'No. You must see with *your* eyes, not mine. Perhaps I can help you to see with your eyes.'

'If you could help me to see with my eyes, I would be grateful to you.'

'I do not want gratitude. I want you to stay a little time with us, to come when you want and learn what you need. That is all.'

And then he said, as he was walking out of the room back to his own quarters, 'Come and see me again this evening.'

He looked so young that morning it was almost uncanny, especially since I remembered clearly how, the evening before, he had seemed weary and fragile. His skin shone. He saw me looking at him, and laughed.

'Whose eyes are you looking at me with? Mine or yours?'

There was still an hour to go before morning prayers began. Already, people were arriving from Shey and the surrounding villages. I sat on the steps and watched them climb the long path to the monastery doors — the old men with their still springy steps and flowers in their ears, the old women gossiping together, carrying baskets of fruit and bread.

Nawang came up to me and said, 'Have you seen the painting of Shamunatha we have here? He founded the monastery of Hemis and his portrait is one of the glories of Ladakh.' He said 'glories of Ladakh' in such a self-important way I had to laugh.

'Why are you laughing?'

'You said "glories of Ladakh" so pompously I thought you were a tour leader.'

'Don't laugh too soon. If things go on as badly as they have done, that is exactly what I might have to become.'

He laughed. 'Think what a pompous tour leader I would make. I would be very famous. I would give long lectures. Especially to the French people. They like long lectures very much.'

'I know exactly what you would do. You would repeat the lectures of the Rinpoche, steal all his images, probably even try to imitate his deep voice.'

'Of course. How did you guess?' Nawang said in a dark, slow voice, before laughing. 'I would be best of all on Karma. I made a big study of Karma when I was in Benares. I could make an insect weep, I am so eloquent on Karma.'

We were in the shrine-room now, and Nawang was directing me to the far left wall, where there was a small altar. He lit the lamp that had gone out overnight, and pointed to the left. There on the wall was the painting.

And I saw Nawang fold his hands in prayer and bow to the painting, gently and ceremoniously. 'Now I shall leave you alone with him.'

Nawang had not said 'it'; he had said 'him', and he had chosen his words well, consciously or unconsciously. The painting was alive with the presence of the Teacher it was made to celebrate. I stood in front of it. Nawang reappeared and handed me a small lit lamp, without saying anything.

The painting I was standing in front of was, in its way, as moving a spiritual portrait as the one of the Rinpoche of Stakna;

but it was a portrait of a very different kind. There had been something stark, intense, in the Stakna Rinpoche — an almost frightening austerity of line and gaze. There was nothing austere about Shamunatha. Seated on a red cushion, lightly embroidered with gold squares and circles, he is wearing a loosely fitting white cotton robe; in front of him, there is a table with flowers, a bell, a small kettle, a vajra; behind and around him there are lotuses and chrysanthemums and a trellis of small intensely red apples, half-hidden in circles of dark-green leaves. Two large black ring earrings hang from his ears, symbols of the perfection of consciousness; a necklace of white stones burns softly around his neck. The Rinpoche of Stakna is painted alone in a circle of green light; Shamunatha breathes out of the life that surrounds and sustains him. Everything is alive in him, even the delicately swirling folds of his cloak; devotees in miniature are arriving from behind his throne, moustached and coiffed and bearing gifts; the great red flower to the left of him and the two white flowers on either side of his head both seem to be opening in the warmth of his presence; his body is golden, half-exposed, sensuous, the body of a Prince as well as of an ascetic.

Nawang had returned and was standing beside me. I asked him:

'Why are there so many people and flowers in the painting?'

'Shamunatha was a Great Tantric Master. The Way of Tantric Buddhism is the Way of Acceptance, the way of working with all the energies and powers of living, refusing and denying none of them, but using all of them, transforming all of them into wisdom. That is why he is shown surrounded by living things. His is a mind, we say, that makes the world flower; his is a mind that has denied nothing and transformed everything within him and within the world into harmony and spiritual power. This is the way of Tantra. It is the hardest way.'

'Why?'

'Because it is the most dangerous. Because it has so many temptations — to hedonism, to the relish of worldly power. It is also the most *effective* way. The man who can travel it successfully, we believe, can attain Enlightenment in one lifetime.'

Then Nawang said, 'I am happy you like this painting. Whenever I leave Ladakh, it is this painting that I remember. I

meditate on it in the winter in Darjeeling. It expresses everything that I wish to become. When I was younger I wanted to
renounce everything. Now I understand that that was vanity,
and a desire for safety. The Tantric way is harder and demands a
greater purity and fearlessness. It is harder to love the world
than to leave it; it is harder to accept with joy and gratitude than
to renounce; it is harder to work with our emotions of greed and
desire and anger, to face them and transform them slowly into
loving power, than it is to cut them off, to deny them. And
because it is harder the rewards are greater. The Tantric Way is
one of discipline without dogma, renunciation without con-
tempt.'

'Nawang, you are preaching!'

'Yes, but I'm doing it rather well, don't you think? Why
shouldn't I go on about him? I love him!'

People were coming in through the great doors to begin
morning prayers. Nawang raised his small lamp higher so that
it was almost under Shamunatha's face.

'If only I could grow a moustache like that!' Nawang said. 'It
is such a beautiful moustache, such a fine moustache. But the
most I can ever grow is a dirty ragged beard. Perhaps I am not
evolved enough yet.'

'What would the Rinpoche say if you grew a moustache?'

'He would say, "Aren't you content with trying to be a
film-star? Why do you want to pretend to be a Master as well?" '

All day I watched the Rinpoche and slowly the feeling grew
within me, no, not the feeling, the emotional certainty
that the man I was watching was, in some exhilarating sense,
both the Rinpoche of Stakna, and Shamunatha; I do not mean
that he was in any real or even mystic way the combination of
the two of them, but that he combined what I had seen and felt
from both paintings. He was the austere fierce Master of Meditation of Stakna and the Tantric Master, the joy-giver, the
celebrator of all living things, the genial impresario of love of
Shey. He was both remote and present, abstract and immediate,

stark and tender, fierce and hilarious, immensely, almost frighteningly, disciplined, and the most unforced and unaffected man I had ever seen. All day what Nawang had said the night before ran through my mind:

'We call a man a Rinpoche, which means diamond, when he has achieved perfection. We do not believe that man is a flawed animal; we believe he is capable of perfection. Buddhists do not believe in God; they believe in man, in the transforming powers within man. We call a man a diamond when he has transformed every evil in himself into wisdom, every dark energy into an energy of light, every movement of hatred or impatience into a blessing. We know that it is possible. Many men have achieved it within our tradition and that is how we know that it is possible. We have seen it and we have felt it from living men. It is not a fantasy, it is an experience, as real as lying on this bed in this cold room, as watching those shadows on the wall, as hearing the snores of the monks from the other room. We call a man a diamond also when he has gone beyond himself, beyond his old identity and personality. He becomes not just a man, but a woman and a child as well, a Mother and a boy and an old woman and an old man, a Prince and a Yogi, a King and a beggar and a girl. A man who no longer wants to be anything becomes everything; a man who is free of desire and self-consciousness enters with love into all things and all people, and all things and people come to him without fear. I have spoken with so many Westerners. They say, "All this is beautiful — but it is not realistic, it is not truthful." I say to them, "Are you certain that you and your culture know all that is real, know all the limits of reality? Are you certain that you have exhausted the truth?" They are frightened. They are frightened that they do not know everything, that they have been cheated. You see, they were told that their culture was superior, knew the answers to all ills and injustices . . . and now it is collapsing. They have been told, "Trust to the Intellect! Trust to Reason!" and it is good to use both, it is good — but how can either penetrate to truth? It is in the spirit and in the heart that perfection is found, and when it is found there it irradiates the reason, makes the intellect perfect. We call a man a diamond when his heart is a mind and his mind is a heart, when there is no separation between the two, when both are illuminated. I am not a man like that; I may never be. But I have seen men like that, I have known them and loved them and they have given me faith — not in any God, but in myself, in the powers I have hidden within myself, that we all have hidden within ourselves and must uncover and realise. And now I must sleep. Even a great Tantric yogi must sleep — ' and Nawang rolled over and slept, snoring almost immediately, his big dirty feet sticking out of the end of his blanket, his dark glasses resting by him on the pillow.

That evening I went again to the Rinpoche's room. I was elated. All day I had been looking forward to being with him again. He was sitting, as before, sipping tea, on a red mattress. He looked vigorous, and only by his occasional rubbing of his eyes could I tell that he was tired.

He welcomed me and blessed me. My glasses did not fall off this time. He seemed disappointed.

'So this time you are keeping your eyes? That is sad. You do not want me to have them.'

'I want you to have them but they do not seem to want to leave me.'

He was amused. 'You mustn't force them to leave. They must come of their own accord.'

And then he was quiet, looking down, as he often did, at his hands folded in his lap. I studied his hands for the first time — they were broad farmer's hands, but they had no lines on them. They looked like the hands of a young man, firm, almost fleshy. And the Rinpoche was in his late sixties. There were no rings on them, no charms, no good-luck twists of hair as on some yogis' hands. They were as strong and unadorned as he was himself. Then he looked up and touched the tip of his ragged white moustache.

'Don't you have any questions? You may ask anything you like.'

So great was the atmosphere of liberty and freedom of spirit that he seemed always to create that I felt I could have asked him anything about myself, about himself. He was not awe-inspiring this evening at all, but intimate, almost conspiratorial.

'You said when we first spoke, I think, that only the perfect can help others. What did you mean?'

'If a man who is still full of anger and desire and greed tries to "help" another, what will his help be worth? It will be dirty, it will be coloured, it will be a burden as much as a help. If you are serious about wanting to be of help to others you should be serious too about achieving perfection of heart and mind. Only when the heart is clear can it feel without greed or possessiveness; only when the mind is clear of all false perceptions, can it guide action. If you really love others and truly see the extent and range and depth of their suffering, and feel it in your heart, then you will want to give them strength and want to bring them peace. If you do not have strength and peace yourself how can you give it to them? If you do not have light, how can you bring light to others? If you are not free of suffering, how can you free others?'

I answered, 'But cannot a man, precisely because he *is* suffering, help others? Cannot a man who is in the world help those in the world more effectively and with greater compassion than someone who has gone beyond the world?'

'The man who really helps is the man who is in the world but not of it, who loves the world but is not attached to it, who lives in the world but is not stained by it. A lotus arises from mud, doesn't it? But it is not made of mud and it has no mud on its bud or petals. A lotus arises from water, but it rises above the water. If it flowered under the water, no one could see it and get pleasure from it. A man who is suffering can have compassion, can be intelligent and humane — but he will not have the power to help others. It is necessary not merely to feel for others, not merely to win a certain kind of wisdom from the trials of living, but also to live the life necessary to acquire the good powers, the healing powers, that can save created beings from torment. Only the perfect can have these powers and not use them badly; only the perfect can acquire these powers without harm to themselves and use them without harm to others.'

'What are these powers?'

'There are many of them. Powers of healing, mental and physical. Powers of transformation, of oneself, and in certain

163

definite cases, of others. Powers of determining one's next incarnation. Powers of acting within phenomena in many different ways to secure the Victory of Enlightened Goodness. These powers are real but they can only be acquired by those who have undergone the most severe disciplines of purification. And they must never be used except to help others. They are not personal powers; they are powers acquired for the benefit of all. The perfection of the use of power rests in an understanding of Emptiness and a limitless compassion for all things.'

'What is it to understand Emptiness?'

'I can answer this question in words but to understand what I mean you will have to experience it. And that you can experience safely only after many years of dedicated meditation. To experience it without that background of meditation might lead to madness, or worse . . . To understand Emptiness is to understand that all things are contingent, that all things arise contingently, that nothing has an absolute reality, only a present, contingent reality. It is to understand that all connections are of the mind, all notions of Selfhood or Personality are fictions created and sustained by the Mind for its own purposes, for the purposes of the Ego, which is itself a fiction. It is not merely to understand these things but to live that understanding.'

'But if all things are empty,' I said, 'if all notions are empty, isn't compassion as empty as everything else, as devoid of absolute meaning? and isn't saying "Have compassion" in the face of so nihilistic a philosophy as Buddhism a kind of sentimentality?'

The Rinpoche laughed. 'You have been studying, I see. You have many words. But what I am talking about is not merely a perfection of mind, a perfection of the ruthless, nihilistic intellect. That perfection must be there, must be attained. But not at the expense of a perfection of heart, a perfection of love. We Tibetans believe that the one cannot exist without the other, that they are linked in a mystery. Have you not seen the paintings or the statues of the Buddha in union with his Shakti? There are some in Lamayuru that are very beautiful. These express the complete unity of all the different perfections, a unity of Awareness and Knowledge, of Consciousness and Compassion, a unity that is ecstasy, that is a unity of all opposites and paradoxes, that is a mystery of the deepest and most abiding joy. When I pick up the bell and the vajra in the ceremony you see every day I am expressing the same thing, the unity of Mind and Spirit, of Wisdom and Compassion. When I sound the bell with one hand, I keep the vajra, the silent vajra, in the other. The ringing of the bell is rooted in the silence of the vajra; the silence of the vajra resounds with the ringing of the bell. Wisdom is rooted in Compassion; Compassion is made sonorous and active through Wisdom. Milarepa said, "Seeing Emptiness, have compassion." The true experience of Emptiness, of Sunyata, is also, at the same time, an experience of compassion, of love. And the deepest compassion is the one, as Nagarjuna said, that is "unfounded", that has "no support", no justification, no philosophical structure and framework, because the mind has undermined them all, seen through them all — but which exists, simply and completely, as a horse exists, as a jug exists, as this kettle exists, as the night sky outside this room exists. This is the compassion of the Buddhas, and this is the end of wisdom and the foundation of true power! You will only glimpse it through words; to enter it you will have to meditate on it, and learn to become it.'

As he was speaking, his hands, consciously or unconsciously, were moving in the gestures of the ritual, the sacred mudras. One of the candles had guttered and gone out. Nawang lit it. The flame hovered uneasily for a while, before taking hold and burning clearly and steadily.

It was time to leave him.

What moved me in the Rinpoche and in Nawang was their faith in man, their belief in the innate and possible perfection of the human spirit. It was that faith that illuminated everything they said and did, and was, I understood, at the heart of all the joy of the art of Ladakh — the Buddhas and mandalas, the Rinpoche of Stakna, Padmasambhava himself, master of Transformations. It was not a sentimental faith.

Later that evening I asked Nawang about the loss of his family and home in Tibet.

'For a long time I was sad. For a long time I missed everything — the fields, the smells, my friends, my house. But then I said to myself, "I am a Buddhist. I know that all things pass away. I know that nothing lasts or can last. Why am I mourning? Why am I wasting my life in mourning? I am here in India. I must live. I must live to be worthy of the belief I chose when I was very young." And then I came to learn more about Tibet. I learnt about many things I had not known — about the oppression of the people, about the cruelty of some of the old customs. So I felt, "It is not Tibet that is important, not the old system — but the philosophy of Tibetan Buddhism, and that philosophy is not Tibetan only, it belongs to the world, and perhaps it has unique things to tell men." And then I even thought, "It may be a good thing that Tibet has fallen, has passed away. Now the philosophy that was confined to Tibet can be shared with others. And perhaps it is specially important to share everything that can make for peace at this moment, at this time of so much pain and terror and war. Perhaps Tibet fell for a purpose — that its wisdom could be given to anyone who wanted it and was prepared to study and train to understand it!" And so I was not sad that I was no longer in Tibet; I was happy to be given the chance by history to live outside, to test my faith, to live my faith without support, without social consolations, to come to a place and time when I can talk to you, when people from such different worlds as we are can exchange our thoughts.

'It is not so important that one small country falls. The danger now is the loss of spiritual vision in a whole world. And our task, whether we are Tibetans or Americans or Englishmen, is to keep that vision alive, to see that it lives through the dark times that we live in, which will get darker.'

'Do you really think that?'

'Oh yes,' Nawang said. 'Certainly. This is Kali Yuga. The Age of Destruction. Everything is ending, everything is falling away. But why should that frighten us?'

'It frightens me.'

'You want a philosophy that says, "Man will get better. Man will change his world. There is hope." That philosophy would

166

be a lie. This world is illusion. But within this world and within man there are great powers — powers of love, of healing, of clarity, that can lead man to liberation. The worse the time, the more we should look for those powers within ourselves, the more deeply we should strive to obtain them and live them, for our own sake and the sake of others. Our terrible time makes the choices clear for us. We will not be able to hide from our spiritual responsibilities; we will not be able to pretend that we can go on living without taking thought for our salvation and that of others. We will have to invoke the deepest strengths of our spirit to survive at all.'

He paused and smiled. 'There is one consolation.'

'What is that?' I asked.

'It is said that at the end of Kali Yuga all the Buddhas and Bodhisatvas will help men with especial force.'

'Let us hope so.'

'You sound doubtful.'

'No, not doubtful. It is hard at this time to believe in any help.'

'That is because you have not yet found where help is.'

We had been lying awake talking in Nawang's small, musty room. It was late — perhaps midnight, perhaps later.

'When I was studying in Benares,' Nawang said, 'reading everything I could get my hands on in English, there was one thing, as a Tibetan and a Buddhist, I could never understand.'

'What?'

'That there were so few good people in your literature. That the only things that seemed to interest any of your writers were evil, cruelty, hatred, passion. That they hardly any of them had any words for describing any other kind of emotion — let alone spiritual emotion, let alone spiritual discovery.'

'Did you read Dante? Did you read George Herbert? There are many exceptions to what you say.'

'Not a great many. And how many in the modern period? Dante believed he was a miserably sinful worm who had to be *saved* by Beatrice and a few hundred thousand saints and angels. All this grovelling before God — I hate it, it is so stupid! We must be reverent before ourselves, before what we have within us, not destructive, not self-hating. And from that reverence for ourselves we will learn reverence for all things.'

Then Nawang said, 'Can you name me one figure of good power in your literature? Isn't it true that nearly every powerful man in your mind is in some way evil, that power must in some way be evil because the man who wields it is always partly evil? Isn't that so? Even Shakespeare. Look at Prospero. Isn't Prospero partly evil, partly a fool? Why couldn't even Shakespeare imagine a man who, while being human, was also wholly good?'

It seemed absurd to be having this discussion in a monk's room in Ladakh, and so I began to laugh.

'What are you laughing at?'

'I am laughing at us.'

'Laughter is the beginning of wisdom.'

'Oh, for god's sake shut up.'

The next day was the penultimate day of the festival at Shey. More people than ever came. Three busloads from Thikse alone, five or six from Leh. Nawang and I watched them arrive from the top of the monastery, perched on the walls like eagles, eating bread and cabbage.

Nawang said, 'The young Rinpoche is coming from Hemis this afternoon.'

'What for?'

'Tomorrow there will be a big ceremony. The two Rinpoches will give Initiation. The Initiation of Fearlessness and the Initiation of Long Life.'

'What is the young Rinpoche called?'

'Drukchen Rinpoche. Have you been to Lamayuru?'

'Yes.'

'Did you see the cave of Naropa?'

'Yes. It moved me. It was so small and simple. Even the clumsy statue in it seemed appropriate. I would have hated a large splendid statue. I thought of Naropa often when I was in Lamayuru.'

'Well, now you can meet him.'

'What do you mean?'

'The young Rinpoche is the incarnation of Naropa.'

I sat silently.

'Don't you believe that a Great Personality can choose his incarnation? Don't you believe that a Bodhisatva can come back to Samsara again and again out of compassion?'

'I don't know. Everything in my tradition denies the possibility of such an idea; everything in my instinct and in what little spiritual knowledge I have says that it is possible. I don't know.'

'You will like Drukchen. He is very clever, very modest. I will see to it that you talk . . . Did you know that it was only two years ago that he was installed as Rinpoche? Did you hear what happened — in front of thousands of people, foreigners too of course, French and German and American? . . . During the ceremony Drukchen received the sacred ornaments of Naropa. As he came out from the central shrine-room on to the balcony to greet the people, wearing the sacred ornaments, three rainbows appeared in the sky. The sky was cloudless. There had been no rain. Everyone saw the rainbows.'

'And what is the significance of the rainbows?'

Nawang smiled. 'The Rainbow is the symbol of Naropa.'

Prayers were beginning. The trumpets announcing the arrival of Thuksey Rinpoche had sounded, and the old man was walking down the small path in front of us from his room at the top of the monastery. The path was lined with Ladakhis of all kinds and ages. When the Rinpoche appeared at the top of the roughly whitewashed steps, everyone started jostling towards him. He moved slowly down the path, very slowly, smiling and concentrated, touching each head that was bowed to him, each hand that was held out to him. The young monks looked bored and impatient behind him, but he would not move any faster. Sometimes he would stop, look around quietly, lean on his stick to get his breath, exaggerating his infirmity a little perhaps to have more time with his people. As he walked towards us, I remembered that I had seen a photograph of him in Nawang's room when he was younger. He had looked very strong, and fierce, then. Now he was old, thinner and weaker, and he used his age, the tender authority his bald head and white beard and slight stoop gave him, to gather everyone to him. Frailty made him vulnerable, and through that vulnerability he drew closer to the world. He seemed to touch each hand and each head with the soft and precise grace of someone who knows there is not much time left. As he passed me, he stopped and said, 'Come and see me this afternoon. There will be a rest before Drukchen Rinpoche comes. We will talk,' brushing my cheek gently with his knuckles. He looked at us both, smilingly, deeply, for a moment, and walked on. As he walked in through the door, the sun suddenly caught the back of his red robe and it seemed to catch fire. He tottered slightly, and leant on a young monk.

That morning, everybody in the shrine-room seemed touched by the gravity of the day to come. It was a brilliant morning and the gompa had never looked more shining than in the light that poured down from the roof on to the Rinpoche and the faces of the monks around him, on to the long necks of the trumpets and the sacred books. The Rinpoche, more even than usual, seemed lost in what he was doing, abandoned to it. Nothing in that morning's ritual seemed remote or hieratic; it grew naturally out of the fresh sunlight, from the flames of the lamps, and the voices of the Ladakhis, rising and falling with the rhythms of the Rinpoche's voice and hands. Nawang turned to me after an hour, and said, 'Today the Buddha of Compassion is present. We have called him for four days and now he has come.'

'So you are a poet,' the Rinpoche said.
'Yes,' I said.
Nawang and I were alone in his room with him, eating a late lunch of rice and vegetables. The Rinpoche ate noisily and with great gusto.

'I have written poetry,' he said. 'I still write it sometimes. I have to wait until the winter. In the summer time there is so much to do. In the winter when I am left to myself, then I write sometimes. I never write very much now. When I was young I used to write all the time.

'Nawang,' he said suddenly, 'is Wangchuk here, the painter?'

'Yes, Rinpoche.'

'Ask him to join us.'

Five minutes later, a smiling old man in very simple Ladakhi robes came through the door, bowing his head.

Nawang said, 'Wangchuk is the best painter in Ladakh!'

Wangchuk looked very embarrassed, but smiled broadly. Four of his front teeth were missing.

'At the moment,' Nawang said, 'Wangchuk is painting a great tanka for Hemis. Of the Buddha of Compassion, Avalokiteshvara. He has come to spend a few days with the Rinpoche because he wants his advice on certain details. Also he wanted to be in Shey for the prayers. He says he cannot paint the tanka until he is in the right spirit. Anything he paints not in the right spirit he says will do evil, will not have the holy power that he wants. Wangchuk and the Rinpoche are old friends. Once Wangchuk had money, but now he is old he has given nearly all of it away to his sons and daughters, and lives alone in a one-room house. Now he never accepts any money for his painting. The monks give him what food and what clothing he needs. Sometimes the Rinpoche will try to give him money, but Wangchuk always says, "What do I want money for? I have everything I need." Sometimes the Rinpoche will tease him and say, "If you were any good as a painter, Wangchuk, you'd demand money for your work. It's only because it's no good that you daren't ask for money." '

As we were talking, Nawang and I, the Rinpoche and Wangchuk were talking among themselves. The intimacy between the two old men was obvious. Often the Rinpoche would pat Wangchuk's knee as if teasing or admonishing him. Perhaps a man like Wangchuk had painted the Shamunatha downstairs. Perhaps four hundred years ago, the painting had grown from talks and prayers and meditations between that man and another Rinpoche, in his room that we were now sitting in.

'Wangchuk has been saying', Nawang said, 'that the hardest thing to represent in a painting of Avalokiteshvara is his face.'

'Why?'

'Because the hardest thing to paint is great compassion. It must not be ordinary pity, he says, it must be sublime pity. It must be a pity as great as the pity of a God.'

'How will he paint it then?'

'The Rinpoche says, "The Face of the Buddha of Compassion is your real face. But to see your real face you must be very calm, you must forget all your other faces, you must be fearless." '

'Why fearless?' I asked.

'Because the face of true pity is so beautiful it is frightening.'

'If they have been having such a holy conversation,' I asked, 'why are they laughing?'

'Because Wangchuk told the Rinpoche that some of his paints had been stolen. And the Rinpoche said to Wangchuk, "You are only saying that because you have no talent and know it, and are too scared to begin." '

Wangchuk bowed to the Rinpoche and to us, and left. I turned to the Rinpoche.

'You asked me, Rinpoche, if I was a poet. Yes, I am, or rather I try to be. But I am afraid. I am afraid that my art draws me away from the spiritual awareness I want, and I am afraid too that if I were to enter a spiritual life more completely my art would end. There is an old Western story that expresses what I feel better than I can express it. There was a monk who had a beautiful singing voice. Such a fine voice, in fact, that everyone wanted to hear it and drew the greatest joy from listening to it. One day a holy man came to the monastery where the man was, and heard him sing. He said, "This is not the voice of a man. This is the voice of the Devil," and immediately, in front of all the monastery, he exorcised the monk, who collapsed into a small, writhing, stinking heap. The monk was nothing without his voice; and the voice was the voice of the Devil; its very sweetness and intensity came from evil. I feel like the monk, though nothing that I have ever written has the power or sweetness of his voice! What can I do? What is there to be done? Should I give up my work altogether?'

I was surprised at the intensity with which I had spoken. I remembered Perec and his saying that afternoon, 'Don't be saved, whatever you do. It will stop you singing.' What power did the old man have, that he drew my deepest fears and thoughts from me and made me confront them so nakedly? I would have been afraid of him then, in that room, had he not made me through the days trust him, had I not felt, continually, in each of his gestures and looks towards me, a great and kind love. Suddenly, I felt that on his answer would depend a great deal, perhaps a whole direction for my life.

The Rinpoche did not answer me for a long time. Nawang looked away at the wall. He knew that I was risking something I had not risked before in any of the talks I had had with him, that I was asking for some guidance in a way I had not asked before, and he was as tense and expectant as I was. We had become friends so easily and his heart opened to those around him so completely that their anxieties were his own. I felt a great warmth towards him, a rush of gratitude for all that he had given.

When the Rinpoche spoke at last he spoke quietly, as if to himself. Perhaps, in some sense, he was speaking to himself — to the young man he had been thirty or forty years ago, struggling with his own conscience in a monastery in Tibet. He spoke quietly and lyrically. I had never heard a voice like his, so powerful in its gentleness, so bare and unadorned in its rhythms and inflections.

'I am happy you told me what you did,' he began. 'It is good that you know that you must choose. That you feel you must change. That you have realised that you must no longer work from anger or bitterness or pride. It is good that you have lived enough and worked deeply enough to know that there is a conflict between certain kinds of work and a spiritual life, a life lived in recognition and knowledge of the spirit. It is painful, but it is good that you know these things. If you did not know them, you would be the slave of your greeds — your greed for fame, your greed to create, your greed to find meaning and significance in things. But it would not be good if you came to believe that there was no work possible that was not evil, that there was no creation that was not in some sense the work of the limited and self-deluding Ego. The story you told me is moving. But it is only partially true, and only true for some people, and I do not believe that it need always be true for you.

It is stupid to imagine that Evil has the sweetest music. Have you not seen our paintings and sculptures in Ladakh? Have you not felt their spiritual grace and dignity? Do you imagine that they were created out of vanity? They were created, many of them, by humble and poor men, who left no names behind them, and who worked on them out of love and in worship. The most beautiful paintings and sculptures, the greatest poetry, have not always been born from torment or bitterness. Often they have sprung from contemplation, from joy, from an instinct or wonder towards all things. To create from joy, to create from wonder, demands a continual discipline, a great compassion. It demands a severity of mind towards all vanity and posturing of the Ego that loves its suffering, and clings to its despairs and depressions and fears; it demands a continual objectivity of spirit, a continual looking out at, and beyond, the world created by the senses, towards a spiritual reality, whose lineaments only emerge slowly, after years of experience and meditation. You do not need to stop working, but you need to strive for a new relationship with your work. You do not need to stop writing, you need to begin to explore another way to write, to build another awareness to write from. You will not be able to find this quickly. You will need patience. Many people will tell you that you are foolish, misguided, ridiculous. You must listen to what they have to say, learn from their criticisms, but not be swayed by them. With time and sincerity you will discover a way to work and write that does not harm you spiritually, that does not tempt you to vanity, that is the deepest expression of your spirituality. You will find a voice that is not your voice only, but the voice of Reality itself, and free from all delusion and stain of personality. If you can be empty enough, that voice can speak through you. If you can be humble enough, that voice can inhabit you and use you.'

We sat in ringing, charged silence. Suddenly trumpets sounded from above us, from the roof of the monastery.

The Rinpoche jumped up. I had never seen him move so quickly. 'Oh my goodness,' he said, 'while I have been talking away like this, the young Rinpoche has arrived! If he finds that I have forgotten him while talking to you he will mock me unmercifully! Please don't tell him!'

'We'd better leave now,' Nawang said. 'The Rinpoche has to change his clothes. The trumpets mean that the young Rinpoche's jeep has been sighted. With luck, the crowd's so great that the jeep won't have been able to get up the hill yet. When Drukchen comes, the whole of Ladakh comes out to greet him. He's the Rinpoche of Hemis . . . I'll explain later. Hurry. I'll take you where you can see everything and not get trampled to death.'

We ran to a small room near the kitchen, with a view across the plain. The trumpets were being played on the roof directly above us, and from where we were standing sounded menacingly loud.

The young Rinpoche's jeep had crawled, its prayer flags flapping in the wind, half-way up the hill. Every yard of its slow progress was impeded by cheering and shouting Ladakhis.

Drukchen got out of the car. He stood, looking up at the monastery's door. I could see very little of him from this distance, except that he was thin, but strong-armed, and wore black glasses, like Nawang. He was shading his eyes to see more clearly. Then he started to stride up the hill. He did not use the winding path, but went straight up, skipping from boulder to boulder like a child. Then he broke into what was almost a run.

Nawang said, 'Drukchen loves to run. He hates being locked up in a monastery. He loves to ride too.'

Drukchen Rinpoche was now half-running up the hill, with a posse of young Ladakhis running with him. His people might believe Drukchen to be an incarnation of Naropa — but they felt no distance from him. He was their Prince, their high-priest, but he was also their brother, their son . . . Nothing separated him from them, no official protocol, no squadron of dark-glassed secret policemen. He laughed as he ran, and the people with him held out their hands to him, and he took them, one by one.

The Old Rinpoche was waiting for him in the crumbling monastery door. He wore a gold cloak and leant on a stick tipped with a large silver dragon's head. Old Tibet was waiting to greet young Ladakh. For a moment it was as if Tibet had not fallen, as if Ladakh were not threatened from within and without, as if all the long continuities of a sacred tradition were not menaced with destruction. The trumpets sounded. The two men touched hands, the young man gathered into the gold bulk of the old. The crowd fell silent.

I met Drukchen Rinpoche alone for several hours that afternoon and evening. We sat in a room on the other side of the courtyard from Thuksey Rinpoche's quarters. It had been filled with flowers. A tanka of a sage hung on the walls, very old and battered, the silk in strips in some places, but still beautiful. When the sun set, Drukchen lit five candles and placed seven bowls of water in front of them. There was a slight wind from the open window, and the water and flames trembled. Drukchen wore nothing but a simple monk's robe.

I had liked him the first time I had seen him — liked his wiry elegance, liked his striding up and across the rocks to the monastery door, liked the warmth and sincerity of his reaction to the Ladakhis' love; being alone for those hours with him made me admire him too. Drukchen is only twenty years old, but his candour, his subtlety, the sharpness and quickness of his mind, make him seem far older. Sometimes, listening to him in the half-dark, I felt that I was talking to a man in his fifties or sixties — and then I would look up and see Drukchen staring across the candles, his face almost gauche in its bony youthfulness, with a shadow of a moustache, small pimples on his face, his eyes not old at all, but brimming with quick young humour. And yet he had a stillness also, a sense of clear repose I have never found in a man so young. When he talked, his hands stayed folded in his lap; his gaze never lost its calm intensity. I felt in talking to him that nothing escaped him of his world; I felt he had not hidden himself from the realities of a modern existence as he could have

176

done, surrounded by a mediaeval adulation, by a people who believed him almost a God. He spoke quickly but quietly, and in good English. His voice was soft and rather deep.

'I had a Western education. I love mathematics. Did Nawang tell you that? I'm fascinated by mathematical puzzles. Sometimes, when I am alone, I play with them for hours. Mathematics is close to meditation. To meditate is to begin to understand the structure of thought, the structure of the self, to begin to see both as transparently as possible; to do mathematics gives me the same sense of composure and delight. I feel as refreshed after an hour of mathematics as I do after an hour of meditation. And I love to put things together too — anything, radios, cars, motors of all kinds, watches . . . Does that surprise you? It makes me peaceful to see how things work.'

I asked him about being a Rinpoche in charge of a monastery so young.

He laughed. 'In charge! I am not in charge! Oh, they say I am, of course, they say they love me and want my good in all things, I am the Incarnation, I am the Rinpoche. All that is true. But as for being in charge . . . I have hardly any real power at all. For one thing, I am still very young, I have very much to learn about my people, about Ladakh, about how to run the monastery itself. For another, Hemis, my monastery, the chief monastery of Ladakh, has been without a Rinpoche for nearly twenty years — my predecessor went to China and was kept there as a prisoner — and, as you can imagine, in the twenty years Hemis had no head many bad things happened — the monks grew slack, records were fudged, or in some cases even lost. I have to go slowly. My monks are wary of giving up the power they have got for themselves in the absence of a true spiritual head. And they are very conservative in all their ideas, unwilling to try new things, unwilling to look at the true conditions of things. Most of Hemis's wealth, for instance, is in land, in land-holdings in the villages. I am always asking my monks, the Treasurer and his friends, to sell some land and invest the money in other ways, but they will not, they will not alter the old pattern of doing things. The result is that the monastery, while being very rich on paper, has hardly any money with which to begin badly needed repairs and restorations. Do you see? I am a Rinpoche, yes, and I think I am loved

— but sometimes I think that is all I am. I am not often listened to. For a lot of the year we are in Darjeeling and not in Ladakh. It is too cold to stay here in the winter; I need those months away.'

'Why?'

'Because I need to rest. Here in Ladakh everyone wants to see me, everyone wants to spend time with me. I have to be on show to my people all the time, continually with them. I want to be with them. I love the traditions of my office and of Tibetan Buddhism; but sometimes I feel unable to give any more. And the truth is also that I am not really old enough yet to bear so much responsibility. I haven't meditated enough, I haven't yet built in myself the kinds of spiritual resources that I need. Thuksey Rinpoche has. He is an old man. He meditated many years in a cave alone. He is a rock, a mountain. He can give endlessly, tirelessly. He is always gentle, always attentive. But he can be like that because he has worked on himself, over many years. It is harder for us now. By "us" I mean the younger monks. Thuksey began his religious life in Tibet, in a world that understood the spirit, celebrated it, and allowed for its unfolding and its growth. I was brought up on the fringes of modern India; I was given a Western education, for which I am grateful in many ways. But I lost something. I lost the peace of mind that I might have had in another generation, the sense of order, the sense that I could develop in my own time and under very composed conditions. Everyone of our generation — you are not so much older than I am — lives in a fragmented, complex, disturbing time, in which it is hard to keep one's spiritual balance, hard to find the time to build that balance in the first place. I feel increasingly that I must go into retreat more, must meditate more, must discipline myself more. Otherwise I shall be of no use to my people.'

He paused. 'I am sheltered from too many things by being a Rinpoche. Sometimes it angers me. I do not want to be treated differently from anyone else. I do not want to be shut away from the world. What is the point of compassion unless it is exercised in experience, at the heart of things, and not from some privileged position? I do not want to be treated as a God; I want to be useful. And to be useful you must have lived variously, complexly; you must have been allowed to feel and see many things.

The Buddha never wanted to be treated as a Special Being. Everyone is Buddha, everything is Buddha. We each of us contain heaven and hell, ignorance and Nirvana. The Buddha always said, "I am not a God. I am a man. And that is why what I say is of use to you — because I say it to you as a man and not as a God, as someone like you." Buddhism is a very human religion, entirely practical. Fortunately my father and mother are with me always. My father is a Rinpoche also and my mother is a very strong, very humorous woman. She never allows me to be proud. She is always laughing at me. And I have Thuksey Rinpoche too as my spiritual father and adviser. To be with him is to be constantly reminded of what I have not yet achieved, of what I am not.'

We fell silent. It was late. We had been talking for two or three hours. The candles were half-burnt. From down below, the soft growl of chanting came up to us. The window was still open and a chill night wind blew through it.

'Autumn is coming,' he said. 'I can smell it in the air. I am happy. It is, for me, the most beautiful season. The trees turn gold against the rock; each morning you wake to a different, colder, purer blue . . . Can you stay?'

'No, I have to go back.'

'I am sorry. There are so many beautiful places to walk near Hemis . . . gorges, streams . . . and round the monastery there are many caves and rocks where you can watch the moon from. The autumn moon is the most beautiful.'

'I am not going yet. I will be here another fortnight.'

'Then you will see one more full moon in Ladakh, before you leave. You must come and see it with us in Hemis.'

'I would love that.'

We fell silent again, happy in the sound of the chanting, in the soft insistent rattle of the wind against the window.

'Drukchen,' I said, 'there is one last thing I must ask you. You are of your world, and yet you have also had a Western education; you are a Tibetan monk and yet you understand Western mathematics, engineering, politics, Western ideas of all kinds; you must have met many Western seekers, here and in Darjeeling and in your travels in India; you must have talked about what I am going to ask you with your fellow monks, with the Rinpoche, with your father . . . Can Tibetan Buddhism survive the fall of Tibet? And can Westerners follow the Tibetan Buddhist way without betraying it or themselves, without falsifying it or themselves?'

Drukchen Rinpoche laughed. 'What a question! So many questions, in fact . . . I don't really think I have the wisdom to answer them properly.'

He sat silently, frowning a little into the dark beyond my head.

'Shall I tell you something that might surprise you? Some of the best Buddhists I know are Westerners. I met two Canadian women last year in Darjeeling whose faith amazed me. And one of the monks I feel closest to in Darjeeling is not a Tibetan. He is an Australian, in his thirties. He came to Ladakh, met Thuksey Rinpoche, and changed his life. He did not worry about whether it was possible or not to be a Buddhist — he *became* one, with courage and sincerity. One day I teased him. We were here at Hemis. Hemis food is very bad. I said to him, "Brian, why are you here? Why have you come so far to eat such bad food?" And he looked at me and he said, "Drukchen, I have tasted every kind of food." I thought about that remark for a long time. Perhaps in fact it is in the West, at this time of the West's development, that Buddhism will find another life. Many Westerners, like Brian, have "tasted every kind of food". They have exhausted most sensations, most of the possibilities of their culture, most of the possibilities of the affluent world. They are schooled, if you like, in unillusion. And to have no illusions is the beginning of Buddhist practice: no longer to believe in any of the fictions of personality or success or desire is the foundation of all true meditation, the beginning of the Path towards Nirvana. Buddhism will flourish in the West, I believe, because the West is coming of age; it is becoming adult, able to bear the radical clarity of the Buddha, hungry for it, in fact; for a wisdom that is without any false hope or consolation, that is rooted in a practical, severe analysis of things as they are, of the mind as it is. Do not forget that Buddhism was not in its origins a peasant belief, a peasant philosophy; the Buddha was a Prince and a scholar; the Buddhist world at the beginning was a sophisticated urban one — the cities of Northern India where Buddhism first began in the fifth century B.C. were great centres of scholarship and commerce; many of the Buddha's first converts were

180

merchants. The West is at the end of its belief in its own values; Buddhism puts in question all values, all judgments. The West is ready for a philosophy that is radical, and in some senses nihilistic — but that also has, at its heart, a vision of compassion as complete as anything in Christianity, and as absolute. Many Westerners tell me that they can no longer believe in Christ as a God, but they can love and follow him as a man. The Buddha was not a God; there are no Gods in Buddhism; the Buddha was a man and Buddhism is a human philosophy of Being. It may be a philosophy that the West will turn to in its despair precisely because Buddhism has always recognised that despair, even celebrated it as the beginning of wisdom, as the necessary beginning of a journey that leads beyond despair, to Awareness, and to a compassionate involvement with all life.'

Drukchen stopped and laughed sadly. 'Many Tibetans, you know, are no longer Buddhist. Oh, they say they are. They come to the Temple in Dharamsala, in Mysore, in Ladakh. But many of the young Tibetans especially are not really interested. They want radios and cars and sex and money. And why shouldn't they? They want to be Western, as they imagine "Western" to be. They really have very little time for their own traditions. The irony is that at the moment when young Tibetans are turning away from their inheritance, young Westerners are turning to it, are coming to men like Thuksey Rinpoche, like the Dalai Lama, for guidance and for new spiritual life. Westerners do not believe in being "Western" as much as young Easterners do; they know what being "Western" means, they have lived the various kinds of depression and deprivation that too great an involvement with materialism brings. They have suffered "being Western", and from that suffering they have grown clearer, sadder, more truthful, more "searching". At the moment when young Tibetans are wanting to become more and more "materialist", many of those who have been brought up with everything that money can buy are turning to the old wisdom of Tibet . . . No, it is not a wisdom of Tibet, or, rather, not of Tibet only. Perhaps Tibet had special conditions, perhaps in a country like Ladakh a certain noble and austere tradition could flourish, could reach a kind of perfection. But that does not mean that the insights that these men of my tradition discovered are for Tibet only; if they are worth anything, they must be valuable and useful in many different circumstances. If Tibet discovered anything truly important, it must be of use to the world. A true Buddhist does not remain attached to one particular tradition or another. He is grateful for what we can learn from the past, but he does not remain addicted to its insights, even to its ways of doing things. He is an adventurer and a pragmatist. He does what is necessary at the time it is necessary to do it. Buddhism will change, it must change, it is good if it changes. Change will reveal a new aspect of its truth, a new possibility in its wisdom. Buddhism in the West will be different in many ways from Buddhism as the Tibetan tradition has interpreted it — but why should we mourn that? We should welcome it. No society, no country, no world has a monopoly of spiritual insight, of spiritual truth. At this time of danger, we all, Buddhists and Christians, and atheists alike, should share all the awareness we have, all the compassion we can find in ourselves, build up every possibility of goodwill that exists within us towards the world. I am a Tibetan, yes, and I am a Tibetan Buddhist. But I am also, first and foremost, a man, and a man of my time, concerned for my time and for the establishment of peace and truth.'

Drukchen stopped and looked at me. 'Do you know the story of the Buddha in the park, in autumn? He was walking with his disciples through a park covered in autumn leaves. I often think of this story at Hemis in the autumn, when all the paths are gold with fallen leaves. The Buddha stopped and picked up a leaf and held it out to his disciples and said, "This one leaf represents what I have told you. Look at all the other leaves. They are what I have left unsaid." Every fresh awareness of Buddhism, every new expression of the Buddhist Way, is another leaf, another of the leaves in that park . . . We must be still within ourselves, still and calm, and yet we must also, at the same time, be moving forward, moving further and deeper towards each other, towards the world. What is not useful for this endless transformation must be abandoned; anything that prevents a finer flowering of our spirit must be left behind; anything that hinders us from dealing with the world as it is, with ourselves as we are, in this place and in this time, with all the dangers and fears and sadnesses of this time and this place, must be renounced, and renounced, if possible, without grief and without nostalgia. Every truthful transformation takes us closer to the world, closer to things, closer to each other; the clearest and wisest man becomes the world, becomes Buddha, becomes "awake", enters without fear and without hope, and without any consolation or protection, into the full presence of Reality.'

Drukchen stopped and put a hand on my shoulder. 'I have been talking too long. Forgive me!'

I could not say anything. We sat together, listening to the wind.

Next morning, preparations for the Initiation Ceremony, the Wang, began early. For days now the monks had been making small votive objects out of barley, squatting round a big tin tub in the kitchen. They had been cleaning and filling the old butter lamps, sweeping the upper courtyard clean, bringing out from their old dusty boxes the oldest and most sacred tankas. Now the last touches had to be put to everything — the last votive figures made, the last rooms swept, the tin tub in the kitchen washed and scoured clean, the food and the tea prepared for the hundreds of people who would be coming from all over Ladakh, the butter lamps carried down to the shrine that already looked as if it was about to break into flame. Banners of red and green silk were placed on the highest wall of the monastery, the wall where the monks had stood with their trumpets the day before, and flapped in the strong breeze; a great yellow prayer flag was placed at the top of the crumbling stairs; a monk was hurriedly painting on one of the rocks on the path up, in green and red and purple, 'OM MANI PADME HUM', splashing the paint around like a child, stamping his feet with impatience when the paint did not run properly. Nawang sat in his room cutting out green and red ribbons from long strips of coarse silk.

'What are those for?' I asked him.

'They are the ribbons of Initiation. After all the ritual objects have been blessed, and all the sacred mantras said, these ribbons will be given to everyone by the Rinpoches. They are very

183

powerful. You must wear them until they fall off, and then throw them away in a stream.'

I seized another pair of scissors, and we sat cross-legged on the monastery floor, cutting and talking. From time to time a monk would come in with a pot of Tibetan tea and tell us to hurry up.

Tantric ceremonies are slow, long, and hypnotic. There is no point in expecting anything to happen. What happens, happens in its own mysterious time, in its own sacred rhythm. The spectator has to open completely to all the sights and sounds around him, or find nothing in the proceedings but monotony and a kind of chaos. A Tantric Master, Trungpa, has written that some meditation should be boring, should be as boring as possible, because in intense boredom all our habitual responses and concepts are dissolved. The mind's terror of boredom is the more acute because the mind suspects that through boredom, through its extreme experience, another reality might be reached that would threaten its pretensions, and perhaps even dissolve them altogether. The Ladakhis are not afraid of monotony, of this kind of boredom; nor are the Indians. It is what in them is perhaps most alien to us. Nothing is stranger to me in India than to see the rows and rows of people waiting for trains hour after hour, without anger, without complaint, waiting without eating or talking, simply waiting. In India I had never managed to surrender to this rhythm, I had never been able to give up my European need to be entertained, and stimulated; in Ladakh, increasingly, I found myself able to be empty, to wait without any expectation, to be bored without being annoyed or afraid at my boredom, sometimes without even calling it 'boredom' and so defining it in my own old terms, giving it a power it need not have. It was a very strange, unexpected, mysterious joy to me, this emptiness, this simple bare surrender. In it I saw and felt everything afresh. Each sound was new to me, each growl on the trumpets, each pouring of hot tea into a bowl, each scrape of a foot on the stone floor. Each look at my surroundings seemed to remake them. I had been in that shrine-room for a week, but that morning it was as if I was seeing it for the first time, with unspoiled eyes. I had had glimpses of this state throughout my stay in Ladakh; I had felt it in the mountains, I had felt it, for moments, staring out at the flowers of the garden in Leh, I had felt it on long bus journeys, rocked by the swaying of the bus; I had tried to grasp it, to understand it, which is probably why it had abandoned me. That morning during the Initiation Ceremony, with Drukchen and Thuksey Rinpoche sitting on small thrones at the centre of the room, in the endless drone of mantras and trumpets and chanting, I felt it unbrokenly, for several hours. I began, in those hours, not merely to understand, but to see and to know what Ananda, years before in Sri Lanka, had told me of the Hinayana meditation technique, known as Vipassyana, 'Seeing without discrimination', 'Open seeing'.

'One moment of pure seeing,' he had said, 'is the beginning of Liberation. If you can see, for a moment, one flower, one face, one dog, as they are in themselves and for themselves, you have begun to be free enough to love.'

Later I found these words in the Mahamudra Upadesa:

Keep your spirit in its nudity.
Let the polluted waters of the mind
Flow away of themselves . . .

If you perceive the true nature and extent of space
All fixed notions of centre and limit will disappear
If the spirit sees into the spirit
All mental games will end . . .

Although you can call it 'empty'
Space is indescribable
Although you can call it 'luminous'
Giving it a name does not prove the spirit exists.
Space cannot be given a name or home . . .

Without changing, rest without attachment
In your state of origin
All your bonds will dissolve.
The essence of the spirit is space
There is nothing that it holds to in the end.

For hours, Drukchen and Thuksey Rinpoche had been chanting, singing, praying, charging with power the objects in front of them, the dorjes and vajras and dandas, the representations in bronze and copper and barley of Supreme Awareness, of Nirvana, of the people of Ladakh, of the monastery of Shey and its monks. In those hours a whole world was being symbolically charged with power, a whole landscape, a whole people. The Rinpoches held each object for a long time, praying and changing over it. Villagers had been arriving, too, from all parts of Ladakh with gifts for the Rinpoches and their monasteries — apples, apricots, bags of sugar, piles of dirty white scarves. The room was packed and sweltering. Trumpets were sounding to announce the end of the first part of the ceremony — great long blasts, louder than I had ever heard before. An old woman close to me burst into tears and started swaying from side to side; her husband held her to him and patted the back of her head. Monks were standing in all parts of the room, trying to establish some order, some decorum in the long noisy lines of people that were forming to file past the Rinpoches and receive their blessing. The younger Ladakhis were shoving and fighting for the best positions, laughing and slapping each other on the back as if at a football match.

Suddenly two long ragged lines had formed and I was in one of them, being pressed relentlessly forward. I could hardly breathe. I was packed between an old man and an old woman, both of whom reeked of old sweat and fruit and farm dung. The heat, the noise, the sense of expectation, the laughter, the shoving and pushing, the mounting hysteria . . . I had never been at anything like it in all my travels in India, not in Benares or Madras or Bombay, not even in the temple ceremonies I had attended in Madurai. For one moment I felt I would die, die of exhaustion, of asphyxiation, of the excitement and passionate faith of those around me, crushing me in and pressing me forward. And yet behind my fear, there was calm. I did not feel truly afraid. Nothing could happen to me here, I felt, that would bring me to any harm. I was in the hands of the Rinpoche, of the Buddhas on the walls. I gave up, I renounced my fear, I let myself drift with the crowd. I began to laugh with the old man in front of me, who laughed back, and the old women behind me, who started laughing too. It was absurd and magical, our laughter, and it spread down the line, down the long crowd. Soon everyone in our section was laughing. The laughter grew and grew until suddenly I found myself at the head of the line, on Drukchen's right. I would be the next to pass before the two Rinpoches and receive their blessing. Just as I was about to move forward, the old woman behind me kicked me, laughed, and ran in front of me. She had won! She had beaten me to the Rinpoche! She was bent double with laughter!

Drukchen leant forward and blessed her. He caught my eye, laughed, and said, 'Aren't you pleased now you had an English sporting education?'

Thuksey Rinpoche said he would see me that evening. I went into his room at about six. Nawang was with him.

'You are wearing your ribbons,' he said. 'Good. They will bring you luck.'

I bowed to him, and again my glasses fell off into his lap. He was delighted.

'When will you really give me your eyes?' he asked.

'How much will you give me for them?' I replied.

'A monk has no money. If you do not give them freely, there will be no merit attached to your gift.'

'If you say you want them, then you are guilty of desire.'

The Rinpoche clapped his hands with delight. 'Yes, I am guilty! I am guilty! I want your eyes!' and handed me back my glasses with a mock-elaborate gesture.

Nawang was laughing, a little uncontrollably. He looked bright-eyed with exhaustion.

Then the Rinpoche said, 'I am returning to Hemis tomorrow for three days. I shall need to rest a little, and so will Drukchen and the monks. But I shall be back in Shey in three days' time, for the festival of the Shey Oracle. You should be there. It is the first year the Oracle has been revived for a long time. It is a historic occasion for the people of Ladakh . . . Go back to Leh now and be peaceful for three days and think on what you have seen and learnt. Then you will return refreshed.'

'If you are going in a fortnight,' he added, 'you should spend your last days with us at Hemis. I will give you the initiation of the Buddha of Compassion. I have watched you these last days. Avalokiteshvara is your Bodhisatva. I will teach you how to meditate on him.'

He was smiling, but it was an order. I thanked him, bowed, and left for Leh.

I had almost forgotten about Leh. I had not been there for almost ten days, and each of those days had been so charged that Leh had almost vanished from my mind, with its drains full of sweetpaper and dogshit, its Indian National Bank and post office . . . Walking about it again, I felt unsteady, peeled and rawly exposed to everything, every noise, every blare of colour, every new face, staring at me out of the dusk. That evening I didn't want to talk to anyone, write or read anything. I couldn't concentrate on anything, even on remembering what had happened in Shey. I wandered about the town disconsolately and then up by the river, where I sat, like a lovesick schoolboy, throwing stones at the moonlit water and frowning. I walked home to my room and couldn't sleep.

Suddenly, I understood: I was afraid. Everything had happened so fast and with such a compelling intensity at Shey, I had had no time to feel fear. I was afraid. I was afraid of everything — of Drukchen, of Nawang, of the Ladakhis, of the painting of Shamunatha, of the mountains, of the moonlight, of the whole wild beauty of the place and its people and its religion. I was afraid for myself, for my identity, for my past, for my understanding, for my art, for my future, for my health, for my sanity, for my sleep . . . As all the varieties of my fear began to appear before me, I was amazed. I had been so open, I had believed, so enthusiastic a listener, so deeply and truthfully moved. But I had forgotten my own inner anxiety, I had forgotten to listen to it, and now it exacted its revenge, it reappeared in all its cruel and most mocking shapes.

I was also afraid, I realised, of Thuksey Rinpoche himself. What was the nature of his power? How could I be certain that it was for good, the great force I felt from him? How could I be sure that he was not some black magician, some Tantric ensnarer of souls? What if all his gentleness were a mask for some inner drive to domination? Scraps of dialogue with him returned in their darkest sense. Exchanges that seemed the highest humour now seemed to reveal whole landscapes of menace, of threat. And what if I had invented the whole experience? That was what I was most frightened of — more frightened, even, than if the Rinpoche had been evil. What if everything I had seen and felt had not been real but my madness, my fantasy? That would be shameful, a shameful repetition of everything I felt most bleak in myself — my desire to dominate experience through fantasy, my old vanity smuggled in as 'spirituality', more corrupt than ever, and more dangerous. And I felt afraid too of the suffering that the exposure of so much new illusion would bring, of the suffering and the despair. If I had come so far, tried so hard, felt so much, and that too had been a fake, an illusion, a corruption — then what hope could I have in myself? What trust could I have ever again in anything, in any power of my judgment? If Thuksey Rinpoche was an illusion of my devious invention and my feeling for him merely a psychological convenience, what belief could I have in anything I felt? Would any resolution of my fear be another flight from truth, another drab and desolate victory for my vanity?

The only thing I could hold to in those days and nights of pain was a belief that fear itself was not stupid and destructive, that, in some sense I could barely glimpse, it was good, a necessary ritual, a necessary rite of passage. The one thing I could do as I shook with fears of all kinds was to struggle to detach myself from them, and watch them, become their inquisitor, seek, with all my strength of love and reason, to unmask them, to get them to tell their true names. Slowly, painfully, they spoke them, receded, dissolved. I saw that they were the inventions of the old self, the self that was changing; that they were the last games of an ego that did not want to acknowledge powers and presences greater than it could understand, the last ruses of a heart that did not want to endure the transformation of love. Their dissolution left me exhausted and empty, but at peace.

I met Charles at breakfast in my hotel the next day. For weeks before I had gone to Shey I had heard about Charles — from the hotel manager, from friends in Leh. He was Swiss; he was an expert on Ladakhi art; he was a Buddhist; all this I knew about him already, so when I walked into the breakfast room of my hotel and saw a shortish man with a paunch, cold blue eyes, and a half-beard, I knew who he was. He wore the old dark blue sweater and crumpled blue trousers I could always see him in, and he was reading a large black book in Tibetan, making small notes in the margin.

We introduced ourselves.

'The manager told me about you too,' Charles said. 'In this country everyone gets to know everyone else sooner or later. The manager says you are almost a Buddhist.' Charles's eyes glittered sardonically at the word 'almost'.

I ignored the half-challenge. 'What are you reading?' I asked him.

'This book', Charles held it up, 'is one of the most incomprehensible ever written. I have been studying Tibetan for twelve years, three of them in Dharamsala; I live in Switzerland in a Tibetan Buddhist community, under the supervision of a Yeshe, a Master — but I can understand very little. It's a meditation manual. On the Sixteen Types of Emptiness.'

'Sixteen?'

'Sixteen! I can just about understand two. What will I do? Will I have to wait another fifteen years? Yeshe says, "Yes. You will have to wait." But I say, "I am impatient to understand *now*." Yeshe says, "Ah yes, that is your problem. That is why you cannot understand. You want to too much." Then I want to

190

hit him, but I restrain myself and smile. Yeshe says, "You see, you cannot understand. You must *experience*." "But how, but when?" "When it is right for you to do so. When your time is right." And the worst of it is, I know he is right. But I'm not giving in that easily. I've come here to be a guide but I read this in my spare moments. I want to surprise the old bastard.'

I asked Charles about how he had come to be a Tibetan Buddhist, about Ladakhi art, about the book he was writing on Ladakh. He was fluent, witty, precise, vain, reciting all the long names of the sutras, all the elaborate technical terms of esoteric Buddhism with excessive panache. But there was a direct, rather harsh, seriousness about him that I liked, and we spent the day together, walking by the river to Sankar.

'There is one thing you must understand if you are going to take Buddhism seriously. You must not use it as an anaesthetic. I did, for years. I travelled, studied, went into retreats, gave up my job to go to Dharamsala, did all the proper things, had the most amazing experiences, insights . . . yes, indeed. I was very proud of myself, really thought I had got there, arrived, done and understood everything by the age of thirty. I was learned; I had met many of the great Rinpoches and had close friendships with them. I had become fluent in Tibetan. And I was happy, calm, suspiciously happy, in fact, suspiciously calm. I see that now. What I was doing was what many searchers do — I was building a great wall of experiences and meditative ecstasies and learning between me and the world. How many wonderful sermons from great Rinpoches I had listened to! How many young girls I had made cry with joy in my courses, my tours, in my lectures before distinguished audiences! and where was I in all that? I was hidden, afraid and hardly transformed, behind a wall of talk. To be a Buddhist is to cling to no insight, no experience, no learning — it is to be simple and unprotected. It is to be practical, in the highest sense, with everything that is around you, with all the energies, good or bad, of the present. Perhaps it will take me twenty years to be practical in this way.'

He was half angry, half laughing at himself, sitting on a rock, his bright red socks showing, throwing apricot stones at the tree to our right. I told him about the Rinpoche. I told him what I had felt and understood.

'You have been lucky. I have met him too, and he is, in my

opinion, all the things you have said he is. To feel that link, to feel that love for a Master like the Rinpoche is a great thing. Do not worry that you have no precedent for it in your Western experience. The West is largely ignorant of the laws of the spirit, the relationships of the spirit. You must find the courage to live beyond that ignorance. You must also remember that this meeting of yours is only a beginning. It is good to have felt all the things you have felt. Do not hold on to them. If you do, you will mythologise them; you will become the prisoner of your own insights. What the Rinpoche has done for you is to start you on a journey, or help you to start; you are at the beginning. You have a long way to travel. You must always claim very little for yourself, very little, as little as possible. And yet you must be faithful to what you have learnt and seen here: you must bear witness to what you have been given. Otherwise, what are you?'

In the monastery of Sankar there is a sculpture of Avalokiteshvara, the Buddha of Compassion. It stands a little larger than life, made of plaster, blotched and darkened by age and candle-grease, in the darkness of the shrine-room. Charles and I each lit a lamp to it.

'Do you know why Avalokiteshvara is always shown as having a thousand hands? The story goes that when he was about to enter Nirvana, Avalokita happened to look back and notice an animal in distress. Some say it was a rabbit, some say a bird. He was so moved by its pain that he could not enter Nirvana. He could not bear to attain release for himself while any other living thing was in anguish. He begged his father, Amitabha, the Buddha of Endless Light, for permission to return and help the animal. Amitabha replied, "Yes, you may go back. When you do, you will find there are many other beings in torment. To help you see them all, I am going to give you a thousand eyes; to help you save them all, I am going to give you a thousand hands." '

As Charles was talking, a memory came back to me. I saw myself at eleven, on a train in South India with my father. The train was filled with light and the smell of oranges. I had come out from school for the winter holidays and my father was taking me to see the paintings and sculptures of Ajanta and Ellora.

'Who made them?' I asked him.

'Buddhist monks. They carved the caves out of the sheer rock.'

And then my memory shifted; I was standing in one of the caves of Ajanta. My father had taken his torch out and was focusing it on the tall, slightly stooping figure of a man on the wall, holding a flower.

'Who is that Prince, father?'

My father didn't know. He turned to our small fat guide.

'Who is that man?'

'That is the Lotus-One, sahib. That is Avalokiteshvara, the Buddha of Compassion. He has so much love for the world, that his face is sad.'

And I noticed that at the foot of the painting, on the floor, were piles of dried white flowers.

'Why are the flowers there?' I asked the guide.

'The flowers are brought by many people for the Buddha. A flower is beautiful. It fades quickly. It is sad that it fades so quickly. A white flower is a symbol of purity.'

And the guide had bent down and given me one of the flowers.

'This is good luck, sahib, this is good luck . . .'

'Why are you smiling?' Charles asked.

'Because I was remembering going as a child to the caves of Ajanta and seeing the painting of Avalokiteshvara there.'

'Were you moved by it?'

'Very.'

'Perhaps that is why you are here now.'

Outside, we sat on the stone steps of the monastery. It was twilight. The sunflowers in the garden were darkening.

'I was in Pokhara once,' Charles said, 'sitting in a coffee house by the lake. It was cold. There was a beggar woman, very old and thin, sitting on the wooden benches outside, who asked me for some money. I gave her five rupees. She bought herself a meal, a soup of vegetables and potatoes. Then she did something extraordinary. There was a particularly mangy, filthy mongrel skulking about the door of the coffee house. The woman sat down on the ground with the dog, and gave it exactly half her food. They ate together. She had nothing, no money, hardly any clothes; the dog was not hers. I did not feel she had said to herself, "I am going to share half my food with the dog." No, she gave her food simply, spontaneously, without any sense, I saw, that she and the dog were different, or yet that there was any obligation on her part to give or on its part to be grateful. *That* is compassion . . .

'Do you know the story of the Buddha and the prostitute? It is the story that moves me most, I think, of any that I know. When he was young, the Buddha was considered very handsome. Some of his enemies wanted to discredit him, and so they sent to see him the most famous courtesan of his time. The Buddha liked her and they spoke of many things. She was very beautiful and witty. She offered herself to him. The Buddha smiled at her and said, "I will love you when no one else loves you; I will love you when every other love has abandoned you." At this, she grew very angry and left him. Almost forty years later, the Buddha was dying and being carried to his final resting-place on a wooden bier. He saw a figure huddled in rags in the shadow of a wall. It was a leper, a woman, an old hunchback with half her face eaten away. The Buddha dismounted from his bier, and walked across the waste between him and the woman and folded her quietly in his arms.'

I felt perverse and said, 'That seems to me an intolerable story. To win like that! To have the last word like that!'

'Is that all they taught you at Oxford — how to be clever and ironic?' Charles said angrily. 'Don't you understand anything? Don't you see that what the story is talking about is the deepest love we can imagine — the love without desire or expectation, the love that pierces all the veils and barriers of the flesh and the world? Don't you understand that to love like that is the end of our existence? Or do you understand and do not have the courage to say "Yes, I understand"? Is that it? Is that what they did to you in England? Make you too cowardly to admit to what you knew?'

We walked upstairs to the last shrine-room in silence. At the top of the stairs, Charles said, 'I'm sorry. I spoke harshly.'

'But you were right,' I said. 'I was being cowardly. We meet at a time when I am in such turmoil I don't know what to think. I am afraid. So much has happened here in Ladakh, I am not certain of anything.'

'Thank god,' Charles smiled. 'If you were certain, nothing much would have happened! Our deepest insights are ringed about with fears, fears we have to penetrate and make transparent by understanding before we can find what they are hiding. If you were not afraid, you would be careless and stupid. The right fear is one of the greatest gifts you can be given.

'Once I tried to leave Dharamsala altogether. I had had enough. I was making no progress. I thought I had been a fool. I thought I would stop the whole thing, stop learning Tibetan, stop trying to meditate, stop the whole thing and go back to Europe and do something simple. Be a clerk or a journalist. Forget about the whole thing. I even began to suspect that the lama whom I had been studying under was a fraud, not at all evolved, not at all wise, just a parrot of the Old Tradition, a kind of decent fool at best. I grew sullen. I sent for some money to get back to Switzerland. I went to my lama and told him everything that I was feeling. Everything. I spared him nothing. I was angry, insulting, eloquent. He listened carefully. Sometimes he would ask me to make myself clearer, to be more precise. Why did I despise him exactly? What precisely had failed me in his teaching? And so on. At the end of my tirade he said nothing. Then he looked up and said, "Is that all?" I lost my temper. "Is that all? I have been telling you about my deepest feelings, I have been speaking to you out of the heart of my life, and you say is that all?" He smiled and said, "Charles, being angry is the one honest thing you have done all year. Why are you now wasting it? Don't you see it is a gift you must not throw away? Think of your anger as a piece of dark marble; you must work it. If you just carry it with you back to Europe, it will make you a hunchback." I stayed.'

We had come into the last room. Charles said, "Don't look," and he put his hands over my eyes. Downstairs, a monk was chanting the evening prayers. Charles led me a few steps, tilted my head upwards, and removed his hands.

There was a vast statue in front of me, garishly lit by several lamps. It was the statue of a Goddess. With a thousand arms and legs. Her face was terrifying — staring bull-like eyes, her mouth parted in savage laughter.

'Who is it, Charles?' It was a ridiculous question, and Charles laughed.

'Who is it? It is Dukar, in her terrible aspect.'

'Why does she carry all those knives and arrows?'

'To kill Ignorance.'

'Who is she trampling? Who are those small fat demons?'

'They are all the forces within us that are proud and vain.'

'It is terrifying.'

'She is dancing the death of the Self. That is terrifying. But She is also called the Saviour, the bringer of Peace, the Mother of Wisdom.'

'Why is she laughing?'

'She is laughing in triumph and in exultation. Her laughter, it is said, crumbles worlds. She is the holy violence within us that will defeat all our fears and illusions, the great laughter that will laugh in the face of our vanity, the inner fire in which it will be consumed.'

Then he took me tenderly to a small statue on her right. It was the statue of a lama, made out of gilded bronze.

'It was made in Bhutan. It is of a very holy lama.'

'His face is gentle and fine.'

'It is a gentleness that has been through the fire of death.'

That night Charles and I got drunk together in the chang shop. Charles sang Swiss songs in a rusty baritone and did imitations, to the delight of the Tibetan boys who were drinking with us, of Charlie Chaplin in *The Gold Rush*. I sang 'Go away from my window', to great applause and was asked to teach the Tibetans disco dancing, which I did. Mama Chang came from next door to watch me. She clutched her heart, wheezed, sobbed, staggered with laughter. She fell on the bed and couldn't be got up from it, she was laughing so much. We had our revenge when she tried to dance too, all nineteen stone of her. The boys egged her on, clapping and beating their thighs and whistling, and then they too started to dance, not Western style this time, but the slow, sensuous dances of Tibet, with much hand-wringing and hip-wriggling and cries of 'Wa Wa Wa *Wa*' and clapping to keep time.

Partly to torment him, I asked Charles to write me a few sentences that for him epitomised Tantric Buddhism. He groaned, but tore a page out of his notebook and wrote them, in great mocking strokes, drawing faces in the corners — fiery faces, like the face of Dukar, gentle faces, funny faces, one face that was meant to be mine, with a bewildered pop-eyed look, a half-moustache and so-earnest glasses. And when he had written the sentences he drew a caricature of himself underneath, in Swiss Alpine costume, with a Rinpoche's cap with two dragons on it, and a pair of very bedraggled wings decorated with floating ribbons. Under the caricature he wrote in capital letters, 'The Betrayer of the Truth that is beyond words.' Out of his mouth floated a ribbon with 'Wa Wa Wa Wa' written on it and a few mock-Tibetan letters.

In Tantra there are no Gods, no external powers. The Gods are your inner energies. When you are invoking them and worshipping them you are invoking and worshipping yourself.

Pride in one's inner divinity without the wisdom of Emptiness leads to madness or megalomania. Everything is 'empty', even one's inner divinity. Even the Gods are 'empty' symbols to be dissolved in the radiance of the Void once they have served their purpose, completed their design.

Tantra is alchemy, the alchemy that turns the filth of the Self into the Gold of selflessness. There's a phrase for you.

My hand's tired.

Now you understand it all perfectly.

Everyone crowded round Charles as he was writing the sentences. A young Tibetan asked him, 'What are you writing?'

'I am writing a letter to my English friend.'

The Tibetan laughed. 'But why are you writing a letter to him? He is here.'

Charles said, 'My English friend has a strange disease. It is a kind of madness. He has to see things written, otherwise he cannot believe them. He will not believe anything anyone says to him.'

The Tibetan replied, 'This is very sad. He must drink some more and then he won't be able to read either.'

'And what will he do then?'
'He will dance.'

Chang is a soft and glowing drink and I was softly, glow-ingly, totally drunk.

Charles held me up and steered me round the stony paths to my hotel.

'Give an Englishman one glass of anything and he can't walk. So much for English Rationalists.'

'Bastard! How do you manage to be still sober?'

'Long meditative training. You may never reach my exalted stage of development. You could meditate nude in the Hima-layas for years and not be where I am.'

Then he said, 'Are you still afraid?'

'No.'

'Why?'

'I don't know. Does there have to be an explanation?'

'No.'

'Thank god.'

'I'll wake you at six-thirty.'

'Six-thirty!'

'Buddhists wake early.'

'I'm not a Buddhist.'

'You are more Buddhist than you know.'

'Well, if I am, I am going to be a lazy late-rising half-Buddhist.'

'But the bus for Shey goes at seven-thirty. We'll have to get there early.'

'I thought you were going to take your group to Alchi.'

'No, I've changed my mind. I'm not going to miss another opportunity of haranguing you. I'm enjoying myself too much.'

'I thought the Swiss found it very hard to enjoy themselves.'

'Their true pleasures are very refined, very exalted.'

'Really?'

'Really.'

I stumbled into my room. Someone had put a big sunflower into a glass and placed it next to my bed. It looked very funny on its long naked stalk, absurdly big and open in the moonlight.

N awang was waiting for us at Shey, at the bus-stop. He had his dark glasses on, and a fresh red robe. He looked fierce, efficient.

'Why didn't you get the earlier bus?'

'We talked too late last night.'

'Well, hurry. The ceremony has already started. We'll watch it and then go and see the Rinpoche.'

We started to walk towards the village.

'This is the first year, isn't it,' Charles said, 'that the Oracle has been revived?'

'The first time for twenty years, I think,' Nawang replied. 'The Rinpoche has had it revived specially. He says that he is trying to make the sun rise again over a dark land. He says that the people of Shey are in danger of losing their spiritual identity and that bringing back the Oracle is one way of helping them to find it again. In the old days the ceremony of the Oracle was the centre of the year in Shey, the Harvest festival, in fact.'

'Oracles date from pre-Buddhist times,' Charles said.

'Yes. But Buddhism has found a way to channel the ancient forces, to give them new expression.'

Charles said, 'I lived in Brazil once. Every year there used to be this wild festival in which devil-dancers would be invited into the Cathedral . . . After they had danced, screamed, gyrated crazily, someone dressed as the Virgin Mary would come in and start singing a hymn. Who is the Oracle, by the way?'

'He's an official of the Agricultural Department. He comes from a long line of Oracles. His father was the last Oracle, in fact. Usually he is a quiet reserved man. But when he's had some drink in him . . .'

At that moment, the Oracle came round the corner in front of us on his horse. He was immensely drunk. He swayed from side to side, his face blotched, his eyes half-closed, a thin trickle of chang dribbling down from his mouth on to his green and red robe. He was carrying in his left hand a small ritual spear, tipped with silver and decorated with silk ribbons, and was waving it about with such unsteady enthusiasm, it was hard not to fear that he would injure someone. But from all sides, despite the spear, the Ladakhis of Shey were pressing him in, waving white scarves at him, flinging them over the back of the horse, throwing handfuls of grain over him and at the flanks of the horse, cheering in relays, and he acknowledged all the brouhaha and rough homage with practised, if tottering, grandeur, smiling hazily at everyone, touching the heads of the children held out to him, running his hands through the dirty white mane of his carthorse, as if he were a Prince on a charger. His face, when I could study it properly, seemed thin, stupid-looking, and very long and yellow, but he had fine hands, the hands of a painter or watch-maker, with long tapered fingers, thick with rings. Often he seemed on the verge of falling asleep. He would slump forward in the saddle, his great Oracle's hat of white and red brocade leaning dangerously. A red-faced man on his right, who held the horse's reins, would then shake him, mutter something in his ear, and produce from a bag yet another bottle of chang. The Oracle had the true reverence of the drunk, and would hold the bottle in the air as if blessing it, and then empty most of it, scattering the rest over the heads of the crowd, screeching with laughter. He had odd socks on, one bright red, the other black, and filthy old shoes, splitting at the sides, held together only by thick red ribbons.

'What is he going to do now?' I asked Nawang.

'He's going to run to the top of the hill and bless it.'

'He'll never make it.'

'Oh yes, he will. He may seem exhausted to you but actually he's possessed. He has the strength of many men, when he is in a state like this.'

The Oracle was being helped from his horse, and looked so dishevelled and broken that it was difficult to imagine him walking, let alone running. But Nawang was right. Suddenly, the Oracle started shouting, in a deep dark voice quite unlike the voice he had been using before. He started shouting and flailing at the crowd, who quickly withdrew, leaving him alone in his own circle, spinning at its centre, wildly. He spun round and round, faster and faster, shouting louder and louder. And then, just as abruptly, he began to run. He began to run up the hill — not up the path that wound round the hill, but straight up the hill, as the young Rinpoche had done on the day of his arrival. Every so often he would stop, bend, turn round, throw his arms in the air, yell something, and then go on running. No one followed him. On the top of the hill, he turned, stopped, and very solemnly raised both his open hands in blessing. The Ladakhis all around me stopped talking, and bowed their heads. This display of reverence seemed to amuse the Oracle, who began to laugh crazily again and stroll up and down on the rock he was standing on, like a lion tamer in a circus, stopping and then strutting again, stamping his feet and tossing his head, brandishing his sacred spear like a whip. This went on for so long and with such variations of fierce energy that I began to fear he would never come down again and just stay up there on the rock, until he collapsed. What would happen then to the day's festivities? Who would dare approach the Oracle in such a state? Would the Rinpoche have to come in person? Would he have to be exorcised with bells and sacred chanting? Just as I was beginning to imagine the whole comic scenario with relish, the Oracle stopped, put his hands on his hips, like a stripper, threw his spear in the air, caught it, put his hands on his hips again, bent double, leapt up and down three times, shouted something, and started to walk down again, as if nothing at all unusual had happened. The crowd was quiet. A man helped the Oracle back on to his horse. He looked around him, as if to say, with a mild surprise, 'What are all these people doing here?'

'*Now* what?'

'He is going to bless the Holy Tree.'

Nawang pointed to a tree on the other side of the road. A less inspiring Holy Tree would be hard to imagine: it stood isolated and gnarled in a small marsh, with only a few leaves clinging to its boughs. The Oracle had to cross a small causeway of stones across a stream to get to it. He did so, picking his great ballooning skirts up out of the water. When he got to the tree, he wove a white scarf around one of its branches, and bowed slightly to it. He seemed exhausted.

'Will he rest now?'

'Only until this afternoon. When the dances begin.'

Then he walked back across the stream, wiped his brow with a silk scarf, mounted his horse, and rode back to Shey, staring in front of him fixedly. A man offered him a bottle of chang. He took it and threw it to the ground with revulsion, shattering it.

'The Rinpoche is expecting us. Come quickly.' Nawang led us through the lanes of Shey to where the Rinpoche was staying — a square, simple stone house with a large garden full of sunflowers and giant tulips. A stream ran through it. Two old horses were grazing in a corner, under a poplar, their coats blotched and moulting like ancient rugs, their backs in deep shadow. Some monks' robes had been spread out on the grass to dry, and the wind had sprinkled handfuls of dry leaves over them. Autumn was breaking. We went to the stream and washed our hands and faces in it. Charles had some apples in a bag, and we ate them sitting between the sunflowers and the stream. From where I was sitting, I could see into the large half-dark kitchen of the house. An old woman was standing peeling vegetables into a bowl. Behind her, a row of pots of all shapes and sizes shone on the wall, their rough silver shining neat and rich in that late morning air. I was watching her, she came over to the window, put her hands over her eyes to shade them from the sun, and called to us, 'Don't sit there. Come in. I've just made some gongurchai. Don't you want any?'

'That is the Mayor's wife,' Nawang said. 'She is a relative. The Rinpoche always stays with the Mayor when he comes to Shey,' and he called back to her that we thanked her but that we had to see the Rinpoche and had very little time. She smiled, waved to us, and turned back to her kitchen. We sat a few moments longer in the grass. She began to sing in the kitchen.

'She is welcoming us,' Nawang said. 'She is singing a Ladakhi song of welcome:

'If you come to my house
In the morning or the evening, or the afternoon,
If you come in spring or winter,
I will be waiting for you.
I will be waiting with tea and tsampa,
So do not wait, my friends, do not stay away.'

'We must go soon,' Charles said, 'or the Rinpoche will think we have not come.'

'He knows you are here,' Nawang said, and pointed upwards. There, on a small balcony, the Rinpoche was standing, alone, looking down at us and smiling. Looking at him, so solid and gentle in the morning, I lost all fear. A young monk came out on the balcony to join the Rinpoche. He brought him a bowl of Tibetan tea and a plate of fruit. The Rinpoche looked down at us, pointed to the bowl of fruit as if to say, 'If you want any, you must come up.'

We went.

The Rinpoche was sitting in a large empty room with bowls of sunflowers and tulips around him from the garden. In front of him there was a small red lacquered table, crowded with sacred ritual objects — a bell, a vajra, his old large rosary. Sunlight filled the room. There was one old brown rug on the floor.

When he had blessed me, he said, 'Your glasses did not fall off today. Does that mean you have definitely decided to keep your eyes to yourself?'

I took my glasses off and gave them to him. He held them up in the air, looked at them quizzically, then looked through them.

'How can you see anything through these?' he laughed. 'I can see nothing.'

He handed them back to me, with two apricots.

'There, you keep them. They are yours. Only you can see through them. Keep them.

'This morning I am very busy,' he added. 'So many people will want to come and see me before the dances after lunch. But stay here with me. We will talk and have lunch together. In between the arrival of my guests you can ask me any questions you like.'

For a moment, no one wanted to say anything. It seemed

enough to be sitting with him. Then the Mayor came in, a large fat man with a red face, and said, 'Rinpoche, the drummers have come from Shey village to drum for you. Will you hear them?'

The Rinpoche nodded.

The drummers, three of them, an old man and his two sons, did not come into the room. They stayed on the small balcony outside where we had first seen the Rinpoche that morning. They played quietly at first, and then more and more intricately and loudly. The Rinpoche followed their beat gently with his right hand on the table in front of him.

It was during the next ten or fifteen minutes that I had one of the strangest experiences of my life. As the drumming deepened, I began to notice that my mind was detaching itself slowly and gently from my body, was hovering, in fact, a little outside my body. I was not frightened. I had had dreams in which the same gentle process of detachment had occurred, and it did not strike me as unusual. In that new state, I looked at everything and everyone around me — at the walls, at the fruit on the plate in front of the Rinpoche, at Charles, at Nawang, at the Rinpoche himself, tapping on the table before him, smiling to himself, at the sunlight in great shining squares and oblongs on the walls. I saw for the first time, not intellectually, not with my mind only, but with the eyes of my whole body and spirit what is meant by 'Emptiness', by Sunyata. Each object looked at once startlingly, intensely real — and completely fabricated, an invention, as if painted, or made out of ricepaper and balsa wood. Even the Rinpoche looked at once imposing and a doll, a sage and a structure of wood and paper, the paper tightest in the severe lines of his face, where the wood almost peeped through. The fruit in front of him seemed at once solid and so fragile that a breath could blow it away or break it. I felt that for all their strength I could put my hands through the stone walls, lean back through them, and through the garden behind them, through the stream, the mountains. I did not feel separated from any of the people or objects I was looking at, I did not feel any more 'real' than they, with any greater right to be taken as solid or absolute. I realised that even the self that was watching all this, revelling in all this, was itself as insubstantial as wind . . . I turned my head and looked out of the window at the mountains. They were paper a child could tear. I looked at the

Rinpoche. He was staring in front of him, and saying a prayer. His face seemed like the face of an old puppet, his hands papier mâché; he too was an illusion, a game, a breath — but the difference between him and me, I saw, was that he had understood that long ago, had meditated on it for years, and made the spaciousness I was feeling for these brief moments a continual experience, the light and quiet ground of all his living. I never loved him more than in those moments when I saw that he, like everything else, was not inherently real — that he too was, like the fruit and the walls and the mountains, like myself, a transitory fiction. I forgot all my fear and self-hatred in those moments, and I knew, as I have never known before or since, that anything but that feeling of joy and spaciousness was unworthy of myself, of everyone and everything that lives, not only unworthy, but a lie, a defamation. The drumming came to a long climax and stopped. I re-entered my body, and my mind grew dull again. Charles and the fruit and the Rinpoche were still around me; I had not gone mad; I felt quiet; the drummers had come in and were receiving white scarves in the sunlight, scarves and fruit; Nawang was leaning over to me and saying, 'Those drummers, you know, are the best in Ladakh. You will hear them again this afternoon'; the mountains in the window had returned to their solidity and were shining in the sun.

The drummers left the room. Charles said to the Rinpoche, 'I wish to ask you a question.'

'What about?'

'About Giving and the Perfection of Giving.'

'Why are you asking me?'

'Because I am sad at my life. I have lived in illusion. I have lived selfishly.'

The Rinpoche said, 'Be sad, but not too sad; grieve, but do not become absorbed by your grief. You cannot change what you have done; but you can change what you will become. Remember that somewhere you are free already. Remember that you are already Buddha. Draw hope from that; live in that hope.'

'It is hard.'

'It is the hardest thing. That is why you must practise. The self wants sometimes to give up, to abandon itself to despair. Despair is one of the last houses of the ego. And that house too has to be burnt down. We must abide in nothing and nowhere. The Heart sutra says, "Let the mind abide nowhere and alight upon nothing, let it dwell without thought-coverings." '

Charles was silent for a moment, and then said, 'There is a text of Chandrakirti I do not understand. Will you explain it to me? "When a Bodhisatva thinks and hears the word 'give' happiness arises; those who live in Nirvana have no such happiness. What need is there to mention to them the joy of giving everything?" What does Chandrakirti mean?'

The Rinpoche smiled. 'I have loved that text since I first heard it, as a boy of twelve in Tibet! I have used it many times in meditation.'

The Rinpoche did not answer directly or at once. He picked up the vajra in front of him and held it in his left hand. With his right, he picked up a sunflower from the bowl next to him. He held both his hands out to us.

'Look at his flower,' he said. 'It gives itself, to us and the bees that take pollen from it, without holding anything back. It cannot hold anything back. It cannot deny us or the bees anything. Do you remember the story of the Buddha and the flower? When the Buddha was old he wanted to choose a successor. He called his monks together, about three hundred of them. He called them all together but just sat there, in front of them, saying nothing. Then he held out a flower to them, still saying nothing. Only one monk, Kasyapa, understood and smiled. He was chosen. On that day he achieved Enlightenment!'

The Rinpoche looked at us. 'Wisdom is needed as well as openness and generosity, and that is why I hold the vajra in my left hand. The wisdom of Sunyata, of Emptiness, is also needed if giving is to be perfect. The only giving that is perfect is the giving by a giver that knows both giving and giver are not real, are empty, and that the receiver is empty too, does not inherently exist. This does not mean that there is no need to give — on the contrary, giving becomes natural, an action so natural that you do not need to call it "giving". The flower does not "give"; it opens, that is all. The giver does not praise himself for giving, does not celebrate his gift, nor patronise in any way the person who is receiving. The wisdom of Sunyata reveals that you cannot give to another without giving to yourself, and also that there is no giver, no receiver, no gift. And so you give spaciously, with freedom, claiming nothing, hoping nothing, planning nothing. The greatest happiness is to give like this. Shantideva said, "Through giving away everything you pass beyond sorrow." '

He put the flower back into the bowl and placed the vajra on the table in front of him. He leant forward.

'In the text you quoted, Chandrakirti is talking to us of the joy of the Bodhisatva — of the joy that is without end because the giving it springs from is boundless. Those who have already passed into Nirvana cannot know this joy, because it is the happiness of giving to living beings that brings it. The Bodhisatva who refuses to enter Nirvana until every living being can also enter Nirvana with him knows a joy that the Released cannot know; he knows, and lives in, the joy of giving everything without thought for himself. We say, in Tibetan Buddhism, that a Bodhisatva is like the risen moon. He abides in a white light that comes from himself and from the wisdom of Emptiness that shines through him; all who look on him are made happy, if only for a moment, and given courage to begin on the long journey towards their own perfection. Shantideva has written that the perfection of pure giving makes a man "like a water crystal jewel destroying and overcoming darkness". To have turned one small part of one's life into that radiance is enough for most lives, more than enough; but those who are really in love with the world, who have the truest insight and pity, will want to become that "jewel". In becoming that radiance they will live in the joy that Chandrakirti speaks of, a joy that nothing will take from them, because it clings to nothing.'

I said, 'There are many in my country who would say that what you have just said is beautiful but without meaning, a dream.'

The Rinpoche smiled. 'As long as there is Samsara, there will be an evasion of the inner perfection that is man's essence. This is perhaps the saddest of all the tragedies of Samsara, and the most painful. A man is starving in one dark room, while in another just across the corridor from him there is enough food for many lives, for eternity. But he has to *walk* to that room, and before he can walk to it, he has to believe that it is there. No one else can believe for him. No one can even bring the food from that room to him. Even if they could, he would not believe in the food or be able to eat it. The Dhammapada says, "Buddhas neither wash away sins with water nor remove the sufferings of being with their hands. They do not transfer their realisation to others. Beings are freed through the teaching of truth, of the nature of things." But to be taught, they have to want to listen, and to learn they have to have the humility to want to change. No one can make them listen or want to change. We are free to become Bodhisatvas or consign ourselves to life after life in pain. Often when men say they are helpless, trapped, imperfect, they are really saying, "I do not want to endure my own perfection, I do not want to bear my own reality." Imperfection is more comforting, more human than perfection. Many men want to believe that man is imperfect because it makes it easier to live with their own imperfection, more forgiving towards themselves. And who can blame them? To understand that even despair at oneself can be a deception, perhaps the most dangerous; and to discover an inner power, that is completely good and gentle, is frightening; it robs us of every comfort, every safety in resignation or irony. Who can live naked to his own perfection? And yet who, once seeing and acknowledging his own perfection, could bear not to try to realise it in living? To see it is hard; to realise it within life is the hardest thing. Somewhere men know that, and that is why they cover up their knowledge. They prefer the nightmare of Samsara which they know to the Awakening which they do not. And in a sense they are right. Once they have acknowledged Reality, they will have to learn how to die into it; they will have nowhere to hide any more, no corner of the world to feel safe in any longer. They will have to "abide nowhere and alight on nothing".'

'The dances will begin in an hour,' said Nawang. 'The Rinpoche must rest.' And so we left him. I turned in the door to bow to him, but he was already abstracted, sitting cross-legged on his threadbare cushions, his eyes fixed on the floor, his mouth moving in prayer. He was holding his rosary in his right hand, the large brown wooden rosary he had been given as a boy and kept with him ever since. Suddenly, he looked old, and exhausted. That was the only moment I saw him as if he were alone, as you might see a person sitting in a room reading, through a window, and in that moment it was clear to me how much of his life was a work of silence, how all the effortlessness and wisdom of his actions and words began so, in a room alone, concentrating on and invoking the power within him. The work would never be over: too many people would need him always. Even as he prayed he seemed to offer himself, leaning so far forward I feared he would fall. His hands moved with long-practised certainty over the beads of his rosary. I saw they were the youngest-looking parts of his body, and the strongest.

'Come on,' Nawang whispered.

We walked out into the early afternoon light and sat for an hour on the balcony where we had first seen the Rinpoche. There was no need to talk, and we didn't want to. Charles sat in a corner with his Alpine hat over his eyes, pretending to sleep. Nawang sat in another corner and meditated between two pots of yellow flowers. The horses stood in their old shadowed silence, sometimes lazily whisking a fly from their backs; the stream seemed slower in the afternoon than it had in the morning, slower and more secretive, and I had to lean towards it to hear it in its soft grasses; villagers from Shey in twos and threes and in their best hats and satins walked up the path to the side of the garden, sometimes singing, sometimes in a silence that seemed as happy as ours was. From where I sat on the edge of the balcony, I could see through a grove of trees, lightly waving in the wind, across the fields of the valley of Shey, the ripening gold fields, and beyond them to the mountains. The smallest shadow on the mountains, the slightest shift of light, rearranged and brought a fresh life to everything, to the horses, the stream, the walls, the trembling yellow flowers. Nawang opened his eyes and looked across to me. His eyes were as clear as that afternoon sky, clear and tender. We smiled at each other.

Charles broke the silence. 'Hadn't we better go to the clearing? We don't want the dances to start without us.'

'Nothing can start without the Rinpoche,' Nawang said. 'But you are right. We should go.'

The clearing where the dances were held was only about two hundred yards from where the Rinpoche was staying. We ate apples as we walked. Charles had some chang in a flask, and it was good to drink it in the heat. Nawang drank some too, looking very secretive and pleased with himself. 'Don't worry,' he said. 'Padmasambhava himself drank. A great deal.'

'What will the dances be about?' Charles asked.

'I feel as if I shouldn't tell you, and get you to guess. But then you would never guess. It is too hard.'

'Well, then, tell us,' Charles said. 'If you don't tell us — no more chang.'

'Well, if you are bribing me . . . The Oracle used to be at Thikse hundreds of years ago. The Kings of Shey wanted it to come to Shey. I have forgotten why. Perhaps because they wanted the prestige of having it. Anyway, the Kings knew that the Oracle was rather childish, and so they sent it an immense toy dragon as a present. This toy dragon had two men inside it who could make it dance. The Oracle was delighted and danced all the way from Thikse to Shey following the dragon. The dragon is Buddhism, the dragon of Wisdom tempting away the Oracle from its old pre-Buddhist ways.'

'What does the Oracle do while all the dances are going on?'

'For a bit he just watches and drinks. And then he blesses some ritual objects that symbolise the village and all its people.'

We arrived at the clearing. On one side the village gompa rose white and imposing, with a large window in its wall about twenty feet up. It was open. Nawang pointed. 'That's where the Rinpoche will sit and watch everything.' To the left of the wall, which also had a small door in it, there was a tent of sorts, in which a small stage had been erected. Apparently there had been plays the night before, local plays. A few children were chasing each other round the stage. In front of us a large ragged circle had been cleared, and people were sitting or standing all around it, Ladakhis and some foreigners too, a sprinkling of Italians with sweat shirts, an American doctor I had met briefly on my return to Leh, with his serious Jewish eyes and camera and large notebook, a Frenchwoman, a psychoanalyst, completely in black with her hair swept back and a bright, darting face, like a haggard sparrow's.

The trumpets announcing the departure of the Rinpoche from the Mayor's house sounded, their long dark blasts echoing from wall to wall, field to field. The crowd surged forward to line the alley that led from the house to the clearing. Ladakh was waiting for its Rinpoche — old men and women, children, clerks, drivers and farmers, old monks with young monks on their shoulders. He appeared, and came slowly down the steps on the side of the Mayor's house. For a long moment, the crowd was so silent that all you could hear was the birdsong in the trees that lined the alley, and the soft low chanting of the monks that had begun in the gompa, where the Oracle and the dancers were waiting. The Rinpoche paused half-way down the steps and raised his hands in blessing; everyone in the crowd raised their hands to him also and blessed him. He came down the steps and walked through the crowd that pressed around him with gentle excitement. I had seen him before at Shey walk among his people, but that had been within the confines of the monastery; now, as he walked in the open, and with all the splendour of late summer Ladakh about him, the dark gold fields, the birds, the flowers running in red and blue and yellow fire along the walls or tumbling down them, he looked more majestic and younger than I had known him before. He walked slowly. He touched everyone he could, sharing himself with all those who asked something of him, advice or healing or blessing. He never seemed hurried. Sometimes, when he was moving in light, he looked so frail that he was almost transparent; at other times, he looked as if nothing could tire or weaken him. He did not only welcome his own people: to as many of the foreigners there as he could he extended a hand or a smile. His walking there, his presence, gathered everyone together, united everyone and everything in that afternoon, the birds, the flowers, the walls, Ladakhi and foreigner alike. Charles said, 'Of all the lamas I have met, only the Dalai Lama inspires such simple devotion.' I said nothing. I wanted to remember each of his gestures, every way his face shone and changed, each look in the faces turned towards him, each stone, each movement of the light.

The Rinpoche walked past the place where Nawang and I were standing, stood silently smiling at us for a moment, then called me to him.

'Today is a happy day,' he said. 'It is the Day of the Oracle. It is the best day of summer. You must be happy today. Do you have days like this in your country?'

'Sometimes,' I said.

'You must invite me,' he said, and walked on into the gompa. A few minutes later he reappeared in the window, where a chair had been placed for him. Two young monks helped him into it. He sat down. He looked around. He raised his hands. At that moment, the trumpets sounded again, this time with a great loud roll of drums; the door to the side of the gompa opened; and the dancers came out. The Rinpoche threw back his head and laughed, and the crowd laughed with him.

All the dancers were drunk. Two old men in rags carrying branches were the drunkest of all. They were old and thin and very drunk, and stumbled and staggered round the circle to the ironic claps of the onlookers, waving their branches around their heads, and sometimes threatening to charge the crowd, but never getting further than the first few unsteady steps. And the dragon was drunk too. The famous fifteen-foot-long green and red and purple-mouthed dragon was drunk — or rather the two men who inhabited it were. Neither of them, I suspect, could see the other — and drink had quite destroyed any notion of rhythm either of them might once have possessed. The back of the dragon dipped and rippled and swayed alarmingly while the front, its pop-eyed, garish, smirking head, constantly threatened to walk off into the crowd. The crowd loved it. Children screamed. Women threw white scarves around its head. The young men, one after another, broke out of the crowd and started prancing mockingly around the dragon, calling it names and putting apples or vegetables into its mouth. Three pairs of old men shambled forward to break spontaneously, if also a little unsteadily, into one of the slow, shoulder-to-shoulder,

Ladakhi dances that the old men love all over Ladakh, because they can dance them without falling down.

The Oracle was the last to appear. Like any prima donna, he waited for the first flurry of excitement to be exhausted before he made his own entrance. And what an entrance! He skipped, he leapt, he moaned, he whinnied, he threw his hat in the air, he made great strange gestures in the air with his hands, he ran up to the old men and took some branches from them and ran with them round the circle, whooping and clucking and wheezing. Children screamed. Women threw white scarves at him. Young men leapt out of the crowd and started dancing around him. Charles, whom I had never seen laugh, was helpless with laughter. The tears were running around his cheeks and he had to lean on me to stand up at all.

'Oh, my god,' he kept moaning, 'oh, my god! What chaos! What complete chaos!' his Swiss heart shocked and delighted by so much pandemonium. Nawang stood under the tree, wiping his dark glasses, his shoulders shaking. He saw me looking at him and raised his hands in a great mock Indian 'What-to-do-Sahib?' gesture, the kind of gesture Indian railway officials make when the train is going to be four hours late.

Slowly things calmed down. The Oracle stopped prancing around, drew himself to his full oracular dignity, walked once in his lion-tamer's walk around the circle, strutting and hawking, and then withdrew to the makeshift throne that had been prepared for him under the big central tree. The Frenchwoman was hovering about him with her camera, simpering and clicking. He loved it, turning all his profiles to her, taking off his great hat three times so that she could see his balding dignified head, holding up to her one by one his sacred objects, the spear, the vajra, the long beribboned dorje that he carried in his sash. Meanwhile, nothing would stop the old men, the two old men with branches, from continuing their aimless fertility-strut round and round the circle. They ran and stopped and stumbled, roughly in a circle, and with the kind of sombre dedication that drunkenness can produce, taking themselves and their function with great and comic seriousness. They were summer spirits, guardians of the village, and they went to each corner in turn, muttering prayers and blessing all the four directions. The dragon, however, never recovered from what it had been drinking in the secrecy of the monastery. It tried, with great earnestness, to make one circuit, but collapsed completely, only three-quarters of the way round the not-very-large circle. The two Dragon-men knew they were beaten and just lay in the dirt, laughing — the green and red stomach of the Dragon wrapped around them like a blanket. One of their friends from the crowd brought them a bottle of chang each and sat drinking with them. The lure of the dragon, evidently, its vast power of temptation, would from now on have to be taken as danced. No one minded. The dragon had appeared at least, the children had screamed, the women had thrown their white scarves, the young men had had a chance to do a little mocking dancing. The two old men and the Oracle were delighted — they now had the stage to themselves.

In the corner, the Oracle was silent for a few minutes, recovering, I imagine, wiping his face with a great red handkerchief. Then he started to chant in a loud voice.

'What is he chanting?' I asked Nawang, who had come over to join me and was still laughing.

'Do you see all those little barley objects in front of him? He is going to bless them all. They are the village and its fields. He is making certain of a good harvest.'

He swayed and chanted, taking, as Nawang had predicted, each of the small barley figures into his hand, one by one. I was afraid that in his drunken enthusiasm he might squeeze one of the figures too hard (what would that bring? Lightning? Hail? The Plague?), but beneath his extravagance the Oracle was a shrewd performer and managed himself well, chanting lustily and blessing everything in sight. As the Oracle blessed the barley objects, I looked up and watched the face of the Rinpoche. His mouth, also, was moving in prayer and his eyes were closed. It was such a strange and luminous contrast — the operatic face and gestures of the Oracle and the devotion of the Rinpoche. And yet it was only superficially a contrast: the Oracle and the Rinpoche were linked in a unity deeper than any difference. The prayer and the presence of the Rinpoche were the ground of that afternoon; everything that happened, all the frivolity and drunkenness, all the comic solemnity of the old men's dances, was touched by his power and by his love. At the heart of all that hilarity, sustaining it and giving it depth, was his devotion, his strength. Slowly I began to see everything that was happening as if in meditation, and nothing appeared ridiculous or garbled. The dragon collapsed in the middle of the circle seemed no longer comic, but a revelation of Evil deflated; the old men wandering with branches in their hands were no longer two drunk old men, but messengers of a new possibility, the new hope of a new year, the more poignant and urgent for being carried by such old dancers; the Oracle no longer looked operatic, I no longer thought of him as an agricultural worker in costume — he became for me the interpreter and carrier of ancient powers and forces that were still alive, still powerful. I remembered all my ironic perceptions, but I also saw beyond them, into a symbolic world in which all fragments were united and all absurdities had their rich and subtle function, in which everything that happened had the inscrutable clarity of music.

Charles announced, 'The Initiation is beginning. People are starting to go into the gompa.'

We joined the long snaking line of Ladakhis and followed its progress slowly, silently into the main hall of the gompa, where there is a huge statue of the Buddha. It was late afternoon and the statue was lit by a rich gold light. The Rinpoche was sitting in his chair in the far corner, receiving everyone in turn. Charles was in front of me. The Rinpoche held his head in both his hands and said a prayer over him. Charles moved to the side and looked at me quietly. It was my turn. I bowed. The Rinpoche put his right hand on my head. I stood up. The Rinpoche held out his left hand and took my right hand. He held it a long time, looking up at me, saying nothing.

Next day Charles came with me to Hemis on the bus. He wanted to see the Rinpoche again, one last time before he left for Srinagar.

He said, 'It is good to see how happy you are. When I met you you looked worn and sad. Now you look young again. Do not cling to your happiness and do not mourn it when it is gone.'

'Charles,' I said. 'I appreciate your Swiss caution and wisdom, and I'm grateful, but nothing is going to stop me enjoying these next days. I don't mind paying for them.'

Charles smiled. 'You are in love. You are in love. As I was, when I first met my lama. He is a short fat man, and I was deeply in love with him. I wanted to go with him everywhere. I think I would have gone with him to the lavatory if he had asked me. I was very un-Swiss in my passion for him. I am happy I knew what it was to believe in someone so much that I could love them with that devotion. I am grateful. It dissolved my cynicism, it melted my coldness a little. But I realise too now that I was asking Yeshe to be things for me that no one can be or should be. I was asking him to save me, and I have to save myself, as you have to save yourself, alone.

'And yet because I loved Yeshe so extravagantly, something could open within me which, otherwise, would never have opened. Because I could believe in him I came to believe a little in myself, in my own power to help myself. Because I had been able to follow my love for him without fear, I learnt how to begin to love others and myself. I still love him. I still ask his advice on many things. But I see him clearly. He irritates me often. He repeats himself, he doesn't wash, he is maddeningly vague and dreamy sometimes. I am grateful that I didn't see that too clearly in the beginning . . .'

Charles paused. 'And yet I sometimes think that what I saw him as in the beginning was his true self, was his essential self, and that I have lost him a little since, lost him in biographical and psychological trivia, as you might "lose" parts of the moon behind rags of cloud. Personal details seem to be authentic, but are they? Is what is happening between Master and Pupil far beyond personality or understanding?'

'Charles, you are as confused as I am.'

'Yes,' he laughed, 'I am. Yes. Things don't get simpler. Each clarity is a beginning of another journey . . . What more complex relationship exists than that between a seeker and his master? Even saying "seeker" and "master" simplifies things too much. At a certain stage of love, there is no "seeker" and "master". The "master" learns from the love of the "seeker", the "seeker" may learn more from the "master" than the "master" himself has learnt. The Tibetans say that the relationship between a man and his Guru is as inexhaustible as Sunyata, as inexhaustible, in fact, as life itself. If you have really met your Guru, you see him in everything and everything in him, you see his wisdom enacting itself in every movement and shift of life. Life becomes the Guru, the Master. First you meet his Power in the form of your master; then, slowly, that form and face dissolve and you are left naked to life itself.'

'Is that how you live?' I asked.

'It is how I try to live,' Charles said, 'sometimes, when I have the courage. It is how I have lived just often enough to know that, for myself, there is no other kind of life I want.'

The room in which the Rinpoche received us, in Hemis, was the last of the rooms I would see and talk to him in, at once the most elaborate and the most intimate. Charles whispered as we entered, taking off our shoes, 'This is the heart of Ladakh,' and I felt what he meant; we were entering the innermost sanctuary of the country, the centre of the mandala that Ladakh had been for both of us. Everything in it looked familiar — the rugs piled haphazardly in the far left corner, the carved wooden balcony windows, the small lacquer table with its kettle and peacock feathers, a rosary, and two small bronze dragon's heads, the zig-zag of the tiled floor where it was not covered by carpet. So familiar did everything seem that it was hard for me to remember in the coming days that I had never been there before. The Rinpoche sat to the right of the door on a small raised mattress covered with threadbare red and golden silk. As we entered, I heard doves outside the window. Nawang, who was sitting by the Rinpoche, took some bread from a bag, stood up, and walked to the window to feed them.

We bowed to the Rinpoche, received his blessing, and sat on two cushions that he placed on the floor before him. For minutes we looked at each other and said nothing. In that silence every sound from outside grew clear, and I could hear as well as the doves the rushing of the large stream that runs past Hemis. At times it seemed so loud and so close that it could have been flowing through the room, and the cool fresh autumn air in the room tasted of snow-water. On the wall above the Rinpoche's head, there was a large tapestry. The light fell on it from the open window and as I contemplated it in that silence it seemed as alive as the birds and the stream.

Woven in still lustrous gold and silver threads against a background of black velvet, the tapestry was of an Emperor and Empress standing in a spring pavilion ringed by courtiers. The Emperor stood to the right, the largest figure of all, old, balding, and gently abstracted, dressed as the Sun; the Empress, slightly smaller and younger, stood to the left, her eyes lowered, her face gently turned away, dressed as the Moon and unadorned except for one jewel at her neck, in the shape of a sun. Near the Empress a group of women stood in stiff elaborate dresses, one of them holding a sleepy Pekinese; below the Emperor, and much smaller in scale, stood a group of young courtiers, handsome, a little rakish, their robes decorated with dragons and chrysanthemums, their chiselled eager heads turned upwards towards the Emperor. In the garden that surrounded the pavilion, birds sat singing in a willow tree; three roses had opened, dew glittering on their tall stems; a stream flowed below them with rushes bending and waving in it; a cherry tree was alight with blossom, and swallows were flying to it from a cluster of rocks.

'What are you smiling at?' the Rinpoche asked me. I had not realised I was smiling.

'At the tapestry,' I said. 'It is so happy.'

'Yes,' the Rinpoche said. 'Our art is happy.'

'What does the tapestry mean?' I asked.

'What does it mean to you?'

'To me the Emperor is the Male Principle, the Will, the Understanding, the Sun; the Empress is Compassion, Awareness, the Moon. When the Male and Female Principles live in peace and harmony, there is spring.'

'What you have said is too simple,' said the Rinpoche. 'The heart and understanding need winter also. They need desolation, unhappiness, even sometimes death. Milarepa said, "A man who is aware finds a friend in desolation and a master in winter." That is why spring does not dominate the whole of the

tapestry. There are suggestions in it of winter — in the silver of
the Empress's cloak, in the emptiness between the rocks. The
harmony of Wisdom and Compassion, Will and Awareness, is
not changeless — to want it to be is a sign of spiritual childish-
ness. The spirit needs spring and winter, beauty and terror,
meeting and parting, needs every experience and every energy
to achieve wholeness. Milarepa said, "Contemplate all energies
without fear or disgust; find their essence, for that is the stone
that turns everything to gold." '

Charles said, 'And what about the Pekinese?' Everyone
laughed.

'I often think about the Pekinese,' the Rinpoche said. 'To me
the Pekinese represents the part of the Self that wants to sleep
through everything, the part of the mind that yawns even when
the Buddha is talking. And look how much the woman that is
holding it loves it! She is so happy, she is ignorant and cannot
hear what the seasons are saying to her; she is safe, worldly and
safe.'

'Do we need the worldly woman and the Pekinese also?'
Charles said.

'Yes,' said the Rinpoche. 'Of course. And why not?'

'Why is the Emperor old and the Empress young?'

The Rinpoche thought. 'Knowledge can make you old. Compassion is a river of youth that will never run dry. Knowledge
can make you tired — bathe in the water of compassion and you
will be refreshed.'

'Why . . . ' Charles began.

'No more questions! No more questions!' the Rinpoche said.
'When you look again at the tapestry forget, as far as you can,
everything that we have said. Perhaps there is another life in it
altogether, another, different meaning. Fix nothing. Throw
away everything you already understand. Otherwise the tapestry will die for you and you will not see it any more, only your
ideas about it.'

'Or your ideas about it,' Charles said.

'Exactly,' said the Rinpoche. 'That is what I do not want. If
anyone points out the moon to you and you see it, do you go on
staring at the finger?'

Afterwards, Charles and I walked past the monastery buildings up a small winding path to a stupa.

'Those peaks over there', Charles pointed to the left, 'are in Chang Tang. That means that Tibet is only a few weeks' walk away. Perhaps one day we will be able to walk there as the pilgrims used to. Lhasa, Lake Mansarovar, Kailasa, all the sacred places . . .'

We sat in the shadow of the crumbling wall.

Charles took my hands and held them gently. 'I shall soon have to hitch-hike back to Leh. I'm going down to Kashmir tomorrow . . . There's bound to be an army lorry . . . I shall miss you . . . Thank you for these few days . . . I find it hard to thank people.'

He leant back against the wall. 'Last year, I did a strange thing. I made my lama read Nietzsche. He has been in Switzerland several years now, and his German is fluent. I said to him, "You are always telling me how wonderful Tibetan philosophy is, but why don't you read a great German philosopher for a change?" He said he would, and read Nietzsche for a month. At the end of the month, he summoned me to his room. I could see something was up from his mischievous expression. He walked round and round the room, pretending to think deeply, and then said, "What a great Tantric philosopher Nietzsche was! What an extraordinarily clear awareness he had of the need and process of self-transformation! What Tantric courage he showed in continually pressing beyond ordinary conventions of thought and morality! Padmasambhava and he would have been friends; he and Milarepa would have understood each other." Then Yeshe paused. "And yet I find a certain hysteria in him, a certain imbalance that is incompatible with the highest spiritual insight. Perhaps he lacked inner discipline, the kind of discipline he could have been helped to through the Tibetan way. He was afraid of his pity. He was afraid to be tender, and that fear drove him mad. He went mad hugging the neck of a horse that he had seen being whipped. What a confession! And that from a man who claimed to worship strength! If he had been helped to understand and bear pity, he would have been perfect. If he had been taught to use his pity and compose his life in a discipline of wisdom and compassion, he would have attained Nirvana!" '

Charles put his hand on my shoulder. 'The West and East are not finally separated. I can speak of what I know — that my love of Eastern thought has helped me to read Western thought and philosophy with a new mind. I even listen to Western music with a new understanding. Before I came out East, I had never listened to mediaeval or Renaissance music with any enthusiasm. Learning to follow the rhythms of Indian music helped me to begin to hear the patient exaltation in Palestrina, in Josquin, in Orlando di Lassus. There is so much in our own tradition that is hidden from us. How few read the Western mystics — Eckhart and St John and Teresa. I have read very little serious modern writing about the relations between spirituality and creativity that have been the inspiration for most of the geniuses of Western art. Almost immediately after I had returned that first time from Dharamsala, I went on a kind of pilgrimage through Europe to visit the great European cathedrals, Chartres, Canterbury, Rheims . . . and as I did so I realised with growing desperation and anger that what we have been most deprived of, as Westerners brought up in a materialistic age, is the richest, most spiritual part of our own culture . . . And it was coming out East that helped me to see that, to become aware of that. Perhaps I should have been able to see it without coming to India. I had to experience India as completely "other", completely "different", before I could begin to discover the many links between Eastern and Western thought and art. I know many others for whom the same experience has been true — that an absorption in Eastern thought has not meant a negation of the West, but a discovery of the West's buried and defaced spiritual identity, an awakening to those parts of our Western past that have been denied us.

'There *are* differences, sometimes very radical differences, between East and West. I have spent twelve years exploring and suffering those differences. But I know now that there is a dialogue possible between the truths of East and West, a dialogue of extraordinary beauty and complexity. Perhaps, from that dialogue, which we are only just beginning, will come truths as yet unformed and unglimpsed by either East or West, truths that may, in some way none of us can foresee, fuse the dynamic intuitions and practice of Western philosophy and science and the transcendental insight of the East. Sometimes, when I am in despair, I think that to pursue this dialogue seriously is the last hope for the West to listen not merely to Eastern voices, but to its own buried and banished voices, the voices it has silenced at its peril — the voices of Plato, of Dante, of Eckhart — all those voices that speak of ecstasy and the long labour of the spirit. There are many ways of beginning this dialogue between East and West, and each person must choose the way that suits his own temperament. I have chosen the way of Tibetan Buddhism because it is a way of fulfilment, of plenitude. I did not want an ascetic path; I know that all the temptations of my personality are towards a cold and proud ascesis; I do not believe that the West can be helped at this stage by an ascetic philosophy, by a philosophy of repression or denial that obscures all the insights of Western psychology. So I chose a way that would make me enter the world, help me to savour it and celebrate it. I realised long ago that the main illness of my life had been repression — repression of my spirit, of my sexuality, of my anger. The men I met and loved in Dharamsala, the Tibetan monks I grew to know there, were not self-torturers; they were cheerful and open and loving. They combined earthiness with refinement of mind and spirit. I knew in those first months I had to try to find out how they became like that. Nietzsche wrote: "It is a sign of having turned out well when, like Goethe, a man clings with ever-greater joy and cordiality to the 'things of the world' for in this way he adheres to the great conception of man that man becomes the transfigurer of existence when he learns to transfigure himself." When I showed it to Yeshe, he was delighted and said, "Who is this Goethe? He sounds a wise man." '

Charles stopped. 'God, I've been talking for an hour at least. It must be the Rinpoche and the mountain air.'

I laughed. 'Charles, you've done nothing but harangue me since we met. You must feel I need my soul saved very urgently. You are probably right. And I've been delighted, moved, instructed, privileged . . . but you can hardly represent yourself as a taciturn Bodhisatva!'

Charles smiled. Two cows appeared from a shed below the stupa and stared at us over the wall. We fed them apples.

'I must go back now,' Charles said, 'otherwise it'll get dark and I'll be stranded on the road. When you see the Rinpoche again tomorrow tell him that I love him and will remember him in my meditation every day. No, that sounds vain. Don't tell him that. Just say . . . no, don't say anything. When one has met a man like him, what is there to say? Even saying "Thank you" seems absurd.'

'Not to him.'

'That's true. Nothing would seem absurd to him.'

Charles looked one last time across the valley to the mountains. 'It is hard to leave a place where you can believe that anything is possible. But that is why one must leave. To see if you were right, to see if your insights can be lived in a different air, at a lower level.'

I met Drukchen Rinpoche again that evening. He had small bare rooms near the room of Thuksey Rinpoche. His mother, a beautiful large smiling woman in her forties, was with him.

'Where is your father?' I asked him.

'My father is in retreat. He sometimes goes into retreat for a few days . . . Often we long to be back in Darjeeling. I love Ladakh, but I miss the silence of Darjeeling.'

'For me,' I said, 'Ladakh is silence itself. What more silence could you want than the silence of these plains and these mountains?'

Drukchen smiled. 'That is because you are not a Rinpoche, my friend. You are here to look, and talk, and be open to all that comes to you; I am here to work and help my people.'

I must have looked a little pained because Drukchen then said, 'I didn't mean, of course, that being open wasn't work too.

It is the hardest work. And I am very happy you find silence here. Any place where we find silence, true silence, is holy.'

His mother put a plate of vegetables between Drukchen and myself with two smaller plates, and left us to talk and eat.

'This room is rather bare,' I said.

'I like it that way. There are many tankas and paintings in the monastery, and I suppose I could have some of them placed up here if I wanted them — but I prefer bare walls. It is good to meditate before a bare wall. You can do many different meditations. You can meditate on Emptiness, on suffering, decay, death. Or you can meditate on the small patches of different colour in the wall, the seas and the faces in the plaster, and then you would be meditating on the variety of phenomena that arise from the Void. You can also meditate on seeing the wall as transparent, on imagining it as having no substance — this is very hard, but it is useful because it teaches you not to believe your senses, not to trust your materialist understanding of things. Once you have learnt how to discipline your perception you can change reality, your experience of reality.'

Drukchen turned to face the bare wall. We sat in silence, watching the shadows made by the three flickering candles Drukchen's mother had placed on a table behind us.

That night I dreamt I was again sitting with Drukchen, staring at the bare walls.

'As a child,' I said to him, 'I used to make the shapes of animals on the wall, using a candle and shadow.'

'So did I,' Drukchen said. 'You can make all sorts of animals. I can make a dzo, a yak, a leopard, an eagle — all the animals of Tibet, in fact. Would you like to see?'

And he made the animals on the wall. The dzo was lumbering and sleepy; the yak stood still; the leopard ran across the wall and disappeared into the dark of the corner; the eagle dived and swooped with disconsolate majesty. At the end of the demonstration, he spread his hands and withdrew them slowly so that they became larger and larger. Then he clapped them once and lowered them, leaving the wall empty again.

'You make some too.'

And so I made for him some of the animals of my Indian childhood, animals I had loved and watched as a child in the plains of India. I did a large deer, the kind of deer I had seen from the windows at school in the Nilgiri Hills; I did a hyena, I tried to do a tiger but failed; I ended with a dog, the Dalmatian of my boyhood, whose wild walk I tried to represent, and the way he used to run along the road snapping at cyclists' legs.

Drukchen laughed. 'Very good!'

'But the tiger was hopeless.'

'You have to do something badly, or it's bad luck. You forgot one thing, though,' Drukchen said. 'You forgot to clap.'

'Does that matter?'

'When you clap like that it is a reminder of the drum of Tantric Ritual, of the sound of the Damaru. And it means, "Listen to the Law. Listen to the Law that says all things are transient, all things are the moving and dissolving figures of a dream." To clap is very important.'

Drukchen raised his hands again.

'What are you going to make this time?'

'You'll see.'

For a moment, he did nothing and seemed to be concentrating. Then he rubbed his hands.

'Drukchen,' I said, 'you are being mysterious.'

He smiled but said nothing.

Then he made a figure on the wall. At first I couldn't see what it was.

'Well?' Drukchen said.

'It is you, isn't it? I can tell by the hat. It is a pity you can't do the dark glasses.'

'Yes, it is me,' Drukchen said, and clapped slowly, twice.

I awoke in a deep calm.

After we had eaten, Drukchen and I walked on to the roof of the monastery.

'Tomorrow is the full moon. We will watch it rise together,' Drukchen said.

We sat looking across the valley to the moonlit peaks of Chang Tang and down at the small village of Hemis, with its grove of willows, and its stupas, and its rushing noisy stream. Only a few of the houses had put their lights on. Dogs were barking in the distance.

'So the dogs bark in the same crazy way all over Ladakh,' I said.

'Yes,' Drukchen said. 'Sometimes I think they are expressing our fear for us, our fear and our sorrow. They are as restless in these times as we are. They are worried for Ladakh, for the future.'

'Are you?'

'Not for myself. For my people, for this people, for their way of life, their simplicity, their dignity. But it is no good being afraid. That saps your strength. What I have to try to do is give my people a sense of what they can do, how they can preserve what they are and yet change, and yet adapt. Can it be done?'

We looked down at the stream. Drukchen pointed out a particular stupa.

I said, suddenly, 'Sometimes in these months I have wanted to leave the West and come and live here.'

I had never formulated that thought to myself so directly, and it startled me.

'Don't,' Drukchen said.

'Why not?'

'I do not think you are ready to become a monk. And there is no reason why you should be. There are many other ways of life and many other ways of attaining Enlightenment. You have your work to do in the West. As a teacher, as a writer . . . '

'But I find it so hard to teach or write in the West about the experiences I have had in the East.'

'That is why you must. You must find a way of making what you have lived through believable to others. You must not refuse that challenge. Those who reject the materialism of the West, who despise it and separate themselves from it, are in danger of refusing to look at it, they are in danger of not being responsible to the facts of life as it is lived, and must be lived, now. We must find a way to work within the world, within science, within industry, even within politics; we cannot simply pretend a superiority to those things, for they are the forces that largely shape mankind. To work in the world we will have to be strong, and in the world our inner strengths will be greatly tested. But that is good. That will dissolve any pride we may have, any sense of virtuous invulnerability. It will take away from us any sense that we are "special", that we deserve "special treatment", that we are "unique". So many Westerners who find solace in the East are coming to have their Egos healed, their shattered personalities reassembled in some way. But the East is not a large convalescent home for the West, a sort of enormous recreation room where Westerners can play at being spiritual, at "exploring themselves"; it is a place of power, of new power, a new kind of strength which must be used in the world.'

'But to survive in the world,' I said, 'you need spiritual strength. And to build spiritual strength you need solitude.'

'Make retreats often. Come back here if you can find the money and the time. Make pilgrimages to holy places. But re-enter the world. Re-enter the world and test again and again what you have learnt. If what you have learnt is true, it will hold. Some of the humblest people I have met, the most spiritual, have been drivers or farmers or businessmen, even politicians; some of the most arrogant and useless, monks, so-called "religious" men. Be quietly detached from what you do and dedicate it to the good of all created beings, and you will be safe from disillusion or vanity.'

'But how to do that?'

'By discipline. By prayer, by cultivating the wisdom of Emptiness, by building daily your resources of compassion, by humour! The old way . . . Begin, and you will find out! It is not so very elaborate, you know, not so hard.'

Thuksey Rinpoche was too busy to see me next morning. He sent me two apples and a message that he would see me the next day. I did not mind. I wanted to walk in the hills around Hemis. I wanted to walk to Go-Tsang.

Charles had said, 'Go-Tsang is the highest and loneliest monastery of Ladakh.' And Nawang, 'The Dalai Lama made a special pilgrimage there. The monastery is built around the cave of a hermit who meditated there three hundred years ago. You can still see the cave. It is very powerful.' Even the Italian girl had said, 'Ladakh is a ruin, a fantasy . . . but there is one place . . .'

I walked slowly, idly. It was a brilliant, nearly cloudless morning. For about half an hour the path into the mountains wound above the stream. A donkey moved in and out of the shadows in the willow grove beneath me. I watched it until it went out of sight and then sat on a rock. Three lizards were on the rock beside me. They were not afraid of me. Their speckled leathery bodies collapsed, expanded, with each breath. Even when I got up to move on and dropped my satchel with the Rinpoche's apples and my notebook they did not move. They stood where they were, blinking, staring into the silence, dying and resurrecting themselves in breath after breath. I walked on to the stupa where I had talked with Charles for the last time, and ate the apples, looking over the valley to the snow-peaks, the crisp smell of dung on the air. Snow, apple, dung: their different tangs made me heady. Again and again as I walked on, some small occurrence, some detail, would delight me into stopping — the way a shadow fell on a rock, a feather fallen on to a rock and shining in the light, a calf lying in gold-green grass, kicking its spindly legs in the air, a break of clear, high, rapid birdsong, a patch of rose-bushes, gnarled, windswept, but with a few last roses still on them, marking the place where green ended and rock began. Where had those roses come from? From Kashmir? From the moghul gardens of Srinagar? It was a thought that made me smile — those roses being blown from their sophisticated terraces in the plains, to this wilderness of rock and wind. So many miles of snow . . . and still they clung to their determination to flower, and realised it, against the rock, against the sharp winds. Perhaps the roses lasted longer for being forced to grow against such powers. I stood and watched them shaking in the wind. They were wild red; looking at them long, in that light, hurt the eyes.

Few things could be lonelier than that landscape of storm-beaten rose-bush and rock, and yet I never felt alone. All round me, along the path, in the willow grove, by the stream, on and between the rocks, there were signs that others had passed the same way. Prayer flags shook out their yellow and red rags from the heart of a gully or from the tops of crags above me; stones arranged in half-circles, in sacred letters, in small unsteady-looking heaps, stood in the shadow of trees or in glowing patches of shaggy mountain grass; three large dark stones with the mantra of Avalokiteshvara carved on them were lying in the stream, guarding the small wooden bridge all travellers have to cross, their letters shaking in the light reflected from the rock into the water; at the edge of the clump of rose-bushes, someone had made a small mound of white stones that shone in the sun, and when I took them into my hands, warmed them. I came to the fork in the path Nawang had told me about, and looked up. There, half a mile above me, was the monastery; there Go-Tsang was at last, high in its cradle of rock, with nothing but the wide, burning blue sky behind it.

Nawang said, later, back at Hemis, 'What did you do when you got there?'

'I talked to the monks in the shrine-room. They were cleaning kettles and things.'

'What did you think of them?'

'Not much. They seemed rather dull and lazy.'

'Perhaps you are right. The Abbot is not there enough.'

'But I liked their shoes.'

'What?'

'I sat and tried to draw their shoes. While they were working in the shrine-room they had left a pile of shoes outside in the stone courtyard. They were such worn shoes. Such old, worn, shambling shoes. They spoke to me, everything that is good about this country — its simplicity, its honesty. Each of the shoes was very beautiful to me.'

'Are you teasing me?'

'Yes. Not completely.'

'What did you do with the drawings?'

'I threw them away.'

'Why?'

'Because only the greatest artist could have captured the life in those shoes. Because I cannot draw. Because as I sat there drawing them nervously, the shoes seemed to mock me from their stillness. They were *there*.'

'And were you?'

'For a moment, yes.'

'Then what are you worrying about? If you saw those shoes as they are even for one second, you have been blessed. What more do you want?'

We were waiting on the roof of the monastery for the full moon to rise. Nawang had lit three long thick sticks of incense from a packet of Tibetan incense I had brought him from Leh.

The horizon was dark with cloud. Would we see the moon when it had risen?

'I listened to what you said about the monks' shoes,' Nawang said, 'and I understood. There is a silence in things in which the mind can renew itself. But sometimes the mind grows tired of all things. Even of the beauty of a night like this. Even of the splendour of the moon. Even of a Buddha, perhaps, alive with wisdom. And then the mind wants to go beyond all form, to live in a silence beyond all words or images.'

'Meister Eckhart wrote,' I said, ' "Your soul ought to be without ghosts, to be void of all forms and images that are ghosts. You should strive to keep it so. For if you love God as a god, a ghost, a person, you are not loving Him as He is, One, in Whom there is no duality." '

'You know that by heart,' Nawang said, 'and yet you are a writer. To write is to make ghosts. To write is to add to the noise and clutter of images.'

'Some images are more useful than others because they are closer to the truth that no images can express. Some writing is honest about its ghostliness and can shine with an awareness

230

that is beyond words, as the moon shines with light reflected from an invisible sun.'

Nawang had a cold, and was wrapped in a large black shawl with holes in it. All he needed was an Indian cigarette, a beedi, to look like one of the night-watchmen of my childhood.

'What are you thinking about?' I asked him.

'Two lines by Milarepa:

'If the horse of my mind is cold
I will shelter him within the walls of Emptiness.'

'Isn't "shelter" an odd word there?" I asked.

'Not at all. To have no home anywhere can be to be at home with all things. The mind feels cold and alone in its waste of mirrors. How can light and warmth pass to it directly, when there are so many mirrors to break them up?'

It was at that moment the moon appeared. It broke suddenly from a mass of dark cloud, huge, imperial, and dazzling, flooding the long valley with light. Even Nawang fell silent.

The Rinpoche said that he would see me, but as it turned out he could not see me for several days.

I did not miss him; I felt him in everything. Each painting in the monastery, each stone and each bird, seemed charged with a joy whose source and centre were in him. Looking down from the roof above his room, I saw the long valley of Ladakh as one of his hands, open to all weather, and the mountains as his arm; I saw that his power penetrated and shone within everything. I knew that there was nothing tyrannical in this great power of his; I knew that I was not his plaything or victim. The essence of his gift to me was freedom, and I felt able to accept it and him freely, without fear and without any sense of abasement. I do not know how I could feel so undiminished, while at the same time being aware of his spirit within me, changing me and revealing itself to me in its range and splendour; that strength to welcome him was his gift also, a gift that his love gathered for me from that light and that rock.

I asked the Rinpoche, 'Will you teach me the meditation on Avalokiteshvara?'

'Why do you want to learn it?'

'Because I want to practise it.'

I was sitting in front of the Rinpoche on a small cushion; he touched my right hand gently with his and smiled.

Then he said, 'Do you believe that it can help you?'

'Yes.'

'Will you practise it sincerely and with the right motivation, dedicating your meditation not to your own enlightenment but to the welfare of all created beings?'

'Yes.'

'Will you renew each time before you meditate the vow of the Bodhisatva – to take all the suffering of the world on yourself and to give all your joy to others, not to enter Nirvana until every creature can enter with you?'

'Yes.'

'Then I will teach you.'

I found that tears had come to my eyes. We looked at each other a long time without saying anything.

Then the Rinpoche said softly, 'Do not be afraid. There is nothing to fear.'

'I have never been less afraid in my life.'

He walked to the window and opened it. The morning light broke into the room, lighting up the tapestry of the Emperor and Empress about his small throne.

He stood before it, smiling. 'The old Emperor looks young again in this light.'

He sat down, folding his robes quietly around him. 'Although it is nearly autumn', he said, 'and the leaves are beginning to fall, this morning is so fresh it could be spring.'

'It is spring,' I said.

'I chose the Bodhisatva of Compassion for you,' the Rinpoche said, 'because it is that part of you that he represents, that force inside you that he is, that will help you most. Each personality is moved and sustained by different images and different ideals. What make one man progress can baffle or even destroy another; what to one man is a sun, to another is a maze in which he may wander darkly all his life. But I have seen that the images that will help you order your heart and mind are images of love; that the energy you need to bring peace to your life is an energy of love. There are many Ways that lead to Enlightenment, and no one is better than another, and all are hard to travel; the Way for you, I understood when I saw you, is the Way of Compassion, the way of Avalokiteshvara. I saw when I met you that your heart has been baffled and embittered and that your mind is proud; the Way I will teach you will crumble the pride of your mind, and call out the sun that is your true heart from behind its clouds of fear and anger. What I am going to teach you is not special and not specially elaborate; it is simple. You will need a simplicity and humility to follow it. You have both within you, but you will have to work hard to find them, and then live them. The true journey of your life is towards the enlightened self, and you are that already. You came, across your life, across Ladakh, to this room, to this morning, to me, and now another journey is beginning, the journey which you travelled here to begin.

'Now I shall teach you the meditation. First, as I said at first, you must dedicate the merit of it to the joy and happiness of all created beings. The practice of meditation is not a selfish one, and is not undertaken for the personal satisfaction of the self. It is important always to remember this, otherwise you will become vain and the meditation will be of no use to you or anyone else.'

The Rinpoche gave me the vows in detail and made me repeat them after him in Tibetan.

'The next stage of the meditation is to visualise the Bodhisatva. You must visualise him so intensely and with such fidelity that he is more real even than I am, sitting here in front of you, more real, in fact, than anything else that exists. And you must remember as you visualise him that He is the divine part of yourself projected out of yourself, your most sublime energy of love given external and living expression.'

The Rinpoche gave me in great precision each detail of the Bodhisatva's dress, the way his hands must be imagined, the colours of his robes and jewels.

'It is a mistake,' he said, 'to imagine that any of these details are irrelevant. Each of them can be a source of ecstasy; each of them, properly contemplated, can reveal another part of the nature of compassion.'

And he repeated again each detail and invited me gently to repeat them with him. I did so. Sometimes he would stop me and correct me. He repeated each detail again and again until he was satisfied that I had remembered them.

'At first you will find the process of visualisation hard. You have not been trained to it. You have been trained in a material-ist way of imagining and seeing, which has its beauties and precisions, but has not accustomed you to the kind of inner projection that I am asking you to do. But the harder you work at it, the more the power will come to you. And with it will come an extraordinary joy and confidence in the power of your own mind. You will understand, slowly, and in slow stages, that Reality is a creation of the mind. You will understand it not with your intellect or even with your intuition, but practically, because you will be growing within you the power to alter Reality. You must work every day. You must not be dis-couraged if for many months you can visualise very little. What you are beginning is a journey into a different world, into an awareness of a different reality; you cannot expect to make that journey quickly. Nor, in a sense, should you want to. The journey itself has its joys; the hardness of the journey has its lessons also, of perseverance and trust and humility, which you will need to learn.'

He paused. 'And when you have imagined the Bodhisatva in all his splendour, seated on his lotus, in his jewels, in the many colours of his robes, with the sacred syllables of his crown radiating thousands of beams of light on which exalted and sacred beings are seated in meditation, when you have visualised all this so powerfully that you feel you could reach out your hand and touch the Bodhisatva himself who is looking into your eyes with a look of immense love, then you are ready to begin the most exalted stage of all. In this, you offer yourself to the Bodhisatva — you offer him your senses, your body, your heart, your spirit. You make a sacrifice to him of everything that you are and then you merge with him, you melt into him. You become your highest self, which is He. And in this state you will see everything with his eyes, hear all sounds with his ears. You will see the world as his body and you will hear all sounds singing his sacred mantra. Even the noise of a car will be singing his mantra; even the whirr of an aeroplane; even the singing of a farmer in the fields; even the barking of a dog.'

The Rinpoche seemed to enter as he was talking into a kind of ecstasy. For a long time he could not speak. He sat with his eyes closed, the sun lighting up his body and the wall behind him.

'You must understand that this merging with the God that you have projected out of yourself, that you have visualised from your own deepest energies, is not an ecstasy that the ego can claim for itself. It is an experience of power, yes, of immense power, but of a power transformed and purified by love and dedicated to all beings, to the salvation of all life. And to save yourself from any possibility of vanity, there is a final stage in the meditation which you must also perform. You must dissolve the meditation; you must dissolve your own projection; you must unmake your own ecstasy; you must rest your mind in all emptiness that has no form, neither your own, nor that of the Bodhisatva that your mind has visualised. You must enter in this last stage into the Sunyata that is the mother of all projections, the Emptiness from which all forms are born, yours, mine, and all the imaginations of our minds and hearts. There must be nothing left of yourself or of the experience of the Bodhisatva or your delight in his splendour, and in your own, nothing but Sunyata, and the clear radiance of the Void.'

We were silent again a long time. The doves had returned to their station under the window, and the room filled with their sound. The sun had passed along the wall, leaving the tapestry above the Rinpoche's head in glowing shadow.

'You are going tomorrow?'

'Yes. I have to.'

I noticed for the first time the two small roses the Rinpoche had placed on the table beside him. He saw me looking at them, blew on one softly to bless it, and gave it to me.

'It is from the pass below Go-Tsang.'

I told him that I loved him and would keep him in my heart all my life. I told him I hoped I would live to have been worthy of his kindness.

He shook his head, smilingly. 'You are worthy already. I do not want your gratitude; I want you not to allow the bond between us to break.'

'It will never break,' I said.

The Rinpoche was silent for a moment and then said, 'We will do the first part of the meditation I taught you together.'

We sat together quietly. After some time, he said, 'Was your visualisation good?'

'Of course not,' I smiled. 'I could hardly visualise anything. I feel a fool. In my mind is a dark stone.'

'Well then,' the Rinpoche said, 'practise and wear it down.'

Afterword

When I first suggested writing an account of my visit to Ladakh in summer 1979 to my then editor — a brilliant, caustic Englishwoman in her early sixties who had discovered V. S. Naipaul — she looked at me with ill-disguised amusement, put down her glass of white wine in the restaurant we were lunching in, and drawled, 'Darling, forget it. No one on earth is going to be interested in what you have to say about some unwashed tribe in the Himalayas. As for trying to describe some old Tibetan sage — well, you might just as well put a stone around your neck and jump into the Thames. The English don't give a fig for mysticism; they think it's something for Americans. If you must write a travel book, do it on Italy or Iceland.'

I was hurt by what she said but soon understood that my sincerity was being tested. If I was going to write the book I wanted to, I would have to separate myself from all the games of English society and all the sophisticated prejudices of Western intellectual and literary life. I would, in fact, have to begin to become my real self, and damn the consequences. There was no precedent I knew of for the kind of book I wanted to create — but why should that stop me? I realized that if I really believed in the power of what I had come to know in Ladakh through my relationship with Thuksey Rinpoche, I must also believe that the power to describe it would be given me.

Deciding that I would have to write *A Journey in Ladakh* or permanently stifle something essential in my true nature liberated a wild joy in me. No book I have ever written gave me such clean rapture. All the sights, smells, and sounds of Ladakh seemed to surround me in the poky attic room my Oxford college lent me. Many times as I walked from downtown Oxford, where I was staying, to my college in the early morning, I would feel surrounding me a huge ecstatic Presence. On one early November dawn in particular, which I shall never forget, the whole world seemed drowned in a brilliant unearthly golden light that gave a divine beauty and splendor even to the puddles at my feet and the worn, sad faces of passers-by. I knew I was being helped and supported by powers not my own, and started to intuit, with greater and greater joy, that my destiny, both as a human being and as an artist, lay in a dedication to the mystical search and to trying to help others discover what was inspiring and transforming my own vision.

Two years after finishing *A Journey in Ladakh* I returned to the Himalayas and to Hemis monastery, and saw Thuksey Rinpoche for the last time. He was dying from diabetes, visibly sick and frail. I had been scared of seeing him again, frightened that I had 'invented' him out of an unconscious need for a 'good' father or that a romantic love of old vanishing worlds had led me to imbue him with a greater wisdom and power than he in fact possessed.

I need not have worried. His force and inner beauty radiated with an even greater intensity than before, brought into high and poignant relief by the quiet drama of his illness. There weren't many other people in Hemis that summer, just a few anxious monks and a small motley crew of Europeans, an intense hawk-faced German girl, a scuba diver from Marseilles and his cabaret singer wife, and myself. Knowing that the Rinpoche was dying brought us all extremely close. Every word Thuksey spoke, every look he gave us, every encounter with him had the luster of a final transmission.

What moved me most about the Rinpoche during that last time was that he seemed utterly unconcerned by his increasing frailty. Nothing would stop him teaching, not even the sudden terrifying bouts of coughing that racked him, nor his inability at times to sit up straight or walk without help. Watching him and being with him I was reminded of the sublime words of Shantideva that describe the inner motivation of a Bodhisattva, a being that has pledged himself or herself to the redemption of all beings from suffering:

'For all creatures, I would be a lantern for those desiring a lantern, I would be a bed for those desiring a bed, I would be a slave for those desiring a slave.'

238

Again and again, the Rinpoche would interrupt his teaching to impress upon us the necessity of continual spiritual practice. When I told him, for example, that I had written a book about him, he didn't say anything but immediately asked me how far I had progressed with my mantra practice and visualizations. When I told him, he shook his head angrily and said, with a sternness I had never before seen in him, 'Writing books is all very well, but spiritual practice is the essential activity of a true seeker. You may write a hundred wonderful books, but what will they matter if you never find out who you are?'

I was, in fact, reassured as well as shaken by his sternness, because it showed me just how authentic his love for me really was. That I had written about him meant nothing to him; what mattered was that I should become wholly earnest in my search for truth. He himself never stopped praying; when he was eating or sitting quietly or waiting for guests his lips would always be moving. It was obvious that in his last days he was keeping himself constantly immersed in the sacred stream of truth. I understood from this one of the most important lessons of the Path: enlightenment is not a 'static' state but one of constant inner commitment to, and growth in, love and concentration.

I don't want to give the impression that our last summer together was in any way depressing. Nothing could darken the deep joy that radiated from the Rinpoche. One afternoon, I remember, all of us were waiting for him to return from a doctor's visit. We were standing at the top of a staircase. The car bringing him home drew up; he got out; he looked up at us gazing down anxiously at him, laughed a great leonine laugh, and then proceeded to climb the stairs towards us in great pain but looking at each of us in turn with such naked and tender compassion that we all had tears in our eyes. It was clear that he was far more concerned about our fears for him than he was afraid for himself. My scuba diver friend said to me afterwards, 'When he laughed, I felt he was saying to all of us, "Do not identify me with the dying man you see, I have gone beyond both what you call life and what you call death, I am living in a freedom beyond both."'

Two extraordinary incidents that happened soon after confirmed what my friend had intuited. The first occurred during an elaborate and moving long-life ceremony that was held in the central shrine room of Hemis in Thuksey's honor. At one moment, the Rinpoche had to get down on his knees before his pupil, the young Drukchen Rinpoche. We all watched in anguish as he struggled to kneel. As Thuksey struggled back to his feet, something astonishing happened: he laughed and a terrific sound like a clap of mountain thunder reverberated round the room. I and two other Europeans present heard the thunder distinctly 'speak' the word 'Tongpanyid.' 'Tongpanyid' is Tibetan for 'emptiness.' The entire universe was signaling and celebrating the Rinpoche's liberation from all forms and concepts, from matter and 'biography.' I can see his beautiful laughing face now as I write, white with strain but suffused with ecstasy and, for that moment, hallucinatorily young-looking.

The second incident occurred on my last evening in Hemis. I was sad to be leaving, because I knew that I would never see the Rinpoche again. With my scuba diver friend I climbed a hill behind Hemis and sat silently looking down at the monastery. Suddenly — both I and my friend heard it — the sound of sacred chanting filled the air around us. That evening I noted in my diary, 'I felt as if all the monks who had ever lived and studied at Hemis were singing for the Rinpoche and as if the very rocks we were sitting amongst were also singing for him.' Many years later I described this experience to a Tibetan monk I met while co-writing for Sogyal Rinpoche *The Tibetan Book of Living and Dying*. For a long while, the monk said nothing, studying my face; then he whispered, 'What you heard that night is one of the Signs that our texts say signal the dying of an Enlightened One.'

The last time I saw Thuksey Rinpoche was not in any way remarkable or emotional. He held my hand briefly, gazed deep into my eyes, and said, 'Go on practicing,' and then looked down again at the text he was reading. Almost a year later, he died in India serenely, with little pain. One of the monks who had been with him at the end told me years later, 'He died with a half-smile on his face. Everyone knew a Buddha was passing.' As he said those words quite matter-of-factly, the full grandeur of the blessing I had received from seeing and knowing so great a man broke upon me and I wept not from grief but from joy and gratitude.

Death does not interrupt the inner conversation of two hearts that have met in the Light of Reality. If anything, it makes that conversation even more subtle and profound. I have many times seen Thuksey Rinpoche in dreams; I feel his protection with me always. When I come to die myself, I know I will have before the eyes of my spirit the image and wordless instruction of the way the Rinpoche met his own dying. What more can any human being give to another than the inspiration he gave and gives me still?

If someone had told me when I finished *A Journey in Ladakh*, almost twenty years ago, that at the end of the millennium Tibet would still be under Chinese domination and more threatened than ever, that Ladakh would be increasingly corrupted by commercialism and menaced by the still angry strife between India and Pakistan over Kashmir, and that the Tibetan spiritual tradition itself would be severely compromised and damaged in the eyes of many seekers by a series of terrible sexual scandals and abuses, I would never have believed him or her; I would have accused them of a lack of vision and faith. The tragic facts remain, however. The old Tibet that Thuksey Rinpoche embodied with such natural splendor is now almost totally extinct; the master system he represented with such power has shown itself to be incapable of resisting Western temptation and corruption in all but a handful of lamas. The Dalai Lama himself, marvelous sweet being though he undoubtedly is, has himself delivered depressingly regressive teachings on sex, made homophobic remarks, and espoused an anti-contraception stance in India; the apostle of nonviolence has even saluted India's development of a nuclear bomb! Feminist critiques and modern historical scholarship have revealed the patriarchal bias of much of Tibetan civilization and tradition and the limitations of their misogyny, elitism, and hierarchies restricting access to spiritual truth and power.

There are many sincere and intelligent Western Buddhists who continue to idealize Tibet, the Tibetans, and the Dalai Lama. This serves neither truth nor the cause of a free Tibet. Eventually, the true nature of the many scandals that have shaken the Tibetan world and the foundations of the Tibetan system itself will be exposed, and the disillusion that will follow will be far more dangerous to the Tibetan cause than any 'revisionism.'

What will never die, however — and of this I am more and more convinced — is the brilliance and importance of the sacred technology — the great treasury of visionary practices and philosophies — that the Tibetan mystical schools developed and preserved. The social and religious systems that formed around these teachings will die; the teachings themselves will go on living and will inspire and shape and awaken seekers of all paths and persuasions.

And in remembering such beings as Thuksey Rinpoche we will keep alive and alight the Sign of what such teachings can produce, as a reassurance and a challenge to us all, whatever path we are on.

Andrew Harvey

Nevada,
November 1999

20516998R00148

Made in the USA
Lexington, KY
09 February 2013